God's Word and Our Words

Preaching from the Prophets
to the Present and Beyond

"*God's Word and Our Words* is a rich feast, and a delight. Time after time we see that God raises up preachers in order to bring renewal, revival, and new life to his church. May he do it again as we remind ourselves of our history, and learn its lessons!"

—SIMON VIBERT, Vicar of Christ Church, Virginia Water

"Just as 'Jesus came preaching' (Mark 1:14), so the church has had preaching as a central focus of its life and work through the centuries. In *God's Word and Our Words*, a stellar team of contributors walks the reader through the history of Christian preaching in an engaging and readable way. Growing out of a symposium held at Baylor University, each chapter takes a portion of the preaching story, from the Old Testament prophets to contemporary evangelicalism. Any student of preaching will find this to be a must-have volume."

—MICHAEL DUDUIT, Clamp Divinity School, Anderson University, Executive Editor of *Preaching* magazine,

"There are seasons in every preacher's life when discouragement strikes in the pulpit. We wonder whether preaching is really worth it. In *God's Word and Our Words*, Gloer and Boyd assemble leading voices from the fields of biblical studies, church history, and homiletics to remind and inspire preachers of the past, present, and future significance of preaching—its joys and its challenges. . . . Be prepared to have your fire for preaching rekindled!"

—MATTHEW D. KIM, Gordon-Conwell Theological Seminary, author of *Preaching with Cultural Intelligence* and *A Little Book for New Preachers*

"Packed into this succinct volume is the story of Christian preaching, told by some of the more able scholars of our day. The essays provide critical insights into the biblical, theological, and homiletical genius of preaching. Some writers address the glorious past, others speak to strength in diversity, while some point the way forward for preaching in an uncertain post-Christian world. This should be required reading for lovers of preaching everywhere."

—CLEOPHUS J. LARUE, Princeton Theological Seminary

"This book is a valuable resource that brings together a wide range of preaching perspectives. The topics as much as the voices you'll hear are rich and varied. Each contributor shares a common love for homiletics, the listener, and the Lord. Readers will benefit from their years of pastoral and pulpit experience."

—Patricia Batten, Gordon-Conwell Theological Seminary

"The contributors bring a variety of styles and perspectives as they focus on particular historical and cultural expressions of preaching. Some chapters are introductory, some apologetic, and some exploratory. Each chapter stands in its own right while helpfully being part of the wider discussion on the nature of preaching past, present, and future."

—Stuart Blythe, Acadia Divinity College

"*God's Word and Our Words* is a unique and richly informative guide to preaching in the Bible, church history, and the contemporary world. Remarkable in scope, it contains much to stimulate and challenge teachers and students of preaching, to think deeply about the practice of preaching past, present, and future."

—Julian Gotobed, University of Roehampton

"Whether you are interested in the history or the future of preaching, *God's Word and Our Words* is an essential read. As a homiletics professor, this will be my go-to guide for educating the next generation of preachers. Every chapter reflects the expertise of the contributors with insights that go beyond historical dates and names. This book is beautifully written by the top homileticians of today. A brilliant piece of work!"

—Chris Rappazini, Moody Bible Institute, President of the Evangelical Homiletics Society

God's Word and Our Words

Preaching from the Prophets
to the Present and Beyond

EDITED BY

W. Hulitt Gloer and Shawn Boyd

September 11–12, 2017
Sponsored by
The Kyle Lake Center for Effective Preaching
Baylor University Institute for the Study of Religion,
George W. Truett Theological Seminary
Baylor University
Waco, TX

☙PICKWICK *Publications* • Eugene, Oregon

GOD'S WORD AND OUR WORDS
Preaching from the Prophets to the Present and Beyond

Copyright © 2019 Wipf and Stock Publishers. All rights reserved. Except for brief quotations in critical publications or reviews, no part of this book may be reproduced in any manner without prior written permission from the publisher. Write: Permissions, Wipf and Stock Publishers, 199 W. 8th Ave., Suite 3, Eugene, OR 97401.

Pickwick Publications
An Imprint of Wipf and Stock Publishers
199 W. 8th Ave., Suite 3
Eugene, OR 97401

www.wipfandstock.com

PAPERBACK ISBN: 978-1-5326-4609-6
HARDCOVER ISBN: 978-1-5326-4610-2
EBOOK ISBN: 978-1-5326-4611-9

Cataloging-in-Publication data:

Names: Gloer, W. Hulitt, editor. | Boyd, Shawn, editor.
Title: God's word and our words : preaching from the Prophets to the Present and Beyond / edited by W. Hulitt Gloer and Shawn Boyd.
Description: Eugene, OR : Pickwick Publications, 2019 | Includes bibliographical references.
Identifiers: ISBN 978-1-5326-4609-6 (paperback) | ISBN 978-1-5326-4610-2 (hardcover) | ISBN 978-1-5326-4611-9 (ebook)
Subjects: LCSH: Preaching—History. | Preaching—Congresses. | Preaching—Study and teaching. | Preaching—Sermons.
Classification: LCC BV4207 G6 2019 (print) | LCC BV4207 (ebook)

Manufactured in the U.S.A.

"... with its preaching, Christianity stands or falls."
P. T. Forsyth

Table of Contents

Introduction
W. Hulitt Gloer. *At the time of the symposium, Dr. Gloer was the holder of the David E. Garland Endowed Chair of Preaching and Christian Scripture at Baylor University's George W. Truett Theological Seminary. He is currently the Scholar-in-Residence at the Second Baptist Church, Little Rock, Arkansas.*

1 **The Preaching of the Prophets: Holy Intrusions of Truth and Hope**
Walter Brueggemann, *William Marcellus McPheeters Professor Emeritus of Old Testament at Columbia Theological Seminary*

2 **The Preaching of Jesus**
Thomas G. Long, *Bandy Professor of Preaching at Candler School of Theology at Emory University*

3 **Paul the Preacher and Preaching Paul: The Rhetoric and the Reality**
Ben Witherington III, *Amos Professor of New Testament for Doctoral Studies at Asbury Theological Seminary*

4 **Preaching in Pre-Nicene Christianity**
David E. Wilhite, *Professor of Christian Theology at Baylor University's George W. Truett Theological Seminary*

5 **Preaching from Augustine to Aquinas**
Paul Scott Wilson, *Professor of Homiletics at Emmanuel College of the University of Toronto*

6 **Preaching and the Reformation**
Timothy George, *Dean of Beeson Divinity School at Samford University*

7 **Preaching in the Victorian Era in England and Scotland**
Joel C. Gregory, *George W. Truett Endowed Chair in Preaching and Evangelism at the George W. Truett Theological Seminary of Baylor University*

8 **Preaching in Early America: The Preaching of George Whitefield**
Thomas S. Kidd, *Distinguished Professor of History at Baylor University*

9 The African American Preaching Tradition
   Claybon Lea Jr., *Pastor of the Mount Calvary Baptist Church in Fairfield and Suisun City, California*

10 The Preaching of the Great Evangelists: Finney, Moody, Sunday, and Graham
   Winfred Neely, *Professor of Hermeneutics and Homiletics at Moody Theological Seminary*

11 Preaching in Mainline Protestantism
   Elesha J. Coffman, *Assistant Professor of History at Baylor University*

12 Preaching in American Evangelicalism
   Scott M. Gibson. *At the time of the symposium, Dr. Gibson was the Haddon Robinson Professor of Biblical Preaching at Gordon-Conwell Theological Seminary. He currently holds the David E. Garland Chair in Preaching at the George W. Truett Theological Seminary*

13 The Significance of the "New Homiletic"
   Eugene L. Lowry, *Professor Emeritus of Preaching at Saint Paul School of Theology*

14 Prophesying Daughters (Acts 2:17): Women in the American Pulpit
   Carolyn Ann Knight, *Founder and President of "CAN DO!" Ministries*

15 Predicting the Next Trends in Evangelical Preaching: Retrospect and Prospect
   Dennis L. Phelps, *J. D. Grey Professor of Preaching; Director, Alumni and Church Minister Relations at New Orleans Baptist Theological Seminary*

16 The Future Shapes of Preaching
   Leonard Sweet, *E. Stanley Jones Professor of Evangelism at Drew Theological School at Drew University and Visiting Distinguished Professor at George Fox University*

THE SYMPOSIUM SERMONS

When Our Words Become God's (Acts 2:32-41)
William H. Willimon, *Professor of the Practice of Christian Ministry at the Divinity School, Duke University*

Don't Stop Preaching (Amos 7:10-17)
Jared E. Alcántara. *At time of the symposium, Dr. Alcántara was Associate Professor of Homiletics at Trinity Evangelical Divinity School. He currently holds the Paul Powell Endowed Chair of Preaching at the George W. Truett Theological Seminary*

Introduction

ON SEPTEMBER 11-12, 2017, a group of the world's leading biblical and homiletical scholars gathered for two amazing days of presentations and conversations on the significance of preaching from the prophets to the present and beyond. This volume contains those presentations. A quick glance at the table of contents reveals the importance of the symposium by the names of those who participated—a "who's who" of nationally and internationally known scholars. Each one was given the charge to discuss the significance of preaching for a particular person or period of history. They were given the freedom to approach their topic as they so desired in order to highlight the contributions of the person or period. As you will see, this has resulted in a volume of presentations that are both highly informative and richly creative. Here then is a survey of the history of preaching delivered in a way that is academically sound and, at the same time, extremely interesting. Who could ask for more?

Our journey through that history begins with Walter Brueggemann's seminal treatment of the prophet/preachers of ancient Israel: "The work of the prophets in ancient Israel involved delivering a truth-telling, hope-evoking word in a society that wanted neither the truth that was too hard to bear nor hope that was impossible to entertain." Focusing on Jeremiah, whose book he suggests gives us the "best access to the issues that concern us in prophetic preaching," he offers a cogent analysis of the issues the prophet addressed, reminding us that the prophetic mandate consists of destruction and reconstruction, and the truth-telling exposes "the termination of all reality not in sync with God's purpose" while the hope-telling utters, anticipates, and imagines a new historical reality being birthed by God. His prescription of how we might do this kind of preaching today is provocative and compelling, to say the least, but at the same time encouraging.

In chapter 2, Thomas G. Long focuses on the Markan account of the Jesus who "came preaching." Mark 1:15 is a programmatic statement of the character and content of his preaching. With urgency in His voice, Jesus' preaching was not merely the offering of a new set of ideas but an "event," the event of God's kingdom breaking into history. Any attempt "to summarize Jesus' preaching as a system of thought or set of ethical wisdom sayings domesticates both Jesus and His preaching." He was as "a weather forecaster announcing the impending arrival of a category-5 hurricane, a prophet proclaiming and embodying the in-breaking of the very reign of God." The goal of preaching (both Jesus' and ours) is to enable people to repent and believe the "good news," so "one test of a Christian sermon is whether it has the character-breaking news: God is doing something in our midst, the time is now, the event of God is imminent, and because of this everything has changed, so repent and believe in this news." The nature of His preaching stands out most clearly in the parables, which "turned the world upside down" and are "the nuclear reactor of Jesus' own preaching." While recognizing that Jesus preached in other forms, whether it was a parable or beatitude, proverb or story, it "had a parabolic imagination, intent, and flavor."

Ben Witherington argues in chapter 3 that there is sufficient evidence in Paul's epistles and the Lucan account of his sermons in the Acts narrative to enable an examination of the preaching of Paul. In the book of Acts, we have "rhetorically apt outlines" from Luke's hands: "Luke knew Paul was a good preacher, despite his physical impediments and funny way of speaking. And Paul's letters, of course, show that Luke was indeed right." Paul's letters *are already the preaching and they are in the form of ancient rhetorical sermons.*" Paul's rhetoric is reflective of the Greco-Roman rhetoric of his day, which focused one's attention on ethos, logos, and pathos. Indeed, "Paul knew the conventions of Greco-Roman rhetoric very well and used them to good advantage—both orally and in writing." Witherington demonstrates that Paul makes good use of all three and suggests that today's preachers would do well to do the same.

In chapter 4, David Wilhite explores preaching in pre-Nicene Christianity, a period too long overlooked, in spite of the fact that it is foundational for all preaching that follows. While acknowledging that there are few surviving sermons, Wilhite argues that "virtually every surviving source from this early period is derived from and still reflects 'sermonic' material." After a helpful description of the varieties of sermonic materials that are reflected in the sources and a most interesting discussion of the

INTRODUCTION xiii

development of early Christian tradition "from *kerygma* to *paradosis* to *regula* to *credo*," he then offers a brief survey of preaching from the early centuries by examining the surviving homilies: 2 Clement, the Easter sermon of Melito of Sardis, along with those sermons penned by Clement of Alexandria, Hippolytus of Rome, and Origen. He also includes the works of apologists like Justin Martyr and other sources that are likely to have been delivered orally, such as many of the works of Tertullian, Cyprian, and Irenaeus. He notes that some sources also refer to women preachers.

All of this sets the stage for a most helpful identification of the characteristics of the preaching of this period. Wilhite is not afraid to counter "accepted" views, and even argues that surviving sources from groups deemed heretical should be studied because they reflect the various topics, concerns, and content of early Christian preaching.

Paul Scott Wilson takes on the daunting task of discussing the significance of preaching, from Augustine to Aquinas. While he gives pride of place to the homiletics of Augustine, Anselm, and Aquinas, he also gives careful attention to historical developments and figures throughout the period. Much attention is given to the development and use of multiple meanings in Scripture (which he terms "a brilliant insight") as well as discussion of three keys to fourfold exegesis and its significance for preaching. Acknowledging that Augustine was "the most important person of this period," he highlights six of Augustine's "innovations" for preaching. Based on Aquinas' 155 biblical sermons, he describes him as "one of the foremost pioneers of elaborate, reasoned point-form sermons." Wilson summarizes Aquinas' homiletical method concisely and offers a sample sermon, suggesting that his view on the literal sense of Scripture paved the way for the Reformers.

While the Holy Spirit is the principal interpreter of Scripture, there are three subordinate means that may help us: the analogy of faith, the circumstances passage, and the comparison of different passages (a method for which Wilson gives numerous examples). He offers a comparison regarding the way Augustine and Calvin exegete Ps 3:1-4.

In chapter 6, Timothy George addresses the preaching of the Reformation, focusing on the preaching of Martin Luther. Suggesting that the late Middle Ages was marked by a "gaping hunger" for the verbal exposition of the Bible and hence a great hunger for preaching (as evidenced by the increase of mendicant friars and *Leutpriesters*), the time was ripe for the preaching of the Reformers. He portrays the dialectical nature of Luther's preaching by mirroring his personal inner struggles with law and gospel, grace and wrath, God and Satan, etc. Ever battling Satan, his deep awareness of sin led to a need for a deeper doctrine of grace and thus, justification by faith.

This insight led to the transformation of worship with preaching as the centerpiece (especially chapter-by-chapter, verse-by-verse continuous preaching through a book of the Bible). Preaching came to be understood as an indispensable means of grace, resulting in the view that "the preaching of the word of God is the word of God" (Bullinger). George puts it this way: "It is a performative word . . . a means by which God breaks into our mundane everyday world, and shakes it up, and transforms it." As such, preaching became and remains the centerpiece of worship in the Protestant and Free Church traditions.

Joel Gregory asserts in chapter 7 that "a dozen preachers in nineteenth-century England and Scotland made an impact unequaled in the history of English-language preaching." Choosing to discuss this period by featuring representative (exemplary) preachers rather than by making generalizations, he first sets the context and then focuses on the lives and preaching of six preachers chosen because of their "abiding influence, representation of state church and free-church traditions, Oxford men and self-taught, and—in the case of one—sheer genius." In each case, helpful and interesting thumbnail sketches of their lives that feature both their personal struggles and successes are followed by evaluations of their individual sermon styles reflecting their impact both then and now. The six preachers are Henry Liddon, Frederick W. Robertson, Charles Haddon Spurgeon, Alexander Maclaren, Joseph Parker, and Alexander Whyte. Gregory's insightful analyses of the sermons are helpful for understanding the preaching styles of these six preachers in their context, the role context plays with regard to preaching styles, and the necessity of contextual awareness for preaching—whether one is in Victorian England or twenty-first century America.

In chapter 8, our attention shifts from the continent to the colonies as Thomas Kidd explores preaching in early America with a focus on George Whitefield, whose background as an actor prepared him for "a fabulously successful preaching career." His skillful, powerful presentation of his message ran counter to the lengthy doctrinal sermons read from a manuscript. Methodologically, he "revolutionized the sermonic form with a rhetorical style which captured the imaginations of the Anglo-American people," which included his use of a skeletal outline he fleshed out "as his own feelings and a sense of duty prompted"—plain language that anyone could understand, words that could reach the hearts as well as the minds of his hearers. His mastery of the use of publicity and promotion of his preaching tours gave rise to pundits calling him "Anglo-America's first religious celebrity." Kidd argues that Whitefield was the key figure in the first generation of Anglo-American evangelical Christianity with its emphasis on conversion, the new birth, the work of the Holy Spirit, and the preaching of revival. His innovative preaching style, his out-of-church open field meetings, and his use of the latest forms of media communications all contributed to a ministry that brought the continent and colonies together under the banner of the cross.

"African American preaching, in the expanse of Judeo-Christian preaching, is unquestionably unique. Its significance in the history of preaching in America is undeniable." So begins Claybon Lea Jr.'s treatment of the significance of the African American preaching tradition. He likens it to jazz music, "which is intriguingly diverse in its numerous expressions but obviously distinct from all of the other major music genres." Emphasizing the central role the preacher plays in the African American community, he suggests that the preaching cannot be understood apart from the preacher. Indeed, the relationship between the preacher and the community is absolutely necessary, for the communal affirmation of the preacher's call creates an equality of the voice of the preacher with the voice of God.

The content of this preaching is practical theology emerging from a particular contextual reality: "The experiential realities of inequitable existence and unjust society birthday for preaching that is simultaneously redemptive and hope-filled, biblical and instructive, creative and engaging, artistic and argumentative, rhetorical and theological, spiritual and practical, moral and ethical, worshipful and joyful, comforting and accountable." He offers a helpful treatment of nine characteristics of African American preaching and closes with comments about the future of this tradition.

In chapter 10, Winfred Neely discusses the significance of the preaching of the great evangelists in nineteenth- and twentieth-century America. While focusing his attention on Charles Finney, he also devotes some attention to Dwight Moody, Billy Graham, and Billy Sunday. He emphasizes that the power of the preaching of these evangelists is born out of their own personal experience. Neely sees Finney as a most important figure in the Second Great Awakening, and describes him as both an evangelist and a revivalist whose homiletical aim was revival—divine visitation leading to the churches renewal and consequent awakening, conviction, and conversion of lost people. While known as a "fiery preacher," Finney employed homiletical methods, believing that without some plan of operation, along with some strategies enabling listeners to hear the message and inducing them to pay attention, preaching can never be effective.

Neely also discusses Finney's homiletical insights that mark effective preaching. He suggests that the most significant factor in Finney's preaching was his break with old-school Calvinism and his emphasis on human responsibility to believe the gospel. To Finney, if Christ died on the cross for all people, all people are free to choose for or against Him. This conviction is at the heart of all evangelism and resulted in the inclusion of the "invitation" (an opportunity in the service when people respond to the message in a public way). Neely also highlights Finney's attention to social reforms such as his opposition to slavery.

Elesha Coffman discusses preaching in the white mainline tradition (noting that the African American tradition is discussed by another writer). While recognizing that there is room for disagreement with regards to the makeup of this tradition, for the purpose of this paper she identifies it with the "Seven Sisters of American Protestantism": the Episcopal Church, the Evangelical Lutheran Church in America (ELCA), the Presbyterian Church (PCUSA), the United Methodist Church, the American Baptist Church, the United Church of Christ, and the Disciples of Christ.

Emerging in the late nineteenth century, the preaching of this tradition reflects an "alliance with higher education," or, as she puts it, the reading of books. She finds evidence for this in four developments. First, the tradition embraced modernism with its commitment to higher criticism, or the historical-critical method. Second, (and obviously related to the first), is its embrace of historical consciousness: "To get a handle on all this, you must learn to read books: History books. Philosophy books. Anthropology. Comparative religions." Thus, mainline preaching values erudition and academic credentials. Second, the tradition embraced psychology and self-help books. Third, there is the "perceived" need to preach on political and social issues (the Bible in one hand, the newspaper in the other). Fourth, there is the increased use of the lectionary. All throughout her discussion, Coffman illustrates her assertions with representative preachers and studies that would support her views.

After offering a definition of American evangelicalism, Scott Gibson turns to the place of preaching in this tradition, stating that it is the place of preaching in evangelicalism that distinguishes it as a movement: "Preaching is the mark of the evangelical's commitment to the Bible and spread the movement, and rises as the unique feature of evangelicalism." In fact, "Evangelicalism is preaching." It is in its preaching that its commitments are most clearly manifested. He sees these commitments as, at the same time, the contributions of evangelical preaching.

Gibson highlights three. First, its commitment to the Bible as the authoritative Word of God. Second, its commitment to the high place of preaching. He notes that it has been said evangelical ecclesiology is a "proclamation ecclesiology." This proclamation results in conversion and Christian growth. There is an emphasis on expository preaching that he defines not by propositions but by the great expository preachers, both past and present. Third, its commitment to scholarship that is reflected in publications, indicated by the formation of the Evangelical Homiletics Society, which publishes a peer-reviewed journal, *The Journal of the Evangelical Homiletics Society*. Gibson concludes with a warning: American pragmatism has distilled preaching into what works best, resulting in sermons that are neither theologically sound nor sufficiently nourishing.

In chapter 13, Eugene Lowry surveys the development of the "New Homiletic" by reviewing the work of its five most prominent representatives in chronological order. Charles Rice highlighted the power of story as the medium through which revelation is conveyed in both the Old and New Testaments. He emphasized the "event" nature of the preaching moment and argued that the dramatic form of the biblical text should determine the sermon structure. Fred Craddock argued for the use of the inductive method in which "the preacher provides early promise, but the fulfillment is delayed until the folks are ready."

Based primarily on the work of Søren Kierkegaard, Lowry's argument says that indirection was the best strategy for preaching to those who have already heard or think there is nothing more to hear. Henry Mitchell analyzes the differences between African American preaching that features the whole person and the primarily intellectual approach of Anglo preaching. Rather than the largely "cerebral" Anglo approach that focuses on the production of an idea, the African American preacher targets the whole person and seeks the combination of intellectual and less rational but equally valid processes.

Tracing his own journey, Lowry pays tribute to the influences shaping his own thinking and leading to his writing of *The Homiletical Plot*, in which, moving beyond the principles of induction, he seeks to isolate the steps in a plot that can serve as the form of the sermon. Drawing a distinction between narrative and story, he expands the concept of narrative to include time: "A sermon is a movement in time which begins at a given moment, ends at a given moment, and moves through of the intervening moments one after another."

David Buttrick argued against treating the text like a still-life photograph in which some things may be found. The preacher must attend to the composition of the picture, the narrative structure, the movement of the story, the whole question of what, in fact, the text wants you to preach. Sermons are made up of a series of "moves," which, taken together, form a "conceptual understanding and communal consciousness." For Buttrick, preaching should be a speaking *of* the Scriptures and not *about* the Scriptures.

In chapter 14, Carolyn Ann Knight traces the history of women preachers in America to 1656 when British Quaker "Public Friends" Mary Fisher and Ann Austin landed in the Massachusetts Bay colony, only to be arrested, imprisoned, examined for marks of witchcraft, and shipped back to England. The struggles of women called to preach have continued to the present time. Yet there have been women who have ignored what has been termed by some "the restraining thinker, the unyielding institution, the bastion of male domination that had behind it the force of centuries-old traditions usually reinforced by a 'thus saith the Lord' in order to claim their right to preach."

The path, position, and place of women in the pulpit in our day remains just as challenging in many ways as it was in centuries past. Knight illustrates this powerfully from her own experience. Yet in spite of the struggles, women have persevered, and the last century has witnessed "tremendous shifts in women's ways of preaching," resulting in a great diversity of styles, both in preparation and delivery. To draw attention to the significance of preaching women, she gives a long litany of those gifted orators and expositors who have had great significance on the local, national, and denominational levels and have also written about their own struggles in following the call to preach.

While some progress has been made in the affirmation of women preachers, Knight argues there are still adjustments to be made and resistance to be overcome. She mentions that today's women preachers have many advantages over their forebears, including a rich repository of literature comprising biographies, testimonies, and sermons, as well as many conferences that focus on preaching for women. She challenges women to be "deliberate and intentional" about bringing their unique perspectives as women to the hermeneutical process and their preaching, remembering that they wrestle with texts from different worldviews (e.g., feminist, womanist) when dealing with issues of race, class, power, and culture. She calls for much more attention to be given to those texts in which women are named and play central roles.

Dennis Phelps turns our attention to the future of evangelical preaching. After discussing the identity of evangelicals and their significance in American life, he presents a fascinating and thorough decade-by-decade review of the emphases and issues that dominated evangelical preaching, beginning in the forties and fifties. Turning to the next twenty-five to thirty years, Phelps suggests that evangelical preaching will retain a focus on the New Testament *kerygma*, which he defines as "the gospel without adjectives (e.g., social, prosperity, full) including the call to personal repentance from sin, expression of sincere faith in the person and work of Jesus, necessity of individual conversion to Christ, and demonstration of compassion and love toward others."

Exposition, both topical and textually consecutive, will continue to be the method of choice, especially in light of biblical illiteracy. "Preachers will work to stay true to the intended, plain authorial meaning and purpose of the text" while the sermon moves "meaningfully" between its historical and contemporary significance. Linguistic philosophy will help set the original meaning and intended action of the text within the original social and rhetorical context: 'The rich textures of the Old Testament will ascend with their narrative theology, prophetic challenges, poetry for spiritual formation, and foundation for understanding of Jesus in the New Testament."

Prophetic preaching, both missional and incarnational in nature, will result from the churches' partial participation in culture and the inevitable secular hostility that nonconformity to all aspects of the dominant culture will bring. "Ubiquitous technological augmentation" will enable effective evangelical preaching to offer "a reasonable framework within which to understand individual life experiences, cultural movements, search for meaning in chaos."

While challenging preachers to realize that they are already preaching to the twenty-second century, in chapter 16 Leonard Sweet argues that preachers must do three things to gain a hearing. First, they must learn the language of that culture. Thus, while they are tied to a culture of words, the culture forming around them communicates in two basic forms: narrative and metaphor, from which he coins the term *narraphors*. "One of the biggest discoveries to emerge from cognitive science, cycle neurolinguistics, and cognitive studies is that the last thing the brain comes up with is words. . . . The mind is not made up of words but rather metaphors which it turns into stories." Words are the result of a long process, which begins with metaphors that bring about metamorphosis. The true child of the twenty-second century will not be involved with "words and principles and points and propositions" but with metaphors, which have the real power to change, transform, or metamorphose. The metaphors and stories are in the Bible.

Second, the preacher must listen to the story of that culture until they're able to retell the story to the satisfaction of that culture or person. Finally, the preacher must find ways to tell the culture that there is only one story you can trust your life to, and that is the Jesus story and the Jesus song. The future, according to Sweet, belongs to the Eastern Orthodox and African Pentecostals, who are "addicted" to story and metaphor.

The Symposium Sermons

Two worship services were held during the symposium, and the two preachers demonstrated the effectiveness of two very different styles of preaching. On Monday night, William Willimon took as his text Acts 2:32-41. Titling his sermon "When Our Words Become God's," Willimon states his theme as follows: "The best, most frightening thing about preaching is the theme of this conference: when God takes our words and makes them God's word." Citing the Second Helvetic Confession and Karl Barth, he suggests that Peter's Pentecost sermon is, "by my assertion, the worst sermon in all of church history—no illustrations, culturally insensitive, no connections, no bridge from there to here," yet thousands of people responded. He also uses the story of Philip and the Ethiopian eunuch in Acts 8 and the story of Jonah, along with several anecdotes, all in support of his main thesis. He concludes with an "invitation" from Ivanka Trump to come and preach at the White House. No spoilers here, you'll have to read it for yourself.

Taking as his text Amos 7:10–17, Jared E. Alcántara's sermon brings the confrontation between the prophet Amos and the priest Amaziah up to date. Amaziah serves "the powers that be" (King Jeroboam) and the institution that is (the Temple). Unpacking the nature of his ministry, he reveals its dangerous implications for today. When Amaziah orders Amos ("the wrong kind of preacher on the wrong side of town defending the wrong sort of people") to stop preaching and stop prophesying, Amos answers, "I cannot stop prophesying. I won't stop preaching." His lack of credentials notwithstanding, Amos makes it clear that he answers to no one but God, and it is this God who calls him to Bethel. So, when Alcántara asks, "Why should you not stop preaching?" his answer is simple: Because God has called you to this work and saying yes to this call is saying yes to the God who calls you and empowers you and brings results you cannot even imagine.

Thus ends the preview. Now . . . take up and read!

—W. Hulitt Gloer
David E. Garland Chair of Preaching
Director, Kyle Lake Center for Effective Preaching
George W. Truett Theological Seminary
April 2018

Chapter One

The Preaching of the Prophets

Holy Intrusions of Truth and Hope

WALTER BRUEGGEMANN

THE WORK OF THE prophets in ancient Israel involved delivering a truth-telling, hope-evoking word in a society that wanted neither the truth that was too hard to bear nor hope that was impossible to entertain.

******

The world in which these ancient prophets did their work was one of concentrated power and wealth that sought a monopoly on technology and imagination. The purpose of that wealth and power, on the one hand, was to *control all technology* in a way that ensured military domination and economic mastery. On the other hand, the purpose of wealth and power was to *control all imagination*, a control accomplished by liturgic hegemony in the performance of the temple. The royal hegemony intended to create a comprehensive world in which nothing was thinkable, imaginable, sayable, or doable outside the confines of that control. The best word for such an all-comprehensive system that I know is "totalism." I appropriate the term from Robert Lifton, who over time has studied some of the great totalisms of the modern world, including the cult of National Socialism in Germany and the war machine in Japan.[1]

---

1. Lifton, *Witness*, 67–68, 381.

The totalism of the royal period of the Old Testament is embodied in the Jerusalem establishment of king, temple, and scribal culture founded by Solomon, which lasted for four hundred years. Thus, all of life became contained within and defined by the categories of the regime. Consequently, the regime could readily think of itself as an absolute match for the will of God, with the priests on the royal payroll having ready access between the earthly domain of Solomon and the heavenly domain of YHWH.

The extended historical narrative of the Davidic dynasty is the defining example of totalism in ancient Israel. It is, however, only one of a series of totalisms in the memory of Israel, each of which could pretend to absolutism—thus, Pharaoh's Egypt, Nebuchadnezzar's Babylon, Cyrus's Persia, and on to Alexander and Rome. The Roman Empire entailed totalism in the midst of which the Jesus movement had its inception. We are aware of the way in which Roman military, judicial, and tax-collecting power permeated even the remote territory of Galilee. Each of these totalisms in sequence operated in roughly the same way. When necessary, the regime used raw power, but it preferred softer persuasion to establish the legitimacy and necessity of the regime. In order to maintain this claim and practice, it was necessary to refuse and resist any thought, imagination, utterance, or action to the contrary.

Of course, some of them did not subscribe to the dominant ideology and benefit from the concentration of wealth; instead, they engaged in alternative thought and action of a subversive nature. Moses embodies such a force that Pharaoh must first restrain and then finally, in desperation, expel. The memory concerning the regime of Solomon is not different. From the outset, the regime had to constantly be on guard against those who dared to imagine that life possibilities existed beyond the sphere of the regime. Solomon's violent seizure of the throne, according to the narrative, required him to forcibly eliminate opponents: Adonijah, Joab, and Shimei. But then, as recorded in 1 Kgs 11:29, the prophet Ahijah the Shilonite evoked in Jeroboam a thought about leading a revolution against the house of Solomon, which came to fruition in the next chapter (1 Kgs 12:1–19). In the subsequent royal narrative, we know that Ahab and Jezebel, in the northern kingdom, regarded Elijah and Elisha as enemies of their regime and killed many prophets (1 Kgs 18:4, 13). Moreover, Amaziah, the priest in the royal sanctuary of Bethel, banished the prophet Amos (Amos 7:10–17). Manasseh contradicted the commands of Moses and "shed much innocent blood" (2 Kgs 21:16), and King Jehoiakim sent a posse to arrest Jeremiah (Jer 36:26).

A totalizing regime cannot tolerate dissent or subversion. Thus, as is necessary, totalizing regimes must silence dissent, prohibit subversion, control artists, banish poets, and when necessary, kill prophets. Such brutality is required because dissenters, subversives, artists, poets, and prophets invite thought that the regime is not absolute, its claims to legitimacy are not ultimate, its policies are not beyond criticism, nor its practices beyond destabilization.

Do I need to alert you, before I move on, that it is increasingly in such a totalism of military consumerism, endorsed by uncritical exceptionalism, that we now live? As a successor to Rome, the U. S. Empire prefers the soft legitimacy of liturgic imagination (NFL), but when necessary, will resort to coercive practices. Take a knee during the national anthem, and you'll end up unemployable! Witness our public ambiguity concerning torture! Closer to home, witness the silencing vigilance of adherents to the totalism in our own communities and congregations!

******

It is important that the regal timeline of the Davidic house in the Books of Kings is not given to us in a royal chronicle. It is rather given to us in a theological commentary that footnotes the royal sources (1 Kgs 11:14; 14:19). That theological commentary is commonly termed "Deuteronomic" because behind it is the book and tradition of Deuteronomy. It is clear that in the final form of the text, the prophetic sequence over the centuries of the royal house in Jerusalem cannot be understood apart from the book and tradition of Deuteronomy, which provides interpretive categories and evokes the imagination of the interpretive community.

The Book of Deuteronomy offers the classic structure of the covenant, through which the prophets can be understood. The defining point is that "Moses" traffics in the defining "if" of Sinai: "Now therefore, if you obey my voice and keep my covenant, you shall be my treasured possession out of all the peoples" (Exod 19:5 NRSV).

The "if" is a statement of conditionality that substantively amends (corrects?) the unconditional promise of YHWH to Abraham, which becomes the grounding of the Davidic covenant. The "if" that permeates Deuteronomy binds future blessings and curses to the obedience or disobedience of the commandments (Deut 30:15–20). Obedience to the Torah determines whether Israel will live long in the land. Conversely, disobedience to the Torah will lead to land loss, the abrogation of the promises, and the disappearance of Israel, which will become absorbed into the Canaanite culture.

Two commandments in particular may be noted in this regard. First, in Deut 17:14–20, the only commandment in the Torah concerning monarchy, the acquisitive capacity of the king is curbed so that he is not free to pursue the accumulation of horses, chariots, gold, silver, or wives—five commodities that occupied the acquisitiveness of the urban establishment of Jerusalem. Second, in Deut 15:1–18, Moses preaches "a year of release," during which debts are cancelled, most particularly debts held against poor people. This tradition is determined to prevent any permanent economic underclass in Israel.

With this general imperative for holiness and justice, the tradition of Deuteronomy asserts that the future wellbeing of Israel does not depend upon wealth (gold and silver), power (horses and chariots), or sexual predation by the powerful, but upon a viable neighborhood that requires inconvenient attentiveness on the part of the powerful—that is, the ones who occupy and benefit from the urban establishment of Jerusalem. Thus, the covenant articulated in Deuteronomy is demandingly counter-intuitive for those who know how to take advantage of commercial dealings. The "if" of Moses is uncompromising.

From that tradition, we have a theological presentation of the royal history of Jerusalem in 1 and 2 Kings from the time of Solomon to the period when the city is destroyed. In his classic study, von Rad observes that this narrative recital of kings is an ongoing contestation between the claims of the royal covenant taken as an unconditional blank check by David and the Torah "if" of Deuteronomy.[2] The narrative constructed according to the royal timeline nevertheless includes particular interruptions of prophetic assertion. In this "if-then" horizon, the future of Jerusalem depends on Torah obedience. Moreover, the writer ends the narrative with the destruction of the city, taken as a vindication of the Deuteronomic claim.

The tradition of Deuteronomy represented by the Torah and Deuteronomic royal history of 1 and 2 Kings together constitute the ground through which the role of prophetic preaching can be understood. The

---

2. von Rad, "Studies in Deuteronomy," 74–91.

royal history presents a *totalism of power, wealth, technology, and imagination*. But the narrative allows for episodic intrusions that *disrupt the totalism*. I shall suggest in what follows that it is the burden of prophetic preaching in ancient Israel to make intrusions into the royal totalism in order to interrupt and subvert the illusion of ultimacy in Jerusalem. I intend to imply that this intrusion continues to be the test of prophetic preaching. The marks of holiness and justice expose the illusion of absolutism in a self-satisfied system of easy self-sufficiency. As a child of Deuteronomy, that is what Jesus does amid the Roman Empire, sustained by Jewish collusion. And it continues to be the test for every instance of contemporary totalism.

******

Because the totalism wants to silence, banish, or eliminate every such unwelcome intrusion, the tricky work is to find standing ground outside the totalism, from which to think the unthinkable, imagine the unimaginable, and utter the unutterable. The proponents of this totalism would have us think that no such possible standing ground exists outside of it, so that the claim of these ancient prophets involves speaking a word that comes from elsewhere without the approval or consent of totalizing authority. It consists of making a claim of authority that will not be contained within the totalism, an authority that dissents from and contradicts the absolutism of the totalism.

Two quite familiar formulae asserting prophetic authority do not seek to receive any endorsement from the totalism. First is the formula, "The word of the Lord came to me." The formula, in fact, explains nothing. Behind the formula is the imaginative, poetic, mythic claim of having been in the very presence of God. The mythic device for this claim is a "divine council," a meeting of the gods over which YHWH, the high God, presides.[3] When the council of gods makes a decision, dispatched messengers—variously angel-messengers, but also human agents who have been in the council—now bring the divine decision to earth. The tradition thus insists that the word spoken by the prophets is not the prophet's own word, but a word given by God outside the totalism. It is from elsewhere! It cannot therefore be dismissed but must be heeded.

3. Miller, "Genesis 1–11," 9–26.

The second formula operates to the same effect: "Hear the word of the Lord." This standard introduction to a prophetic oracle is an assertion that the word to be spoken is not "my word," but a word given by God not from within the totalism and thus not subject to the consent of the totalism. These two formulae, "The word of the Lord came to me" and "Hear the word of the Lord," are elusive assertions that attest to a deeply inexplicable compulsion, albeit a divine compulsion, in which the prophet is called beyond the human self to run great risks, exercise daring boldness, and engage in imagination that finally transcends the person of the prophet. One example involves the German Reformer, Martin Luther, who once cried, "It is not my word!" Thus, he confessed, "I cannot do otherwise." Another is Martin Luther King Jr., who, in his "kitchen experience," reported that God spoke to him, "Martin, do not be afraid."

What else would propel Desmond Tutu to defy the apartheid government with such joy? What else would evoke a readiness in Dan Berrigan to suffer long-term imprisonment? What else would cause any contemporary local preacher to tell the truth about racism or economic inequality? Such utterance is not cost effective, even if it is as cunning and careful as possible. Moreover, that word is always spoken into a resistant totalism that wants to silence it. It was a profound question then as now: Is it possible that there is a word, an utterance not contained within the totalism of power, wealth, imagination, and technology? From this perspective, preaching not from elsewhere, in fact, is religious kitsch that functions, just as Karl Marx said, as an "opiate of the people," a religious exercise safely contained within the comfort zone of the totalism.[4]

******

I will focus on the prophet Jeremiah because I believe his book gives us best access to the issues that concern us in prophetic preaching. Jeremiah appears as an outsider in Jerusalem at a moment of acute crisis—a crisis not unlike our own in which public leadership and public assumptions of chosenness brings huge trouble. I will comment on these matters.

1. The editorial introduction to the Book of Jeremiah is quite remarkable. It locates the words of Jeremiah according to the royal timeline: "It [the word] came in the days of King Josiah son of Amon of

---

4. On "kitsch" as numbing conformity, see Friedlander, *Reflections on Nazism*; Kundera, *Unbearable Lightness of Being*; and "On Kitsch," 338–431.

Judah, in the thirteenth year of his reign. It came also in the days of King Jehoiakim son of Josiah of Judah, and until the end of the eleventh year of King Zedekiah son of Josiah of Judah" (1:2–3). The report alludes to three kings: the father Josiah, the good king; the son Jehoiakim, the evil king; and the brother Zedekiah, a pitiful cowardly figure.

The culmination of the royal timeline is destruction, dislocation, and displacement, which exposes the illusion of particular chosenness. Moreover, the prophet Jeremiah is identified as one belonging to "the priests who were in Anathoth." The reference serves to remind every knowledgeable reader of the episode in 1 Kgs 2:26–27 wherein King Solomon banishes Abiathar, a priest from Anathoth, back to his hometown because he has backed the wrong royal candidate. That means Jeremiah belongs to a four-hundred-year brooding resentment for the way in which his priestly family has been mistreated by the crown. Beyond that, the editor identifies the words that follow in the book in this way: "The words of Jeremiah, son of Hilkiah, of the priests who were in Anathoth in the land of Benjamin, to whom the word of the Lord came."

When we bracket these details, we observe this revelatory formulation: "The words of Jeremiah . . . to whom the word of the Lord came." The phrasing makes an *intimate connection* between the prophetic word and God's word possibly given in the divine council. In the face of that intimacy, however, the phrasing also makes a *clear distinction*. The two are not the same. We are put on notice that we are dealing with the divine word factored out as the human word. The word is given with all the specificity of locale, grudging, and resentment, but linked in an intimate way to a word beyond human words.

1. The situation of Jeremiah is presented in his stylized call narrative. After Jeremiah is summoned by God and resists YHWH as much as he is able, YHWH responds with this mandate: "See, today I appoint you over nations and over kingdoms, to pluck up and to pull down, to destroy and to overthrow, to build and to plant (1:10 NIV).

This assignment permeates the final form of the text of Jeremiah (18:7–9; 24:6; 31:28; 45:4). It charges the prophet to perform acts, not mere utterances, in the conviction that words matter, because words generate reality—which is why words are so dangerous. The mandate consists of two parts: *destruction*, which is described by four words and phrases ("pluck up, tear down, destroy, overthrow"), and *construction*, which is portrayed by two words ("plant" and "build"). Of the four negative verbs, two match the two positive ones; so "pluck up" goes with "plant" as an agricultural image, and "pull down" goes with "build" as an architectural image.[5]

The different uses demonstrate the enormous plasticity of the tradition because these uses serve very different intentions. But they are, taken together, the sum of prophetic preaching. It is the work of honest truth-telling to utter and expose the *termination* of all reality not in sync with God's purpose. It is the work of buoyant hope-telling to utter, anticipate, and imagine the *emergence* of new historical reality being birthed by God. So that you can easily connect this to our preaching task, I provide the following clues:

a) The negative verbs in the New Testament have morphed into *the crucifixion of Jesus*, which exposed the world of Caesar, Herod, and Pilate as a non-world that could not be sustained. The crisis is God's great plucking-up of an illusionary world filled with fear, scarcity, greed, and violence. We have no better articulation of this ongoing work of plucking up and tearing down than the summons of Paul to the divided congregation at Corinth: "God chose what is low and despised in the world, things that are not, to bring to nothing the things that are" (1 Cor 1:28 ESV). Does it take your breath away? This little community—not rich, not powerful, not of noble birth—had as its vocation the nullification of the illusionary world of power, wealth, and nobility.

b) The positive verbs in the mandate to Jeremiah in the New Testament have morphed into *the Easter of Jesus*, which becomes the inexplicable starting point for a new world of peace and justice in which the blind see, the lame walk, the dead are raised, and the poor rejoice. We have no better articulation of that ongoing work of anticipating and welcoming a new life than in the doxological articulation of Paul in his assurance to the congregation

---

5. It is worth noting that Paul, in his affirmation of his ministry, utilizes exactly these two images of restoration: "I planted . . . like a skilled master builder, I laid a foundation (1 Cor 3:6, 10). He asserts to the Christian congregation: "You are God's field [planted], God's building [built]" (v. 9). This coheres with Paul's readiness to allude to Jeremiah.

in Rome: "in the presence of the God in whom we he believed, who gives life to the dead and calls into existence the things that do not exist" (Rom 4:17).

Both the bad news of plucking up and tearing down and the good news of planting and building fall outside totalism. Totalism does not believe it will be plucked up and torn down, nor that there can be real newness. Thus, I propose that in the phrasing of 1:10 (with its reiterations), Jeremiah is a *harbinger of the crucifixion that brings to naught the things that are* and *a harbinger of Easter that calls into existence things that do not exist*. Both acts—"plucking up and tearing down" and "planting and building"—involve the ongoing work of the people of God, and they are the ongoing theme of prophetic preaching. The hard part is that such preaching is located outside totalism while our institutional home base of members, budgets, programs, and pensions is thoroughly located within totalism. It is no wonder that we are all tempted to kitsch.

This poetry has intense specificity. Yet we preachers engage in maximum interpretation. We interpret maximally so that our own exceptionalism of military consumerism powered by scarcity, fear, and greed is deemed as failure. It is not sustainable—not by arms, not by racism, not by rage, not by anything—because God is not mocked. We interpret maximally in order to welcome new planting and building, as God authorizes a new multi-culturalism, ecumenism, and international network of peace and justice. It is all "at hand"! That newness threatens the totalism, which has deployed privilege differently. So it was in ancient Jerusalem. And this Jeremiah, an outsider from Anathoth, dared to say, "The word of the Lord came to me," and "Hear the word of the Lord."

2. What begins with the instantaneous *words of the prophet* become the durable words of the *Book of Jeremiah*. The oracle from the prophet becomes the prophetic scroll through a process of editing. The transposition from oracle to scroll ensures that the utterance of the hard word of the one to whom the word of the Lord came can be transmitted and reheard. This move from word to script is reflected in the remarkable text of Jer 36. We are told that Baruch the scribe wrote on a scroll at Jeremiah's dictation all the words of the Lord that he had spoken to him (36:4).

Baruch wrote it all down. The authorities representing Jerusalem totalism who were astonished by the scroll were also highly suspicious, so they vetted Baruch carefully. Finally, after much care, suspicion, and investigation, they were persuaded of the authenticity and authority of the scroll and took it to the king, Jehoiakim. The king, head of the Jerusalem totalism, did not welcome the scroll. He Immediately recognized the scroll to be a threat. In response, Jehoiakim did two things. First, he ostentatiously shredded the document. "As Jehudi read three or four columns, the king would cut them off with a penknife and throw them into the fire in the brazier, until the entire scroll was consumed in the fire that was in the brazier" (v. 23).

Second, he sent the secret police to apprehend both the prophet and the scribe. He thought to silence the voice from elsewhere that threatened the totalism with its truth-telling, hope-telling alternative. The text laconically reports, "And the king commanded Jerahmeel the king's son and Seraiah son of Azriel and Shelemiah son of Abdeel to arrest the secretary Baruch and the prophet Jeremiah" (v. 26).

The verse adds tersely, "But the Lord hid them." The Lord protected the carriers of his word from elsewhere. We may believe along with biblical scholar Robert Wilson that high officials in the king's own government were sympathetic to the prophet and so alarmed by the king's behavior that they wanted him curbed. Thus, they would have protected both prophet and scribe. Either way, we are told that Jeremiah and Baruch would not quit in fear or be deterred by the power of their totalism: "Then Jeremiah took another scroll and gave it to the secretary Baruch son of Neriah, who wrote on it at Jeremiah's dictation all the words of the scroll that King Jehoiakim, of Judah had burned in the fire; and many similar words were added to them" (v. 32).

This is an amazing account of how prophets submitted to the scribes.[6] The scribes are not prophets! They are the ones who wrote, kept, and interpreted the prophetic text.

I tell you this because I think it is reassuring to us. (I assume that many of you are like me: you do not want or intend to be so daringly prophetic.) The scribal scroll gives us an alternative possibility

---

6. Davies, *Scribes and Schools*.

for faithfulness. We do not need to generate dangerous oracles. It is sufficient, in my judgment, to be interpreters of the scroll we already have in hand and let the people of God have informed access to the scroll.

I cannot tell you how important this is. Given institutional reality, not many of us will be ready or able to be prophetic as was Jeremiah. So if you are like me and do not want to be excessively prophetic, then consider scribal work, which by bold, imaginative interpretation exhibits the alternative that lies outside totalism. It is an alternative to illusionary Jerusalem and military consumerism. But it requires different preaching to help the community of the baptized realize, in contrast to our totalizing culture, that our tradition concerns "bringing to naught the things that are" and "calling into existence things that do not exist." Prophetic preaching is the news that a public zone of wellbeing exists that is not sponsored, managed, or controlled by or limited to the claims of totalism.

******

The reality of the prophetic text preserved in the biblical canon is that it has a future. Scholars term this the *Nachleben* of the text—its afterlife, or continuing influence. The text continues to evoke a stream of counter-interpretation of lived reality. Later texts quote and allude to the old remembered text, resituating it in quite new circumstances where it may speak afresh. No prophet, certainly not Jeremiah, anticipates or aims at such an afterlife for prophetic words. Passionate prophets are intensely fixed on the historical crisis in which they find themselves. But the word is remembered and heeded with continuing pertinence and vitality. Such texts have an afterlife because such truthful words continue to ring true in new contexts.

With the text of Jeremiah, the oracle becomes the scroll and has a powerful afterlife that is quite explicit five times in the Old Testament: in grief over the good king Josiah (2 Chr 35:25), in a continuing judgment on the cowardly king Zedekiah (2 Chr 36:12), and in the anticipated length of the exile (2 Chr 36:21–22, Ezra 1:1, and again in Dan 9:2). His words were found to be continuingly compelling.

In the New Testament, Jeremiah continues to be alive and well. In the Gospel of Matthew, Jeremiah is cited by name three times:

- Most important, in Matt 2:17, Jeremiah's allusion to Rachel weeping over destroyed Jerusalem (31:15) is reiterated as Rachel weeping over the slaughter of the innocents. In this way Jeremiah anticipates the contradiction that the baby Jesus is to the kingdom of Herod: "She refused to be comforted."

- In Matt 16:14, Jeremiah's presence is so palpable in the imagination of this society (or of this evangelist) that Jesus (among others) is considered to be a returned Jeremiah. Tradition judges that it is not yet finished with the powerful voice of Jeremiah.

- In Matt 27:9, Jeremiah is credited with a quote concerning the blood money paid to Judas: "Then was fulfilled what had been spoken through the prophet Jeremiah, 'And they took the thirty pieces of silver, the price of one on whom a pride had been set, on whom some of the people of Israel had set a price, and they gave them for the potter's field, as the Lord had commanded them.'" What interests us is the quote attributed to Jeremiah does not come from Jeremiah, though it may allude to Jer 32:6–15. Some manuscripts have the quote credited to Isaiah or Zechariah, and Richard Hays judges that at best "it only very roughly approximates Zechariah 11:13."[7] Jeremiah, however, is so compelling that he draws the attribution to him.

In all, Hays cites thirty-nine allusions to Jeremiah in the Gospel of Matthew. Among these citations, a great many concern Jeremiah's "temple sermon" (Jer 7), through which Jesus critiques the Jerusalem temple as "a den of robbers." Moreover, great emphasis is placed on the promises of Jer 31 concerning the end of exile. Hays allows that Jeremiah's imagery of the "Torah written on the heart" (31:34) in important ways anticipates Matthew's treatment of the demands of the Torah, with special attention given to the Beatitudes.[8]

******

Beyond the gospel uses, I cite two other elements of the *Nachleben* of Jeremiah in the New Testament. First, in Paul's lyrical rendering of the "theology of the cross," he concludes with this counsel to the Corinthian

---

7. Hays, *Echoes of Scripture*, 159–60.
8. Hays, *Echoes of Scripture*, 120.

congregation: "As it is written, 'Let the one who boasts, boast in the Lord'" (1 Cor 1:31). The words are "written" in Jer 9:23–24 wherein the prophet castigates reliance on wealth, might, and wisdom, instead commending steadfast love, justice, and righteousness. It turns out, in Paul's articulation, that Jeremiah is a voice of the "theology of the cross."[9]

And finally, in Heb 8:8–12, the writer quotes Jeremiah's "new covenant" from 31:31–34. The writer does so in order to assert the "new covenant" in Christ that abrogates the old covenant, but the writer could not do so without referring to Jeremiah. Even if the text borders on supersessionism, it could do so only by the writer's use of this citation.

Now, I have dwelled this long on the *Nachleben* of the prophet's oracles becoming the scroll for two reasons. First, when we preach prophetically, our words have an afterlife. They linger in the ears of the congregation of listeners. That may be to our detriment because we would rather that such words might be forgotten. But they also linger to fuel the imagination of the community so that prophetic possibility continues in force. Thus, such preaching generates a world of imagination stitched together by word, gesture, and image that may resurface in other contexts we little suspect. One never knows, as Jeremiah did not know.

The other reason I comment on *Nachleben* is that such afterlife from a text requires an imaginative alternative interpreter who has the capacity to carry remembered prophetic utterance into new circumstances beyond the horizon of the prophetic speaker. Imagine that! We may be a part of the afterlife of a prophetic text! We may carry remembered cadences of a prophet into new circumstances to permit the prophet to again speak the original "spokenness."

******

All of this is very difficult, as it was then. I am under no illusion about prophetic preaching in local congregations that are most often themselves proponents of totalism. This is surely true of both liberal Christians and conservative Christians. Such prophetic preaching requires deep communion and sly imagination, but finally there is no escape from the vocation of truth-telling and hope-telling. I would not be honest if I did not report that I believe our moment calls for such truth

---

9. For a very different accent on "crucifixion" in Jeremiah, read Robinson, *Cross in the Old Testament*.

and hope. Cathleen Kaveny, in her book, *Prophecy without Contempt*, says this about prophetic preaching:

> Chemotherapy can be dangerous. It kills healthy cells as well as diseased ones. To improve the overall health of the patient, therefore, it must be used accurately and sparingly. The same can be said of the moral chemotherapy of prophetic discourse. More especially, as I argued earlier, the use of prophetic language in a particular context disrupts the normal functioning of a deliberate community. It renders the normal interactions of mutual reason giving impossible because the audience's only avenues of response to prophetic statement are either to acquiesce to the prophet's demands or to engage in what amounts to an ad hominem attack. Prophets, therefore, need to acknowledge and take responsibility for the troublesome side effects of their moral chemotherapy.[10]

Kaveny also notes "ordinary moral language" that is generally acceptable must sometimes be disrupted by "extraordinary forms of moral discourse." It puts the expositor at risk, but is indispensable for the saving of life. So imagine the danger to all parties in such prophetic discourse, a danger to be run only if to counter sickness unto death. Prophets characteristically appear in such a time as our own when sickness to death is seen to be at hand.

I conclude with this word from Ezekiel, who was given a very difficult vocation as God's sentinel. In the tight logic of the God of Ezekiel, it is explained this way to the sentinel:

> Whenever you hear a word from my mouth, you shall give them warning from me. If I say to the wicked, "You shall surely die," and you give them no warning or speak to warn the wicked from their wicked way, in order to save their life, these wicked persons shall die for their iniquity, but their blood I will require at your hand. But if you warn the wicked, and they do not turn from their wickedness, or from their wicked way, they shall die for their iniquity; but you will have saved your life. (Ezek 3:17–19)

The lives of those in God's company are at risk. It ill serves them to withhold from them the word of truth along with the word of hope, which is the word of life.

---

10. Kaveny, *Prophecy without Contempt*, 315.

Bibliography

Davies, Philip R. *Scribes and Schools: The Canonization of the Hebrew Scriptures*. Library of Ancient Israel. Louisville: Westminster John Knox, 1998.
Friedlander, Saul. *Reflections on Nazism: An Essay on Kitsch and Death*. Bloomington: Indiana University Press, 1993.
Hays, Richard B. *Echoes of Scripture in the Gospels*. Waco: Baylor University Press, 2016.
Kaveny, Cathleen. *Prophecy without Contempt: Religious Discourse in the Public Square*. Cambridge: Harvard University Press, 2016.
Kundera, Milan. *The Unbearable Lightness of Being*. New York: Harper Perennial, 2009.
Lifton, Robert Jay. *Witness to an Extreme Century: A Memoir*. New York: Free, 2011.
Miller, Patrick D. "Genesis 1–11: Studies in Structure & Theme." *Journal for the Study of the Old Testament* Supp. 8 (1978) 9–26.
"On Kitsch," *Salmagundi Magazine: The Symposium* 2, no. 50 (Summer 2015) 338–431.
Robinson, H. Wheeler. *The Cross in the Old Testament*. Philadelphia: Westminster, 1955.
von Rad, Gerhard. "Studies in Deuteronomy." SBT 9 (1953) 74–91.

Chapter Two

The Preaching of Jesus

Thomas G. Long

The Gospel of Mark introduces the public ministry of Jesus with great drama. Only a few verses in, the drumbeat of decisive events begins to sound loudly, steadily, and rapidly. Abruptly, John appears in the wilderness dressed like old Elijah and thundering a call to baptism and repentance. Quickly, he baptizes Jesus in the Jordan, and the Spirit descends upon Him like a dove. Immediately, that same Spirit drives Jesus deep into the wilderness to be tested by Satan, and shockingly John is felled like an oak when he is arrested by Herod. Then Mark writes, "Now after John was arrested, Jesus came to Galilee, proclaiming the good news of God."

As George Buttrick observed in his 1931 Lyman Beecher lectures, *Jesus Came Preaching*, Jesus could have come as a writer, but instead He entrusted "His most precious sayings to the blemished reputation and the precarious memory of His friends." He could have come as a scribe. Many "had traced on papyri their interpretations of the Law." But no, Jesus came *preaching*, said Buttrick, and His spoken word "was sharp to pierce where the written word would have made no mark. The Gospel was and is a living impact."[1]

Mark's description turns out to be more than an announcement that Jesus was a preacher who began His ministry with a sermon. It is also a programmatic statement of the character and content of His preaching.

---

1. Buttrick, *Jesus Came Preaching*, 16–17.

Distilled to the essence, the sermons Jesus preached said, "The time is fulfilled, and the kingdom of God has come near; repent, and believe in the good news."

What Mark's description of Jesus' preaching does first of all is to clarify that it was an event. Jesus does not emerge from the wilderness with a novel insight, but with an announcement. Something momentous has happened and is still happening—the time is now, the kingdom has drawn near—and the emphasis in Mark is not on the new ideas of Jesus' preaching but on the event of the kingdom to which He gives voice, the event of God's in-breaking to which His preaching pointed. As Richard J. Dillon, writing in the *Catholic Biblical Quarterly*, said, here in Mark, the "'gospel' is a *nomen actionis*,"[2] a noun of action. Interestingly, this effectively thwarts all attempts to say in abstracted, compressed, and logical form exactly what Jesus' message was. We have books on the philosophy of Hegel and Kant, and the thought of Descartes and Nussbaum, but, even though some have tried (even with silly results, like *Jesus the CEO* or *Jesus the Entrepreneur*), it doesn't quite work to imagine a book on "the philosophy of Jesus."

Richard Lischer has pointed out that when Martin Luther King Jr.'s sermons were published as the book, *The Strength to Love*, the local and time-bound references were edited out and the sermons polished to make King sound like a popular philosopher and to be read "as timeless masterpieces of the pulpit." Gone were the cadences of "the African-Baptist gospel in which King was nurtured." Gone was "the prophetic rage that often seized him." Gone was the context of a social order at the breaking point, and gone was King's passionate conviction that God was at this moment marching across the land and surely doing a new thing in our very beholding. In short, what was gone was King as a gospel preacher, along with all the things that made his preaching urgent and powerful. As Lischer observes, "In their printed form, [King's sermons] are scarcely distinguishable from the liberal commonplaces of the white, mainline pulpit in the Eisenhower era."[3]

Just so, we could lift all the red words out of our red-letter New Testaments, assemble them as "the sermons of Jesus," and yet lose the connection to the event of God that propelled those words and gave them power. Ask people what Jesus taught and preached, and they recall

---

2. Dillon, "Mark 1:1–15," 12.
3. Lischer, *Preacher King*, 4.

memorable phrases—"Love your enemies," "Judge not that you be not judged," "Come unto Me all you who labor and are heavy burdened," and so on—but the attempt to summarize Jesus' preaching as a system of thought or set of ethical wisdom sayings domesticates both Jesus and His preaching. Jesus was not merely a sage making astute observations about life. He was a weather forecaster announcing the impending arrival of a category-5 hurricane, a prophet proclaiming and embodying the in-breaking of the very reign of God.

As Mark put it, Jesus essentially came preaching, "The *kairos* is at the bursting point.... Something is happening.... The pregnancy has come full term.... Her water has broken.... Everything is changed and new.... Act now."

In *The Message in the Bottle*, Walker Percy imagined a group of scientists, philosophers, and artists gathered at a conference in Aspen, Colorado, to read learned papers to each other. Percy said, "[I]f during the meeting a fire should break out, and if then a man should mount the podium and utter the sentence, 'Come, I know the way out!'—the conferees will be able to distinguish at once the difference between this sentence and all the other sentences which have been uttered from the podium.[4] The others are information, this is *news*.

Just so, Jesus came into Galilee with news, and any sermon that follows in the stream of the preaching of Jesus should be newsworthy. There is *news* in the "good news." One test of a Christian sermon is whether it has the character of breaking news: God is doing something in our midst, the time is now, the event of God is imminent, and because of this everything has changed, so repent and believe in this news. When we preach a biblical text, the primary goal is not to *explain* the text, but to *proclaim* it. Or, perhaps we could say even say *exclaim* it. We do not look back at the text to find information to relay; instead, we look through the text to see God at work in the world and exclaim what we see.

We also note that Mark's statement about Jesus' preaching is bookended and framed before and after by the word *euangellion* (the gospel; the good news). What Jesus preaches is the *euangellion*, and what He calls those who hear Him to believe is the *euangellion*. But what is the *euangellion*, "the gospel"? In a seminal article on the introduction to Mark's Gospel, Leander Keck, building on the exegetical work of Julius Schniewind, notes that by far the most common usage in the Hellenistic

---

4. Percy, *Message in the Bottle*, 138.

world of words that share the root of *euangellion* "is associated with news of victory,"[5] news from the battlefield or from the world of political contest. Keck goes on to argue that this understanding of *euangellion* as news of battle victory is a consistent theological theme in the beginning of Mark's Gospel.

John the Baptist preaches in the wilderness that the one coming after him is the strong one, "more powerful than I." After His baptism, this strong one (Jesus) is tested by Satan, but in Mark, says Keck, not tested in the sense of moral temptation, but that of combat. The Spirit drives Jesus into the wilderness to take on the Evil One. "Mark's Jesus," says Keck, "is the victorious Son of God who returns from the testing-ground with the *euangellion*." He walks out of the wilderness and into Galilee and preaches the good news of victory: "The time has come at last. The power of sin and death has been vanquished, so turn around and trust this good news."

Some years ago, I was at the Montreat Conference Center in the mountains of North Carolina speaking at a congregational retreat. Saturday afternoon was free time, and, as one of the optional activities, the church had rented a small bus for anyone who wished to take a sightseeing trip along the Blue Ridge. It was a beautiful fall day at the peak of leaf season, so I signed up for the ride.

When I boarded the bus, most of the seats were filled with couples, but I noticed a man sitting near the back by himself whom I had not yet met, so I slipped into the seat beside him and greeted him. We chatted pleasantly, but we were not far down the highway when the tone of the conversation changed. The man looked me straight in the eye with a strange intensity and suddenly offered up this personal revelation: "I used to be an evangelist," he said. I nodded. "Yes, I was an evangelist." His voice began to rise. "I preached at many meetings and revivals all through these hills." I was beginning to have second thoughts about my choice of seats when the man added, "But I stopped preaching." When I asked why, he said, "Because I discovered I wasn't preaching the gospel. I was telling people that they had to believe this and they had to believe that in order to be saved. But I discovered that's not the gospel. I finally found out that the gospel is the good news that, hey, we don't have to live this way anymore."

---

5. Keck, "Introduction to Mark's Gospel," 361.

In his own way, he was saying what Mark said. The gospel is indeed good news from the battlefield. The power of sin and death has been defeated. Its lies have been exposed. Its grip has been broken. The death camp has been liberated and doesn't have to live in slavery to the power of death anymore.

This is what is gathered up in the word "repent." Jesus says, "Repent and believe the *euangellion*." We could say that the goal of preaching—Jesus' preaching and ours—is to enable people to repent and believe. But here, repentance is stronger than simply feeling remorseful for one's sinfulness and pledging to do better in the future. Repentance is more like a change of citizenship. Indeed, Jesus' call to repentance is not a demand but an invitation to leave the laws and customs and oppressions of the old land behind, instead embracing the ways and enjoying the liberation of the new land.

Theologian Arthur C. McGill once reminded preachers that moralistic preaching is bad not simply because it's bad theology but primarily because it's a stupid strategy. It doesn't do any good, McGill said, to stand in the pulpit and attack selfishness or exhort people to get to work helping others. If we live, as comedian Bill Hicks once put it, in the "United States of Advertising," if we are permanent citizens of a dominion where all that we have is commodified, where those not like us are by definition our enemies, where words cannot be trusted because they are so often twisted into lies, where even those close to us are finally threats to our abundance, and death is holding a ticking stopwatch as the lord of time, then being unselfish and serving others would be downright foolish. McGill writes,

> [W]hether people serve themselves or serve others is not in their power to choose. This is decided wholly in terms of the kind of world in which they think they live, in terms of the kind of power they see ruling the roost. The issue lies at the level of the god they worship and not in the kind of person they may want to be. In New Testament terms, they live or die according to the king that holds them and the kingdom to which they belong.[6]

And so, Jesus comes into Galilee with good news to preach. "I have been out in the wilderness going toe-to-toe with the power of this world, kingdom versus kingdom," He announces, "and I have good news. The kingdom of death you believed would hold you forever in its grip has

---

6. McGill, *Suffering*, 92.

been destroyed, and a new kingdom has come near. Pick up your green card, change your citizenship, and live in its freedom and joy. You don't have to live this way anymore."

In the ancient church, the ceremony of the mystery of baptism was a piece of liturgical theater that could be understood as an enactment of Mark's description of Jesus' preaching. In a beautiful catechetical sermon from the fourth century, the old bishop Theodore of Mopsuestia told those who were about to be baptized what was going to happen to them. He said,

> You will kneel on the floor, and you will face the West, the region of evil and darkness, and you will point your finger at the accuser, and you will say, "Satan, I renounce you and all your vanities, and all your angels and all your ministries." Then you will face the East, and you will find that the Bishop is in new clothes which are resplendent and dazzling with light, a symbol of a new world which you are entering. They dazzle because you will shine in that world. They are graceful and delightful for you will be graceful and delightful.

And Jesus came into Galilee preaching, "Good news, the old kingdom of Satan has been destroyed! Turn around and live in the resplendent and dazzling gift of God's life."

When we think of the preaching of Jesus, we also think of the most prominent form it took—namely, the parables. Mark, who introduced us to Jesus the preacher, says later, "With many . . . parables he spoke the word to them; he did not speak to them except in parables" (4:33-34). That is hyperbole, of course—Jesus preached in other forms, too—but we get the point: Jesus' preaching, whether it was parable or beatitude, proverb or story, had a parabolic imagination, intent, and flavor. John Dominic Crossan has even argued that in the parables we find the shape of Jesus's own faith, His own experience of God. For Crossan, Jesus' ministry was not a message and a set of deeds that He illustrated and explained with parables. It was the other way around: "[T]he parables are cause and not effect of Jesus' other words and deeds. They are not what Joachim Jeremias called 'weapons of warfare'; they are the cause of the war and the manifesto of its inception."[7]

It is an overstatement, but not one without merit, when Crossan claims that Jesus was not crucified because He preached in parables, but

---

7. Crossan, *In Parables*, 32.

because He believed parabolically and the experience of the God presented in the parables caused Him to act in ways that *did* get Him crucified.[8]

It is not easy to say what a biblical parable is. The word "parable," along with the Hebrew *mashal* before it, represents a multi-faceted literary constellation, an actual cluster of genres, so "parable" can be and mean a lot of things. But "riddle" is not a bad partial definition. Parables are riddles, not so much in the sense of puzzles to be solved, but in the sense that they require angular vision and a change of perspective to see one's way through. The humorist Calvin Trillin once said that he failed high school math because his teacher never understood that he meant his answers ironically. And when Jesus comes preaching in parables, He is addressing a world where 2+2 = 4 pretty much seems to say all that can be known, but He is asking us to rather look at it from a new and odd angle of vision.

From time to time over the years, I have taught a course on "Preaching the Parables of Jesus." The course always begins with bold claims and ambitious goals, namely that the parables are the nuclear reactor of Jesus' own preaching. The parables Jesus preached turned the world upside down, so the aim of the course is to express that power anew in our preaching. And then, of course, the students and I create sermons about those parables that are pretty much the same as all the other sermons we craft—no worse, but no better; no more revolutionary or powerful. Part of this is to be expected. No sermon fully taps the power of the text from which it is drawn. But I have come to believe that some of the lack of power in these sermons on parables comes from a flaw in our understanding of Jesus' parabolic preaching.

It is perhaps unfair, but I am going to point the finger of accusation at Adolf Jülicher, who, in the late nineteenth century wrote a massive and highly influential two-volume work on the parables. He argued in meticulous detail that the church had misunderstood Jesus' parables by distorting them as allegories, when in fact the parables were similes, simple side-by-side comparisons—"the kingdom of heaven is *like* . . ."—each intending to convey one broad moral point.

Parables research has moved on from Jülicher, partly because an interest in metaphor has now replaced the focus on simile as well as the opinion that Jülicher's own interpretation of Jesus' parables was so insipid. "Wise use of the present is the condition of a happy future" is what

---

8. Crossan, *In Parables*, 32.

Jülicher found to be the moral of the unjust steward, and "A reward is only earned by performing well" is what the parable of the talents is all about.[9] People who say things like this do not get crucified; instead, they only get tenure.

But what Jülicher set in motion was a fascination in the world of parables study with the literary form of Jesus' parables, as if we could release the power of a parable by discovering how the springs and levers of the literary form work. So, for Norman Perrin, a parable is a simile or a metaphor referencing a tensive symbol called "the kingdom of God . . . a symbol of cultural range, a symbol having meaning for people in cultural continuity with ancient Israel and its myth of God acting as king."[10] For Bernard Brandon Scott, a parable is "a short narrative fiction [referencing] a transcendent symbol."[11] And, of course, there is the famous definition of C. H. Dodd, "[A] parable is a metaphor or simile drawn from nature or common life, arresting the hearer by its vividness or strangeness, and leaving the mind in sufficient doubt about its precise application to tease it into active thought."[12]

So, in the view of these literary-oriented critics, the parable as literary device either teases the mind to thought or references a tensive symbol, "the kingdom of God," which functions in some settings like the tensive symbol "the American dream" functions in our culture, giving structure, hope, and meaning. And what made Jesus a radical preacher were the ways that His parables undermined conventional understandings of this commonly held symbol. But what tends to get washed out (or at least reduced) when parables are seen as metaphors referencing a symbol—no matter how rich—is the very fact for Jesus that the kingdom of God is not a symbol but an *event*. God was, is, and will be doing something by breaking into our assumed reality, and the parables position us toward experiencing this advent. This brings us full circle back around to Mark's introduction: "The time is full to the bursting, the kingdom is at hand."

The kingdom breaks in like a thief in the night, and what Jesus' preaching in parables does is orient us toward those events of in-breaking by heightening our expectation for them, sharpening our perception of

9. See the discussion of Jülicher's interpretation in Jeremias, *Parables of Jesus*, 18–19.
10. Perrin, *Jesus and the Language*.
11. Scott, *Hear Then the Parable*, 8.
12. Dodd, *Parables of the Kingdom*, 5.

what the kingdom is like when it is revealed, and deepening our participation in it. In other words, the power in Jesus' parables is not in their literary form alone but primarily in the kingdom of God, in the event of God's life breaking over us, to which they point and in which they participate.

In his provocative book, *The Difference Heaven Makes,* theologian Christopher Morse surveys the use of the term "heaven" in the New Testament. The "most prominent" use of heavenly language, reports Morse, is not some place where we go when we die but the realm from which God comes to us. God speaks from heaven, acts from heaven, and gives manna from heaven. Heaven is that realm from which God's *basilea,* God's kingdom, comes to us.[13] God's life is constantly adventing into our lives, like waves breaking on the beach. God's life, says Morse, is always at hand, but not in hand. This is not about human potential or secular progress. In sum, Morse says, those who hear the preaching of Jesus are "called to be *on* hand for that which is *at* hand, but not *in* hand."[14] Or, as Jesus put it, "The time is ripe, and the kingdom of God is at hand; repent, and believe in the good news."

New Testament scholar Mary Ann Tolbert has observed that even though many translations of Mark 1:15 render the verbs in the present tense ("the time *is fulfilled,* the kingdom *is at hand*"), both verbs are actually in the perfect tense, indicating action "already well in process and on the verge of completion." At first, Tolbert says this verbal usage "casts an atmosphere of urgency over everything . . . the time is already almost past."[15] But then, Tolbert's language breaks into an unexpected theological confession when she says, "Mark's narrative has no time; all is rushing toward imminent conclusion." What a phrase!

Jesus' preaching voice was urgent. "The time is ripe," he preached, because the kingdom of God was breaking in, which is beyond all time. It gathers up and affirms our faithful memory, but it is not a creature of the past. It revolutionizes the present—everything is changed!—but it is not a creature of the present. It opens up a new and glorious future, but it is more than a promise of better things to come. It is Easter time, eternity, intruding into history. It is God's great Sabbath rest coming as a gift into the restless march of time.

---

13. Morse, *Difference Heaven Makes,* 10, 21.
14. Morse, *Difference Heaven Makes,* 122.
15. Tolbert, *Sowing the Gospel,* 117.

The poet and Yale professor Christian Wiman has been battling a rare form of cancer for several years. In an essay in *The American Scholar*, he describes a summer he and his family spent in Seattle as he rested from a recent bone marrow transplant. He writes,

> Time had a texture that summer, an hourly reality that we could taste and see.... We had the same nightly ritual that we do now. I'd read to [our little girls, who were two years old then] and tuck them in before my wife took over, and the last thing I'd say every night was "I love you," and they would always reply promptly, "I love you too, Daddy."
>
> But one night after my declaration, Fiona was silent. She just kept staring at the ceiling.
>
> "Do you love me too, Fiona?" I asked, foolishly.
>
> A long moment passed.
>
> "No, Daddy, I don't."
>
> "Oh, Fiona sweetie, I bet you do," I said.
>
> Nothing.
>
> "Well," I said finally, "I love you, Finn, and I'll see you in the morning."
>
> And then as I started to get up, I felt her small hand on my arm and she said dreamily, without looking at me, like a little Lauren Bacall, "I will love you in the summertime, Daddy. I will love you ... in the summertime."
>
> I have told this to a couple of people who thought it was heartbreaking, but I was so proud, I thought my heart would burst. I will love you in the summertime. What a piercing poetic thing to say—at two years old. And for weeks I thought about it.... I will love you in the summertime. Which is to say, given the charmed life we were living there in Seattle and all the grace and grief that my wife and I felt ourselves moving through at every second: I will love you in the time where there is time for everything, which is now and always. I will love you in the time when time is no more.
>
> Now, do I think that's what my Athena-eyed and mysteriously interior two-year-old daughter meant by that expression? No, I do not. But do I think that sometimes life and language break each other open to change, that a rupture in one can be a rapture in the other, that sometimes there are, as it were, words underneath the words—even the very Word underneath the words? Yes, I do.[16]

---

16. Wiman, "I Will Love You," 50–58.

Note the key thought here: "Sometimes life and language break each other open to change, that a rupture in one can be a rapture in the other." And Jesus came into Galilee, preaching, "God's time is full to the bursting; God's life is breaking over us like the dawn. Don't miss it! Turn around. Don't miss it! Turn toward the light and open yourself to the gift of shalom!"

Hearing this, we can turn and trust, living now as citizens of a new land who refuse to obey the lies of death, citizens of a new land who can sing that timeless hymn, "The kingdoms of this world have become the kingdoms of our Lord and his Messiah, and He will reign forever and ever" (Rev 11:15).

Bibliography

Buttrick, George A. *Jesus Came Preaching*. New York: Charles Scribner's Sons, 1931.

Crossan, John Dominic. *In Parables: The Challenge of the Historical Jesus*. New York: Harper and Row, 1973.

Dillon, Richard J. "Mark 1:1–15: A 'New Evangelization'?" *The Catholic Biblical Quarterly* 76/1 (January 2014).

Dodd, C. H. *The Parables of the Kingdom*. New York: Charles Scribner's Sons, 1961.

Jeremias, Joachim. *The Parables of Jesus*. Rev. ed. New York: Charles Scribner's Sons, 1963.

Keck, Leander E. "The Introduction to Mark's Gospel." *New Testament Studies* 12 (1966) 361.

Lischer, Richard. *The Preacher King: Martin Luther King, Jr. and the Word that Moved America*. New York: Oxford, 1995.

McGill, Arthur C. *Suffering: A Test of Theological Method*. Philadelphia: Westminster Press, 1978.

Morse, Christopher. *The Difference Heaven Makes: Rehearing the Gospel as News*. New York: T. & T. Clark, 2010.

Percy, Walker. *The Message in the Bottle: How Queer Man Is, How Queer Language Is, and What One Has to Do with the Other*. New York: Picador, 2000.

Perrin, Norman. *Jesus and the Language of the Kingdom: Symbol and Metaphor in New Testament Interpretation*. Philadelphia: Fortress, 1976.

Scott, Bernard Brandon. *Hear Then the Parable: A Commentary on the Parables of Jesus*. Minneapolis: Fortress, 1989.

Tolbert, Mary Ann. *Sowing the Gospel: Mark's World in Literary-Historical Perspective*. Minneapolis: Fortress, 1996.

Wiman, Christian. "I Will Love You in the Summertime." *The American Scholar* (Spring 2016) 50–58.

Chapter Three

Paul the Preacher and Preaching Paul
The Rhetoric and the Reality

BEN WITHERINGTON III

WHEN ASKED TO PRODUCE an essay on "the significance of the preaching of Paul," a cynic might well say, "It will be a short essay—we do not have the preaching of Paul in the New Testament or elsewhere." On the surface of things, it might seem that the cynic is right, for though there is an appalling amount of Paul in the New Testament (thirteen of the twenty-seven New Testament documents are attributed to Paul, and a good half or more of Acts is also about Paul), what we *appear* to have are 1) letters by Paul; and 2) Lucan summaries of Pauline preaching beginning in Acts 13 and continuing on to the end of Acts.

But things are not in fact as bleak as that, for 1) Paul's letters, framed by an epistolary prescript and postscript, actually are *oral* discourses he would have given in person had he been present with his converts; and 2) there is a good likelihood that Luke's summaries of Paul's preaching reflect knowledge of his actual preaching, especially if Luke was a sometime companion of Paul on his second and third missionary journeys.

Certainly, all we have in Acts are rhetorically apt outlines of the preaching from Luke's hand, not full sermons. Eutychus never fell asleep and fell out of a second-story window because Paul preached a five-minute sermon, which is the length of time it takes to read even the longest sermon summary of Paul's in Acts (Acts 13). What then should we think about Pauline preaching and its significance?

In the ancient art of public communication—sometimes called the art of persuasion, and otherwise known as rhetoric—three major areas were attended to in any effective public speech: *ethos, logos,* and *pathos.* Ethos had to do with all things visible—how one spoke, how one looked, how one gestured, and how one held his posture. When an older rhetorician was once speaking in Athens and a wind blew off his hairpiece, it was said that he was having a bad "ethos" day. Ancient rhetoricians knew that for many (if not most) audiences, how one came across, how one looked, how one sounded, and whether one's voice was pleasing or grating mattered. It affected whether one's message would be well received or poorly received.

It still matters today in most cases because the computer age is also the age of visual learners and how things "appear" matter, but you wouldn't know it from the way some preachers act these days. They come into church looking like something the cat dragged in, and thinking, *This is how to show my congregation I'm a man of the people.*

Now, Paul had an ethos problem. The Corinthians brought this up in the context of his discourses with them. Second Corinthians 10:10 says, "Someone says that on the one hand his letters are heavy and strong, but on the other hand the *parousia* (presence) of his body is weak, and his *logos* (word) is contemptible/ineffective." There is a lot here to unpack, and it is relevant not only regarding how we evaluate Paul the preacher, but our own efforts at homiletics as well.

Something about Paul's personal appearance affected the way some people received his oral performance, and something was also not quite right about the way Paul talked. If the Corinthians had been the judges at the speech competitions at the Isthmian games, and had Paul been a contestant, someone would have held up a card that said "2.5 and he can't dance"—not a passing grade.

But what was Paul's *ethos* problem? I would suggest that if we had been paying closer attention to his letters, we would not be scratching our heads about this. Galatians 4:12–16 is quite revealing if you know how to read the signals. The most important remark is, "If you could have done so, you would have plucked out your eyes and given them to me." Now, this cannot be a *random* remark. It means that when Paul reached the Galatians, they noticed he had eye problems. Indeed, as verse 13 indicates, he had a disease or illness that inflicted him. We are not sure what that means, but let's focus on what we do know.

The eyes, in Paul's world, were viewed as the windows on the soul. Unlike moderns, the ancients believed that the eyes projected light or darkness; they were not merely light receptors. There was the "evil eye" convention in the ancient world, such that if a malicious and powerful someone looked at you with malicious intent—you might be cursed. And the way you would avoid that was by turning and spitting. This is interesting because Paul says plainly, "Even though my illness was a trial to you, you did not treat me with contempt, nor did you spit." Again, this is not a random remark. Paul is saying that *despite* his physical issues and how his eyes appeared—presumably, they were oozing—the Galatians treated him as if he were an angel, a messenger sent straight from God.[1]

Now, other passages in Paul suggest that he had such a condition:

1. The story of his conversion tells us he was blinded, and later he regained some sight. We are not told if his previous condition recurred. Perhaps he had a chronic eye condition from then on and had trouble seeing.

2. Although Paul was literate, he used scribes like Tertius, mentioned in Rom 16:22.

3. At the end of Galatians and elsewhere, he says things like "See with what large letters I write my name." What kind of person needs large letters or a large print edition? A poorly sighted person.

4. Second Corinthians 12 refers to his ongoing thorn in the flesh, which God did not remove, but clearly it was not something that prevented his traveling and preaching and teaching.

---

1. The famous second-century physical description of the appearance of Paul, in the Acts of Paul and Thecla, may provide a fragment of historical information about how Paul looked, but there is reason to hesitate on that score because such descriptions were often meant to suggest something more about the *character* of the person than how he looked. For example, a description of a large forehead suggested that the person had wisdom (not just mere intelligence) in the ancient world. What is far clearer from Paul's letters themselves (Gal 6; 2 Cor 10–12) is that Paul's body bore the marks of abuse, of his being beaten various times, which is probably what he is referring to when he speaks about bearing the "stigmata" of Christ in Galatians. More interesting is the painted image in the cave above ancient Ephesus where the second- or third-century church seems to have met, which has an image of Paul and Thecla, and there Paul is portrayed as an itinerant preacher in typical garb, and with eyes wide open.

5. Why would Luke the physician undertake to travel with Paul so extensively on his third missionary journey as well as some on his second one? Perhaps because Paul needed help with his condition. Notice that in the Pastorals we read at one juncture, "Luke alone is with me."

I bring all this to your attention to clarify that *appearance obviously mattered then, and it matters now. Ethos* must be attended to, and Paul knew it.

Second, we learn from this salient passage in 2 Corinthians that the Corinthians whined about Paul's speech. Note that this is not a complaint about whether he was using rhetoric or not. They simply did not like the way he *sounded*—whether because he pronounced Greek in what sounded like a peculiar Eastern-end-of-the-Empire manner, or whether his voice was just not melodious in general. Public speakers like Paul were judged not just on content but also very definitely on form, and I would say to modern preachers as well—*form matters*. Sometimes, whether you persuade someone to believe or behave differently depends on whether you sound convincing to them, as opposed to comical, stupid, or banal. Paul's critics said he sounded "ineffective" or even "despicable."

What about the contrast between the weightiness of Paul's letters and his in-person presentation? Here, the Corinthians had evaluated Paul's letters highly. The issue with his in-person presentations is not that they were lightweight compared to the heavyweight letters. Nor was the issue that Paul preached simply and wrote doctoral level dissertations in his letters. Some have mistakenly taken Paul's remark that he resolved to know nothing but "Christ and him crucified when he came to them" to mean that he would abandon rhetoric and stick to the basic plain, unvarnished presentation of the gospel. Since when is proclaiming Christ and Him crucified a simple or lightweight matter?

Paul is not talking about "form" in that remark, but *content*. The Corinthians needed to hear more about the cross and less about their own wonderful spiritual gifts. What Paul is critiquing there is *mere sophistry*—"words full of sound and fury but signifying nothing." He is indeed criticizing mere verbal eloquence or pyrotechnics, something the Corinthians seem to have been enamored with ever since the beginning of the Second Sophistic before the turn of the era.[2] They had a taste for highly ornamental rhetorical performances, rather like the way Benjamin Franklin was impressed by George Whitefield's oratorical flourishes.[3]

As his letters show, Paul knew the conventions of Greco-Roman rhetoric very well, and he used orally and in writing. In an ancient act of persuasion, one first attended to the issues of *ethos*. If the speaker had an ethos problem, it gave him all the more reason to find some way to make the audience receptive to what he was going to say after the preliminary remarks. This is called *establishing ethos,* and today we might call it "sucking up" to the audience.

The way Paul does that at the outset of a letter is to establish rapport with the audience by saying he is praying for them and always thanking God for them. There is some irony in this. For example, in 1 Cor 1, the apostle says he is thankful for the Corinthians' many spiritual gifts, even though later in the letter he will be dealing with the problems of how the Corinthians are misusing their gifts. If you haven't established some kind of rapport with your audience in the first few minutes of your preaching, you shouldn't expect to hold their attention for long thereafter—especially not in the modern sound-bite and Twitter age. People's attention spans in antiquity seem to have been far longer than they are today.

It was also the task of the persuader to clarify up front his basic issue or thesis (e.g., Rom 1:16-17) the arguments that follow in the discourse are meant to support. So, after the introductory *exordium,* one turns to the issues of *logos.* Make no mistake, Paul believes proclamation that persuades involves the presentation of a theme or thesis, and then arguments

---

2. On this, one should read at length B. W. Winter's fine study *Philo and Paul among the Sophists.* Serious rhetoricians in Paul's age were always conscious of wanting to distinguish themselves from the entertainers who specialized in mere verbal eloquence.

3. Franklin's assessment of Whitefield and his oratory is readily found on the Internet (http://nationalhumanitiescenter.org/pds/becomingamer/ideas/text2/franklinwhitefield.pdf). Notice it includes sentences like, "He had a loud and clear Voice, and articulated his Words and Sentences so perfectly that he might be heard and understood at a great Distance, especially as his Auditors [audience], however numerous, observ'd the most exact Silence. . . . His Delivery of the latter was so improv'd by frequent Repetitions that every Accent, every Emphasis, every Modulation of Voice, was so perfectly well turn'd and well plac'd, that without being interested in the Subject, one could not help being pleas'd with the Discourse, a Pleasure of much the same kind with that receiv'd from an excellent Piece of Music." In short, Franklin's assessment of Whitefield's rhetoric is just the opposite of the effect Paul's *ethos* had on the Corinthians.

for the thesis, followed by arguments removing objections to the thesis. Usually the positive arguments come first, ending with an emotional peroration.

Some modern preachers simply do not understand that it is their job to *convince* the audience of the importance of this or that theme, task, or form of behavior. They think all they need to do is explain what the Bible says, and then *presto*—the congregation will act upon it. Paul knew this was not the case. People need to be convicted, convinced, and converted to the preacher's point of view. And though yes, this is partly the Holy Spirit's job, to judge from Paul's letters, it is also the preacher's job.

Let me reiterate that Paul's letters are surrogates for his oral discourse. They embody what Paul *would have said* in person if he could have been present with the audience addressed in the letter. These are *oral texts*, meant to be heard in their original language, and were surely read aloud *in toto* by someone already familiar with the content of the letter, so that the letter could be presented in a convincing manner that might persuade the audience to change their beliefs or behaviors.

Orality was primary in a world where less than 20 percent of the populace was genuinely literate. Discourses like those we have in Paul's letters were composed primarily *for the ear*, not for the eye. There is a reason why Jesus said, "Let those with two good ears, hear." Far more people could hear than see and read and understand. Since early Christianity was perhaps the only aggressively evangelistic religion on the playing field in the Greco-Roman world, it gave the speaker all the more reason to make his discourse rhetorically acceptable and accessible to as large an audience as possible. How else but by speaking was one going to rescue the perishing, who exhibited all sorts of educational levels and backgrounds? Listening to rhetorically informed speeches was one of the main forms of education, as well as entertainment, in the ancient world.

It should be equally clear that what may persuade one audience may have been completely unconvincing to another one. The speaker has to know his audience if he wants his word to be on target for that particular group of people. Paul knew his people, and it is no accident that his letters are each so different, depending on the audience, situation, problems addressed and a host of other factors. People who trot out old, musty sermons from their sermon barrel, thinking that just any word will do as long as it's biblical, have not learned their lessons from Paul the preacher.

The bulk of any discourse in ancient times consisted of the arguments for one's thesis or case. It was *not* mainly a collection of Bartlett's familiar quotations, illustrations, or stories; rather, it was an exercise in logic and argumentation. Paul knew perfectly well the danger of having a bunch of half-converted Christians, or put another way, immature Christians. So, one's level of discourse needed to match or only slightly exceed the level of maturity and experience of the audience. Yes, by all means, tease their mind into active thought and make their reach extend farther than their grasp. But your job is not to befuddle them with your erudition, nor on the other hand should you insult your audience's intelligence by dumbing everything down.

Paul's preaching and teaching was always challenging, but never merely an example of showing off his education. Much of Paul's *logoi* (which, in a rhetorical context, means "proofs," arguments that prove something) were so heavy and argumentative in character that sometimes he even resorted to the ancient diatribe technique in which a speaker invents an imaginary interlocutor or debate partner, as he does in the sentence quoted earlier from 2 Cor 10: "Someone will say . . ." to which Paul replied with vigor, and at length in the discourse itself. Paul was not the kind of preacher who adopted as his motto, "When in doubt, chicken out. Avoid controversy and debate at all costs."

The third major factor after *ethos* and *logos* that needed attending to in every single act of proclamation was *pathos*, the appeal to the emotions. Paul lived in a highly emotional context, and people frankly were quite used to lengthy emotional harangues attempting to persuade them regarding one thing or another. In our context, some of this will sound like pure manipulation or inappropriate arm-twisting.

Paul and his audience were at the other end of the spectrum from twenty-first century British discourse in which one might hear: "If it's not too much trouble, it would be good if *perhaps* one began to behave a bit better than one used to behave, for instance, by leaving your adulteries behind." No, Paul had no problems appealing to the emotions. At the end of any normal discourse, his job was appealing to the deeper emotions— love or hate, fear or trust, compassion or jealousy, justice or mercy, and so on.

In order to preach like Paul today, the preacher needs to know the emotional temperature of his own audience, and just as important, how different it might be from that of Paul's own audience. Let us study the example of the New Testament letter to Philemon for a moment.

This letter is an example of powerful deliberative rhetoric meant to convince Philemon not merely to accept Onesimus, his runaway slave, back without penalties (or even execution) but, in fact, to manumit him so he could continue to help Paul with his ministry. To this end, Paul pulls out all the stops on his argumentation and plucks all the heart strings he can.

Paul argues his case with these points:

1. He reminds Philemon in his very first words that he himself is in chains, a sympathy plea reinforced a few words later with the reminder that he is an old man. You can almost hear the violins playing in the background.
2. He calls Philemon not merely his co-worker but his *agapeto*—his "beloved," no less!
3. He recalls how great Philemon's work has been used for all God's people.
4. We must remember this letter is read aloud *before the whole congregation* that meets in Philemon's house, perhaps even read by Onesimus himself to them, trembling as he does so. Paul is, to some extent, seeking to publicly shame Philemon into doing the right thing.
5. Paul says his prayer is that Philemon's understanding will be deepened and he will think "of every good thing we share"—surely an allusion to Onesimus, whose name means "useful." Paul makes a rhetorical pun or play on the name by saying, "I want some 'use'/'benefit' from you"; namely, Paul wants Onesimus back.
6. This is the refreshment of his heart Paul is asking for.
7. In fact, he calls Onesimus "my very heart," and he is asking Philemon, "Please don't stomp that sucker flat" when you see him.
8. Onesimus is now called Paul's child or son. *Now* it's a family matter, since Onesimus has been converted by Paul.
9. Paul says he doesn't want to do anything without Philemon's free consent, but then he turns right around and says he is confident of Philemon's *obedience.*
10. He then reminds Philemon that he's willing to pay any debt Onesimus may have to his former master. But just when you thought Paul was going to get out the checkbook, he reminds Philemon, "Not to mention, you owe me your very spiritual life"!

11. If all this were not enough to make sure that Philemon manumits Onesimus and does what Paul wants, he says finally, "By the way, I'm coming (to make sure all is in order), so prepare my guest room"!

Now, all of this letter is written in the typical ancient rhetorical style, including the appeal to the emotions. But I suspect that unless you are pastoring a highly Pentecostal church, this emotional harangue is likely to be way over the top for your audience. The letter of Philemon is a classic study that can be used to help us distinguish between our audience and Paul's, and how preaching should differ in our case. As has been said, "The past is like a foreign country; they do things differently there." Indeed they do.

Today we still need to attend to *ethos, logos, pathos* (form, content, and the emotions). We still need to convince, persuade, and provide good reasons or arguments for our case. The good news about Paul's letters is *they are already the preaching, and they are in the form of ancient rhetorical sermons.* You don't need to turn them into preaching because they *are* the preaching. The question, however, is whether not merely the content but the form and force, the rhetoric and reality, and the emotion and commotion of Paul's letters will communicate and persuade today to very different audiences in very different cultures and times.

Certainly Luke, who put together Acts probably some twenty years after the death of his hero Paul, thought that his preaching would indeed translate to different settings and times. If you study the various sermon synopses of Paul beginning in Acts 13 and continuing on through chapter 28, you will discover that all of those sermon summaries actually feature good rhetorical form or outline, yet still were geared in appropriate ways to persuade various different audiences of Jews and Gentiles, pagans and Christians. Luke knew Paul was a good preacher, despite his physical impediments and funny way of speaking. And Paul's letters of course show that Luke was indeed right.

John Donne, not only a great poet but also himself a great preacher in St. Paul's in London, once said, "Wheresoever I open the letters of St. Paul, I hear thunder, a thunder that rolls throughout the earth." Indeed! And with thunder comes lightning, and people have been struck by that Pauline lightning again and again throughout the ages. It struck Luther through Galatians, about which Luther once quipped that he was married to that epistle. It struck Calvin, especially through Ephesians, with its powerful rhetoric about Christ, the elect one chosen from before the foundation of the universe. It struck Wesley when he was listening to Luther's preface to the epistle to the Romans off Aldersgate Street in London and felt his heart strangely warmed. He said, "I found I did trust in Christ, Christ alone for my salvation. He died for me, even me."

My word to this audience is that I hope and trust you've been struck by Paul's rhetoric somewhere along the line—struck down perhaps, but not stricken; struck down perhaps, but not struck out. Paul's letters are still the living word of God and the gospel, but the preacher needs to learn how to handle such words carefully and prayerfully for very different times and audiences. And in part, this will require that you study Paul's letters with a knowledge of ancient rhetoric, its character and content, and its form and force. It was the ancient art of preaching, and it still has much to teach us.[4]

Bibliography

Winter, B. W. *Philo and Paul among the Sophists*. Grand Rapids, MI: Eerdmans, 2001.
Witherington, Ben, III. *New Testament Rhetoric*. Eugene, OR: Cascade, 2009.

---

4. Witherington III, *New Testament Rhetoric*. One may also wish to consult my Pauline commentaries on each of the Pauline letters.

Chapter Four

Preaching in Pre-Nicene Christianity

DAVID E. WILHITE

Introduction

On the eve of the Council of Nicaea, the newly converted Constantine issued a circular letter denouncing Arius as a heretic. Therein, Constantine declared, "A bad expositor (κακὸς ἑρμηνεὺς) is in very truth the image and representation of the devil."[1] I begin with this quote because it nicely captures, if not the *ipsissima verba* of the so-called Arian controversy, the general tenor of the early Christian debates. It has often been said that the history of Christianity is that of the interpretation of the Scriptures. One could add that this history of interpretation was inherently tied not just to "exposition" in general but to preaching in particular.[2]

The famous, if not infamous, anathemas of the ecumenical councils were believed to be in the direct line of succession to Paul's own anathemas against false teachers (Gal 1:6–9). It is important to remember,

---

1. Epiphanius, *Panarion* 69.9.4; text from ed. Holl and rev. ed. Dummer; Epiphanius, *Panarion*, vol. 3, 159–60; Williams, *Panarion of Epiphanius of Salamis,* 339. It should be noted that the historicity of this later witness to Constantine's letter is questionable. For the present purposes, however, a critical assessment of this source can be left to the side.

2. Bray, *Biblical Interpretation*; Edwards, *History of Preaching*.

therefore, that Paul and other early Christians were not merely concerned with abstract doctrine and the heretical deviations from it, but they were also concerned about the "gospel" that was being "preached" (Gal 1:8). It is noteworthy that the entire controversy that led to Nicaea erupted from the differences between Arius' preaching and that of his bishop.[3]

When looking for "preaching" in the early Christian centuries, one finds good news and bad. The bad news is that very few sermons survive from this period.[4] The good news, however, is that virtually every surviving source from this early period is derived from and still reflects "sermonic" material. Let me take a moment to explain this apparent contradiction.

While a handful of pre-Nicene homilies have survived, one must concede that their survival as written texts has altered them from sermons *per se* into a form of literature, often resulting in significant alterations to their style and even their content. Nevertheless, since the vast majority of the literature from the first three centuries of Christianity can be shown to derive from oral and sermonic origins, we can learn much from this large corpus of material about the sermonic content of early Christians, and sometimes even learn about the sermonic styles of early Christians.

When I say that virtually all of the sources from this period derive from sermonic material, I assume a certain amount of fluidity between the early *kerygma*, oral tradition, and the texts that later codified this preaching and teaching. Many of you will recognize this notion of the *kerygma* as it was championed by Rudolf Bultmann and other scholars from the form critical school of New Testament studies.[5] Bultmann and others argued that the Gospels were *sui generis* in terms of their genre (a

---

3. The controversy began in AD 318, when Arius objected to Alexander's preaching on the Son's equality with the Father. Arius publicly preached against Alexander and offered an alternative view on the Son's pre-existence (Eusebius, *Life of Constantine* 2.61; Epiphanius, *Panarion* 69.6.4 and 69.7.6; Socrates, *Ecclesiastical History* 1.5). For an introduction to the so-called Arian controversy and the historical reassessment of said controversy, see Wilhite, *Gospel According to Heretics*, 105–28.

4. Most studies of early Christian preaching cover a broader time period because of the paucity of sources in the first three centuries. Helpful exceptions include the short study by Salzmann, *Lehren und Ermahnen* 2.59; and the detailed monograph of Stewart-Sykes, *From Prophecy to Preaching*. For general studies of the Patristic era, see Burghardt and Hunter, *Preaching in the Patristic Age*; Cunningham and Allen, *Preacher and Audience*; Dunn-Wilson, *Mirror for the Church*; Mayer, "Homiletics," 565–83; Mühlenberg and van Oort, *Predigt in der Alten Kirche*.

5. Along with Karl Ludwig Schmidt, Martin Dibelius, and others, see Edsall, "Kerygma," 410–41.

view which many later New Testament scholars have rejected), but it is worth remembering that the "forms" this school so eagerly sought were said to be traces of oral tradition from the primitive churches, which is to say, sermons!

Since there has been something of a Bultmannian renaissance in recent years,[6] it is worth recounting how—aside from Bultmann's now outdated views about the genre of the Gospels—he did insightfully place the church's preaching at the center of Christianity. "Christian faith," he says, "did not exist until there was a Christian kerygma, i.e., a kerygma that proclaims Jesus Christ as God's eschatological saving-act."[7] Bultmann later adds, "There is no faith in Christ which would not be at the same time faith in the church as the bearer of the kerygma, that is in dogmatic terminology: faith in the Holy Spirit."[8] If Bultmann is correct on this point, and I think he is,[9] then early Christian preaching represents one of the most important topics of Christian theology and history. This being the case, it is doubly tragic that so little attention has been paid to early Christian preaching by scholars of recent decades.[10]

One of the difficulties in studying the early sermons and even the link between the early kerygma and later written sources is due to the fact that the early Christians did not follow strict rules about what constitutes a sermon, proclamation, prophecy, or oral tradition. We have to admit that in the earliest discernable Christian communities, a scripted homily is not discernable. It is not even clear if there were formal officers who would deliver such a thing in the earliest communities. Instead, scholars

---

6. Congdon, "Is There a Kerygma in this Text?" 299–311.

7. Bultmann, *Theologie des Neuen Testaments*, 1. Bultmann adds, "This first occurred in the kerygma of the early church-community, not in the proclamation of the historical Jesus" (cited in Congdon, "Kerygma and Community," 1–21, 10–11).

8. Bultmann, *Das Verhältnis der urchristlichen Christusbotschaft zum historischen Jesus*, 26; (also cited in Congdon, "Kerygma and Community," 11).

9. Although one should consider the important criticisms discussed in Michael D. Gibson's article, "Does Jesus Have a Say in the Kerygma?," 83–103, I still find Eugene E. Lemcio's studies of the early *kerygma* compelling: Lemcio, "Unifying Kerygma," 3–17, 3–11, respectively. Furthermore, it should not be surprising that preaching is central to the earliest Christian sources since they all agree that preaching was the primary form of communication used by John the Baptist and Jesus (a point made by Fitzmyer, "Preaching in the Apostolic and Subapostolic Age," [19–35] 20–21).

10. For a review of the secondary literature, see Edsall, "Kerygma," 410–41; and Mayer, "Homiletics," 565–71.

speak of the prophetic activity in the primitive church.[11] Even so, we do not need to think of this early prophetic activity as un-sermonic. While there are examples of early Christians defining prophecy in terms of foresight,[12] visions, and/or ecstatic utterances, there are others in which the category of prophecy overlaps significantly with that of proclamation.[13] In other words, anytime prophecy included moral exhortation (and it often did), then said prophecy, or pro-fessing, should be understood as preaching, or pro-claiming (παράκλησις).[14]

Along with the concepts of proclamation and prophecy, we could also point to the overlapping categories of teaching and exhortation. In 1 Tim 4:11, Paul tells Timothy to "pass on the message and teach (παράγγελλε ταῦτα καὶ δίδασκε) [my translation]." Timothy is also commissioned "to the public reading of scripture, to exhorting, to teaching (τῇ ἀναγνώσει, τῇ παρακλήσει, τῇ διδασκαλίᾳ)" (v. 13 NRSV; cf. 2 Tim 4:2). This commissioning, moreover, was given through "prophecy (προφητείας)" and the laying on of hands by the elders (v. 14). Once more, his "teaching (τῇ διδασκαλίᾳ)" is said to be salvific to his "hearers (ἀκούοντάς)" (v. 16). Similarly, in 2 Tim 4:2 (NRSV), Paul urges Timothy to "proclaim the message; be persistent whether the time is favorable or unfavorable; convince, rebuke, and encourage, with the utmost patience

---

11. See 1 Cor 14:26: "What should be done then, my friends? When you come together, each one has a hymn, a lesson, a revelation, a tongue, or an interpretation. Let all things be done for building up" (NRSV; NA28: τί οὖν ἐστιν, ἀδελφοί; ὅταν συνέρχησθε, ἕκαστος ψαλμὸν ἔχει, διδαχὴν ἔχει, ἀποκάλυψιν ἔχει, γλῶσσαν ἔχει, ἑρμηνείαν ἔχει· πάντα πρὸς οἰκοδομὴν γινέσθω). The apparent style of prophecy mentioned by Paul, which is widely assumed to have been ecstatic or at least unscripted, was later seen to be replaced by a concept of prophecy that primarily meant exegesis of the Scriptures (Stewart-Sykes, "Hermas the Prophet," 33–63).

12. It should be noted, however, that these definitions are typically for polemical use: e.g., Irenaeus, Haer, 4.19.5; Origen, Contra Cels. 7.8.

13. The bishops, e.g., are to be regarded as "the mouth of God" (Didasc. Apost. 9.2.28), and as Aaron delivered Moses' message and was thus called a "prophet," so the bishop delivers the Lord's message (Didasc. Apost. 9.2.30). While this example could reflect later institutionalizing developments, other examples will be given below from earlier sources.

14. As made clear by Bauer, Der Wortgottesdienst der ältesten Christen, 54–55. There is, nevertheless, still debate in contemporary scholarship: Forbes (Prophecy and Inspired Speech, 225–28) claims that prophecy is new revelation while preaching is repeating old material, while Stewart-Sykes (From Prophecy to Preaching, 8) rejects this as a false dichotomy in the earliest Christian communities.

in teaching (κήρυξον τὸν λόγον, ἐπίστηθι εὐκαίρως ἀκαίρως, ἔλεγξον, ἐπιτίμησον, παρακάλεσον, ἐν πάσῃ μακροθυμίᾳ καὶ διδαχῇ)."

The late first-century text known as *1 Clement* (1.3) also links instruction (ἐπετρέπετε), exhortation (παρηξξέλετε), and teaching (ἐδιδάσκετε). The *Didache* similarly refers—rather ambiguously—to other individuals who speak in the congregation, such as the teachers (11.1–2) who are to be received "as you would the Lord" (11.2), the same claim stated earlier in the text about the prophets (4.1). Likewise, an apostle (11.3–12) also should be received "as if he were the Lord" (11.4), unless said apostle proves to be a false "prophet" (11.5); some of these "prophets" even chose to reside permanently with the congregation (12.3–13.1). The *Didache* also mentions teachers, possibly as a generic term for prophets and apostles (13.2). Finally, even "bishops and deacons" are said to also "carry out for you the ministry of the prophets and teachers."[15]

In the early second century, Ignatius claims he has "briefly exhorted (συντόμως παρεκάλεσα)" the Christians in Magnesia, but this παράκλησις or exhortation is done in a letter form.[16] Ignatius can make such a claim precisely because his letter was intended to be read aloud in the Christian assembly. This is arguably the case for all early Christian literature. Let us not forget that the root word for "proclamation (παρεκάλεω)" shares the same root as "church (ἐκκλεσία)": both come from the root word καλέω, which means "to call or cry out." The church (ἐκκλεσία) is the called assembly, and as such it receives a "proclamation (παράκλησις)." From these we can see how "prophecy" and "proclamation" are largely synonymous, or at least overlap significantly in content, with *kerygma*.[17]

One last term to mention here is the "homily," from the Greek, ὁμιλέα, meaning "conversation" (the Latin equivalent would be *sermo*, whence we derive our word "sermon"). In Luke 24:14–15, we read how the two disciples "conversed (ὡμίλουν . . . τῷ ὁμιλεῖν)," and then Jesus appeared to them, and "expounded (διερμήνευσεν [from δια- ἑρμηνεύω])" on all the prophets, but they did not recognize Him until the "breaking of

---

15. *Didache* 15.1 (Holmes 366–67: ὑμῖν γὰρ λειτουργοῦσι καὶ αὐτοὶ τὴν λειτουργίαν τῶν προφητῶν καὶ διδασκάλων).

16. *Ad Magnesianos* 14.1 (Holmes 212–13).

17. It is even worth noting the link between the "Paraclete (Παράκλητος)" as the one who gives "proclamation (παρακαλεῖν)." See Cothenet, "Les Prophètes Chrétiens," 80.

the bread" (vv. 30–31, 35). Similarly, Acts 20 reports that at Troas, during the evening service which took place on the "first day of the week" (v. 7, [Saturday night counts as Sunday]), Paul "conversed (ὁμιλέω)" (v. 11) until midnight—this is the scene in which Eutychus fell out of the window after falling asleep during Paul's homily (a passage to which every preacher can relate). In the early second century, Ignatius of Antioch will encourage Polycarp of Smyrna to "preach a sermon (ὁμιλίαν ποιοῦ),"[18] and in the surviving *Life of Polycarp* (22) we read how a series of presbyters delivered "homilies."

Based on the varying kinds of sermons in early Christianity, Wendy Meyer concludes, "At the most basic level, then, all that we can claim is that a homily is something that conforms to a few essential conditions, but whose shape is elastic and changes with regional cultural conditions and with time."[19] In sum, when looking for early Christian preaching, we have to allow for the various forms it took and for the significant overlap between our categories of sermons, oral tradition, prophecy, and teaching.

As part of this discussion, we should recall that even our earliest Christian sources, like the "books" of the New Testament, derive from oral tradition and—I would say—sermonic material. Several scholars have shown that Paul's letters were meant to be delivered orally by one of his trusted associates.[20] The letters, therefore, while epistolary in form, should also be interpreted in terms of their rhetorical style (and—I would add—their sermonic nature). The same is likely true for other New Testament texts, such as some of the Catholic epistles. Similarly, the Gospels in one way or another derive from oral tradition, and as such it should be understood to represent the earliest Christian preaching, or *kerygma*.[21] As Alexander Olivar states in his study on the early origins of Christian preaching, "the New Testament sprang from early Christian preaching, rather than the other way around."[22]

---

18. Ignatius, *Ep. Poly.* 5.1 (Holmes 266–67).

19. Mayer, "Homiletics," [569–71] 570.

20. Witherington, *New Testament Story*, 3–14; further elaborated in his Parchman Lectures delivered at Baylor's Truett Seminary in 2007 (available online at http://www.baylor.edu/truett/index.php?id=927854; also see his transcript at http://benwitherington.blogspot.com/2007/10/sacred-texts-in-oral-culturehow-did.html).

21. For "preaching" or "heralding" (the Greek verb κηρύσσω) in the New Testament, see Rom 10:14; Matt 3:1; and Luke 4:18–19.

22. Olivar, "Reflections," [21–32] 21–22.

Much could be made of this fact, but for now I would like to make one initial observation regarding the continuity between the earliest Christian generations and those that follow. If in addition to evincing the ongoing development of an earlier oral tradition, the surviving sermons retain something of the original content from the earliest years of oral tradition, and if the *kerygma* is understood to describe the core or essentials of Christian discourse believed to be necessarily passed on through oral and written means, then we can better appreciate the link between early Christian preaching and later confessions. In other words, the early Christian faith entailed a development (but arguably a faithful one) from *kerygma* to *paradosis* to *regula* to *credo*—that is, from the apostolic preaching to the early tradition to the rule of faith and to the ecumenical creeds.[23]

Although in one sense all early Christian writings seems to derive from sermons (i.e., oral tradition), it is also perplexing that none were recorded as such. The stenographic recordings of later church fathers, like Augustine, has only one predecessor in the ante-Nicene period, which are Origen's sermons. This raises an important issue: the act of writing a sermon itself changes the genre. In short, the written sermons that survive must have been atypical. Nevertheless, I would suggest that these texts were first written in order to be read as catechetical sermons in other churches. For an example see the Shepherd's command to Hermas to "write these (prophecies) down" (*Vis.* 2.4.3), which is ostensibly why this text was made, distributed, and read broadly.

In short, we have on the one hand a ubiquity of sermons in the first three centuries, because every source is arguably in some sense derived from and/or intended for oral presentation to the Christian gathering. Yet on the other hand, no surviving sermons as such existed until Origen, because the act of writing them ("textualizing") altered them from sermons proper to a literary genre of some sort. To learn more about early Christian preaching, let us now turn to a brief survey of preaching from the early centuries, and then I will offer some observations about the characteristics of preaching from this period.

---

23. For example, the doctrinal content of early Christian "teaching"/"preaching" mentioned above is roughly the *Rule of Faith* or *Canon of Truth* (Irenaeus, *Demonstration of the Apostolic Preaching* 3, 6, and passim).

Surviving Homilies

The number of surviving homilies from the pre-Nicene period is surprisingly low. We can speak confidently of five sources, which I will list here briefly.[24] First, the text known as *2 Clement*[25] (dating back to the early second century) is now widely recognized as a sermon, not a letter.[26] The second is the Easter sermon from the second half of the second century by Melito of Sardis, his *Peri Pascha*.[27] This sermon celebrates the proper meaning of the Passover, which for Melito is Christ's "passion."

The third source for a homily is Clement of Alexandria, who in the early third century authored a sermon entitled *Quis dives salvatur*, or *Who among the Rich May Be Saved?*, regarding the story of the rich young ruler in Mark 10:17–31.[28] Although this is the only surviving sermon from Clement, we should note how much of his "teaching" does survive,

---

24. There are also fragments that appear to be sermons from surviving manuscripts (e.g., PSI 11.1200-LDAB 4669; P. Mich 18.764-LDAB 0562; P. Mich 18.763-LDAB 5071; BKT 9.22-LDAB 4973). To my knowledge, no comprehensive study of these texts has been undertaken to date. We look forward to the forthcoming collection of essays, which should address the topic: Harrower and Bird, *Second Century Christianity*.

25. See studies in Lindemann, *Die Clemensbriefe*; Parvis, "2 Clement," 265–70; and Tuckett, *2 Clement*.

26. First argued by Lightfoot, *Apostolic Fathers*, 1.2:194. See *2 Clem.* 17:3, which speaks to the audience, saying, "Now, while we are being admonished by the elders" (Holmes 160–61). This is during the liturgy when all the presbyters offer a sermon, followed by the bishop. The text may be based on the reading of Isa 54:1 (see *2 Clem.* 2.1). *Second Clem.* also follows the logic of the Old Testament, especially Isaiah, so that Knopf, "Die Anognose zum zweiten Clemensbrief," 266–79, even claimed it was a "Homilet" on Isa 54–66.

27. The authorship has been disputed. For bibliography and discussion, see the studies of Cohink, *Peri Pascha*; Lieu, "Melito of Sardis," 43–46; and Stewart-Sykes, *Lamb's High Feast*.

28. Thought to be a "homily" by Quasten, *Patrology*, 2.15, Buttersworth's *Clement of Alexandria*, 265, states how this text is in the "form of a sermon," but it is too long and so may be "the expansion and elaboration of an actual sermon." Clement mentions how some listen "to the Lord's saying" (τῆς τοῦ κυρίου φωνῆς)" (*Quis div. salv.* 2 [LCL 92:272–73]), which implies—if not a liturgical setting—an audience of Christians who already know the pericope. The same can be said for his statement, "May the Saviour grant us power, then, as we begin our address (τοῦ λόγου) at this point, to impart to the brethren true and fitting and salutary thoughts." (*Quis div. salv.* 4 [LCL 92:278–79: Δοίη τοίνυν ἡμῖν ὁ σωτὴρ ἐντεῦθεν ἀρξαμένοις τοῦ λόγου τἀληθῆ καὶ τὰ πρέποντα καὶ τὰ σωτήρια συμβαλέσθαι τοῖς ἀδελφοῖς]).

which was originally thought to have been delivered orally in his "school" and to the catechumenates.

The fourth source for an early Christian homily is that of Hippolytus of Rome. Here, however, historians have great difficulty navigating the Hippolytus of history (who was a presbyter in Rome in the early third century) due to the numerous works attributed to him—a debate we will largely have to leave to the side for the sake of space.[29] The one surviving sermon that is likely authentic is entitled *On the Antichrist*, a topical survey of several Scripture passages.[30] Aside from this sermon, the other homilies of Hippolytus are only known in fragments quoted by later writers.[31] However, as we said with Clement of Alexandria, some of his other works could be considered in relation to his preaching. The famous anti-modalist treatise entitled *Against Noetus/Contra Noetum* is known in the Greek manuscripts by the longer title, ὁμιλία εἰς τὸν αἵρεσιν Νοήτου— that is, *A Homily on the Heresy of Noetus*. Although this is not a homily as we would define it, we should recognize that ancient Christians did not always draw sharp distinctions between certain genres. Along these same lines, the Hippolytan commentaries should also be considered in this discussion since they may be based on sermons.[32]

---

29. See discussion in Brent, *Hippolytus and the Roman Church*; Cerrato, *Hippolytus between East and West*; Baldovin, "Hippolytus and the Apostolic Tradition, 520–42.

30. Called a homily by Lienhard, "Origen the Homilist," 37. The author does promise "to set these matters of inquiry clearly forth to your view, drawing largely from the Holy Scriptures themselves as from a holy fountain, in order that you may not only have the pleasure of hearing them on the testimony of men, but may also be able, by surveying them in the light of (divine) authority, to glorify God in all." (1) He reiterates this agenda in his closing lines: "These things, then, I have set shortly before thee, O Theophilus, drawing them from Scripture itself, in order that, maintaining in faith what is written, and anticipating the things that are to be, thou mayest keep thyself void of offence both toward God and toward men, looking for that blessed hope and appearing of our God and Saviour, when, having raised the saints among us, He will rejoice with them, glorifying the Father. To Him be the glory unto the endless ages of the ages. Amen" (67). However, the ostensible form is that of a letter to a certain Theophilus (1, opening line; and 67).

31. There are also other sermons attributed to him, but they are disputed by most scholars, which are often difficult to differentiate from the many fragments thought to be authentic. Examples include Psalms (reconstructed from medieval catenae in Nautin, *Le Dossier d'Hippolyte*, 167–83); one on David and Goliath (only surviving in Georgian); and a sermon entitled *On the Holy Theophany* (trans. in ANF 5), which is apparently an epiphany sermon about the baptism of Jesus: "For you have just heard how Jesus came to John" (2 [ANF 5:235]).

32. Salzmann, *Lehren und Ermahnen*, 384–86; Dunn-Wilson, *Mirror for the*

The fifth and last source for surviving sermons from this period is from Origen in the middle of the third century.[33] Whereas each of the previous four authors only left a single sermon to history's records, many of Origen's sermons on various books of the Bible have survived: over two hundred of his sermons are extant,[34] twenty-nine of which were just recently discovered in 2012.[35] Even though Origen is in many ways *sui generis*, it is worth taking a moment to look closer at his preaching because of the sheer number of these sermons.[36]

Origen allowed scribes to record his sermons by shorthand.[37] While Origen is often decried as a rampant allegorist who could make a text mean whatever he wanted it to, his sermons actually belied this accusation and showed that he was an exegete who carefully scrutinized every line and word of the sacred text for its historical, moral, and theological meanings.[38]

Origen preached without a manuscript. His typical practice was commenting (extemporaneously!)[39] verse by verse on the reading and ending with a doxology. (As an aside, this may not be an innovative

---

Church, 36.

33. For the dates, see Nautin, *Origène*, 389–409.

34. *Homilies on Genesis* (text in Doutreleau 1976, SC 7; trans. in Heine 1982, FC 71); *Homilies on Genesis and Exodus* (text in Borret 1985, SC 321; trans. in Heine 1982, FC 71); *Homilies on Leviticus 1–16* (text in Borret 1981, SC 286, 287; trans. in Barkley 1990, FC 83); *Homilies on Numbers* (text in Baehrens, Doutreleau, Méhat, Borret 1996-, 415, 442, 461; trans. Scheck and Hall, *Homilies on Numbers*; text in Méhat 1951, SC 29; *Homilies on Joshua* (text in Jaubert 1960, SC 71; trans. Bruce 2002, FC 105); *Homilies on Judges* (text in Messié, Neyrand, and Borret 1993, SF 389; trans. in Lauro 2010, FC 119); *Homilies on 1 Samuel* (text in Nautin and Nautin 1986, SC 328); *Homilies on Psalms 36 to 38* (text in Prinzivalli, Crouzel, and Brésard 1995, SC 411); *Homilies on the Song of Songs* (text in Rousseau 1966, SC 37; trans. Lawson, and Origen; *The Song of Songs*; *Homilies on Isaiah* (text *Die Griechischen Christlichen Schriftsteller der ersten Jahrhunderte* 33, *Origenes Werke VIII, Homiliae in Regn., Ez. et al.* [1. Aufl. 1925: W. A. Baehrens]); *Homilies on Jeremiah and 1 Kings 28* (text in Nautin 1976–77, SC 232, 238; trans. in Smith 1998, FC 97); *Homilies on Ezekiel 1–14* (text in Borret 1989, SC 352; trans. in Scheck, *Origen: Homilies 1–14 on Ezekiel*; *Homilies on Luke* (text in Crouzel, Fournier, Périchon 1962, SC 87; trans. in Lienhard 1996, FC 94).

35. Perrone, Pradel, Prinzivalli, and Cacciari, *Die neuen Psalmenhomilien*.

36. See "The Scholarly Works of Origen" and "Homilies" in *The Westminster Handbook to Origen*, ed. McGuckin, 28–29, for (mostly older) bibliography.

37. According to Eusebius, *Hist. eccl.* 6.36.1.

38. Lienhard, "Origen as Homilist," [36–52] 38, and 47; following see de Lubac, *Histoire et Esprit*.

39. See Pamphilius, *Apologia pro Origene*, 9.

practice: Eusebius tells us that Origen was influenced by the preaching of Hippolytus of Rome, whose surviving commentaries may also derive from sermons).[40] Once, when preaching as a guest in Jerusalem, the whole of 1 Sam 25-28 was read. Origen explained that there were four distinct pericopes in the reading, and then—apparently unscripted—he turned to the bishop, Alexander of Jerusalem, and asked for which pericope he would like to hear an exposition. The bishop chose the scene about the witch of Endor—undeniably the most intriguing, and so Origen began his sermon.[41]

It is unclear whether Origen's commentaries derive from his sermons or whether his sermons reflect his prior practice of writing commentaries (a bit of a chicken-or-the-egg kind of question).[42] Even so, the relationship between his preaching and written works allows us to address a broader question.

Beyond these few surviving sermons, two other kinds of sources are often consulted when studying early Christian preaching. The first consists of the reports of apologists like Justin Martyr, who describe the early Christian liturgy for outsiders in order to show how benign their "secretive" meetings actually were.[43] These reports for outsiders represent

40. Eusebius, *Hist. eccl.* 6.14.10; and Jerome, *Vir. ill.* 61.

41. *Homily on Samuel* 28, 1. This incident is discussed in Lienhard, "Origen as Homilist," 45.

42. See Armstrong, *Role of the Rule of Faith*, 191-218, for a survey of the primary and secondary sources.

43. See Justin Martyr, *1 Apology* 67.4-5 (emphasis added): "And on the day called Sunday there is an assembly of those who dwell in cities or the countryside, *and the memoirs of the apostles or the writings of the prophets are read, for as long as there is time.* Then, when the reader has stopped, *the president, in an address, makes admonition and invitation of the imitation of their good things.* Then we all stand up together and send prayers. And, as we said before, when we have stopped praying, bread and wine and water are brought, and the president sends up prayers and thanksgiving in similar fashion, to the best of his ability, and the people give their assent, saying 'Amen.' And there is a distribution and a partaking of the eucharistized elements to each one, and it is sent to those who are not present by means of the deacons" (text and trans. from Minns and Parvis, *Justin, Philosopher, and Martyr*, 258-61): καὶ τῇ τοῦ ἡλίου λεγομένῃ ἡμέρᾳ, πάντων κατὰ πόλεις ἢ ἀγροὺς μενόντων ἐπὶ τὸ αὐτὸ συνέλευσις γίνεται, καὶ τὰ ἀπομνημονεύματα τῶν ἀποστόλων ἢ τὰ συγγράμματα τῶν προφητῶν ἀναγινώσκεται, μέχρις ἐγχωρεῖ. εἶτα, παυσαμένου τοῦ ἀναγινώσκοντος, ὁ προεστὼς διὰ λόγου τὴν νουθεσίαν καὶ πρόκλησιν τῆς τῶν καλῶν τούτων μιμήσεως ποιεποιεῖται. ἔπειτα ἀνιστάμεθα κοινῇ πάντες καὶ εὐχὰς πέμπομεν. καί, ὡς προέφημεν, παυσαμένων ἡμῶν τῆς εὐχῆς, ἄρτος προσφέρεται καὶ οἶνος καὶ ὕδωρ, καὶ ὁ προεστὼς εὐχὰσ ὁμοίως καὶ εὐχαριστίας, ὅση δύναμις αὐτῷ, ἀναπέμπει, καὶ ὁ λαὸς ἐπευφημεῖ,

a "positive spin" on early Christian gatherings, and as such do not offer an objective depiction.[44] The other kind of source contains instruction for insiders: the various texts known as "church manuals" describe the proper role and practices of the various officers of the church, including descriptions of preaching. Examples of this kind include the *Didache* from the late first or early second century, the *Apostolic Tradition* from the late second or early third century, the *Didascalia Apostolorum* or *Teaching of the Apostles* from the early third century, and the *Constitutio ecclesiastica apostolorum* or *Apostolic Church Order* from the late third century.[45] These sources for insiders also only offer limited material, since

---

λέγων τὸ Ἀμήν. Καὶ ἡ διάδοσις καὶ ἡ μετάληψις ἀπὸ τῶν εὐκαριστηθέντων ἑκάστῳ γίνεται, καὶ τοῖς οὐ παροῦσι διὰ τῶν διακόνων πέμπεται). Another example is from Tertullian, *Apology* 39.1-4, "I will now at once proclaim the actual occupations of the Christian association, in order that I who rejected the idea that they were evil may show that they are good. We are a corporation with a common knowledge of religion, a common rule of life, and a union of hope. We come together for meeting and assembly, in order that having formed a band as it were to come before God we may encompass him with prayers. This violence is pleasing to God. We pray also for the emperors, for their ministers and those in authority, for the state of the world, for general quiet, for the postponement of the end. We meet to call one another to remembrance of the Scripture, if the aspect of affairs requires us either to be forewarned or to be reminded of anything. In any case we feed our belief on holy words, we raise our hope, we strengthen our confidence, we clinch the teaching nonetheless by driving home precepts. There too are pronounced exhortations, corrections and godly judgments. For our judgment too is delivered with great weight, as among those who are sure that they are acting under the eye of God, and there is the greatest anticipation of the future judgment, if any one has so sinned, as to be banished from the communion of prayer and assembly and all holy fellowship" (Souter 111-13; CCL: *Edam iam nunc ego ipse negotia Christianae factionis, ut qui mala refutaverim, bona ostendam. Corpus sumus de conscientia religionis et disciplinae unitate et spei foedere. Coimus in coetum et congregationem, ut ad deum quasi manu facta precationibus ambiamus orantes. Haec vis deo grata est. Oramus etiam pro imperatoribus, pro ministris eorum et potestatibus, pro statu saeculi, pro rerum quiete, pro mora finis. Coimus ad litterarum divinarum commemorationem, si quid praesentium temporum qualitas aut praemonere cogit aut recognoscere. Certe fidem sanctis vocibus pascimus, spem erigimus, fiduciam figimus, disciplinam praeceptorum nihilominus inculcationibus densamus; ibidem etiam exhortationes, castigationes et censura divina. Nam et iudicatur magno cum pondere, ut apud certos de dei conspectu, summumque futuri iudicii praeiudicium est, si quis ita deliquerit, ut a communicatione orationis et conventus et omnis sancti commercii relegetur*).

44. This is not to devalue these sources, but only to point out their limitations.

45. One could also consult the *Constitutiones Apostolorum* or *Apostolic Constitutions* (c. 380, Syria), which is indebted to these earlier texts. Text/trans. from J. P. Arendzen, *JTS* (1901), 60-73 (cf. Stewart-Sykes, *Apostolic Church Order*.

much is assumed about early Christian preaching,[46] and the bulk of the material focuses on the performance of the Eucharist rather than on the presentation of the Scriptures.[47] From these general sources, historians can identify some of the broad contours of early Christian worship and preaching.

Although we can only identify a few surviving sermons and scattered descriptions of preaching from the early Christian centuries, I would suggest that we can get a much more complete understanding of early Christian preaching if we further consider sources that derive from oral tradition, teaching, preaching, and prophesying.

Other Sources for Early Christian Preaching

As mentioned above, much of the earliest Christian material, especially the texts comprising our New Testament, derive from oral material. When we look outside the New Testament, we find many other comparable connections between surviving treatises and earlier oral and/or sermonic material. For example, in the early second century, Papias of Hierapolis claimed to know tradition from the prior generation of Christians who have connections to the original Jerusalem community, such as the "prophecies" of Philip's daughters.[48] Papias's only surviving work is entitled *Expositions of the Sayings of the Lord* (λογίων κυριακῶν ἐξηγήσεως).[49] While these "sayings" are usually thought to be single sentences, some have argued that the "*exegesis*" is in fact sermonic material, not simply *logia*.[50]

As for other sources that derive from preaching, or at least oral teaching, we have already mentioned how certain authors like Clement of Alexandria, Hippolytus, and Origen left us works that were originally delivered orally in their "schools." The same could be said of Justin Martyr and other earlier apologists, which begs the question about how these

---

46. Similarly, sources like Egeria's *Pilgrimage*, while not recording sermons *per se*, do give us descriptions of how preaching fits within the larger liturgical life of Christian community in the fourth century.

47. This is especially the case for the *Apostolic Tradition*. As what was said previously about apologetic sources, the point is not to devalue these sources, but only to stipulate their limitations.

48. Eusebius, *Hist. eccl.* 3.39.4, 3.39.9.

49. Eusebius, *Hist. eccl.* 3.39.1.

50. See Stewart-Sykes, *From Prophecy to Preaching*, 205–14.

"schools" functioned in relation to the church *per se*. Many of the surviving works from Christian writers[51] like Tertullian[52] and Cyprian[53] reflect material that was almost certainly delivered orally to the congregation.

While these kinds of sources have clearly been converted into literary products meant for wide distribution, and as such cannot tell us much about the form of early Christian preaching, they nevertheless do reflect the various topics, concerns, and content of early Christian preaching. For example, Ireneaus's most famous work, *Against Heresies*, is a polemic against various "Gnostic" groups, and so it is a doctrinal diatribe against unorthodox teachings. But his other surviving work, *Demonstration of the Apostolic Preaching*,[54] while not a sermon *per se*, nevertheless provides us with a nice summation of the doctrinal content or at least the theological parameters of the proper Christian sermon. Numerous other writers like Irenaeus could be considered in the same light.[55]

---

51. For example, the *Epistula Apostolorum* (mid-second century) may have derived from oral exposition, which is certainly used in the *epistula* genre as a rhetorical device; see Hills, *Tradition and Composition*, 14–21.

52. For his catechetical works, like *On Baptism* and *On the Lord's Prayer* as "homiletic discourses," see Barnes, *Tertullian*, 117–18. Dunn-Wilson, *Mirror for the Church*, 36, says they are "clearly homiletic in tone." Although Tertullian is not a "presbyter" *per se*, he likely belonged to the *seniores laici*, a group of "lay elders" only found in North African Christianity, and as such he would have been able to "preach" or speak to fellow Christians (see Wilhite, *Ancient African Christianity*, 112; also cf. Tertullian, *De anima* 9.4).

53. Cyprian's pastoral works originally would have been delivered as homilies (e.g., *On the Dress of Virgins, On the Lord's Prayer, On Works and Almsgiving, On the Good of Patience, On Mortality,* and *On Jealousy and Envy*). Some of the more doctrinal works may have been delivered to the laity before being read at a council and then distributed more widely (e.g., *On the Lapsed* and *On the Unity of the Church*; see Clarke, *Letters of Saint Cyprian*, 2:302; and Bobertz, "Historical Context of Cyprian's *De Unitate*," 107–11). Other (possibly) pre-Nicene sermons also survive in the large pseudo-Cyprianic Corpus: see Psalms-Cyprian, *Orationes* (date unknown); and Psalms-Cyprian, *Sermo de centesima, sexagesima, tricesima* (fourth century).

54. Trans. from Iain M. MacKenzie, *Irenaeus's Demonstration*.

55. For example, Gregory Thaumaturgus (c.213–c.270), whose *Oratio* survives (on Origen), and whose *Ekthesis tes pisteos* is akin to Ireneaus's *Demonstration*; these and other works may have derived from and reflect his oral presentations, but they are all doctrinal and polemical works, not homilies *per se*. Similarly, one could consider Antony of the Desert when studying early pre-Nicene preaching: Antony himself was converted upon hearing the reading of the rich young ruler, and he seems to have preached ("The Lord gave grace-filled speech to Antony" [*Life of Antony*, 14.6 {Greer 93}]), at least to the other "brothers" (*Life of Antony*, 16–43 [Greer 97–151] and 55 [Greer 175–79]), and at times spoke publicly in Alexandria (*Life of Antony*, 69 [Greer

Along with this mention of true versus heretical preaching, we should acknowledge the sources and even some of the surviving works by the so-called heretics. Of course, this begs the question as to who is a heretic and who gets to decide what is heresy.[56] The vast majority of scholarship on early Christian studies has shifted toward an emphasis on "diversity" rather than keeping the traditional binary of orthodoxy and heresy,[57] but this is another debate we must leave to the side for the sake of the current discussion.[58]

Here I will simply list the surviving sources from what have traditionally been deemed heretical groups. There are a few fragments of sermons from the so-called Gnostics, such as Simon Magus's preaching,[59] *The Preaching of Peter*/Πέτρου κήρυγμα,[60] some "homilies (*homiliai*)" from Valentinus,[61] and the *Naassene Sermon*, which is a book used by one sect that allegedly recorded homilies by James, the brother of Jesus.[62] In addition to these fragments, the Nag Hammadi discovery of 1945 included at least three sermons: *The Gospel of Truth*, which appears to be a Valentinian (perhaps even Valentinius's) sermon; *The Sermon of Zostrianos*, which is a third-century discourse by a Persian sage; and *The Letter of Peter to Philip*, which dates to the late second or early third century (and so obviously pseudonymous) that includes a sermon by "Peter."[63]

205]), but these sermons survive almost entirely as fragments. (Twenty other sermons attributed to Antony are thought to be pseudonymous; see Dunn-Wilson, *Mirror for the Church*, 50).

56. Tertullian, *Praesc.* 21.1: "No others ought to be received as preachers than those whom Christ appointed" (trans. ANF).

57. The view of Bauer, *Orthodoxy and Heresy*, xxii. For the reception of Bauer, see Kraft's appendix to the English edition of Bauer (286–316), and Harrington, "Reception of Walter Bauer's *Orthodoxy and Heresy*, 289–98. See also exposition and critique of Bauer in Wilken, "Diversity and Unity," 101–10.

58. For further reading, see Wilhite, *Gospel According to Heretics*, 1–19, 245–56.

59. Irenaeus, *Haer*, 1.23.2. (The reliability of the heresiologists for Simon Magus is highly dubious.)

60. Fragments cited in Clement of Alexandria, but this may not be Gnostic in any sense.

61. Surviving in fragments cited Clement of Alexandria; see Markschies, *Valentinus Gnosticus?*

62. According to Hippolytus, the Naassenes were a Gnostic group who venerated the "serpent" (Hebrew = *nahash*/ נָחָשׁ). He cites a book of theirs called the "Sermon" or "Discourse," which was said to be written by James, the brother of Jesus (see fragments cited in Hippolytus, *Refutation of All Heresies*, 5.1–5 [ANF 5]).

63. Meyer, "Introduction to *The Letter of Peter to Philip*," 231.

In addition to these "Gnostic" sermons, one could consult the surviving Manichaean sermons, some of which date back as early as the third century.[64]

While not strictly along the lines of "heresy," we could also look to the many sources that testify to women's preaching, even though many of the early Christian authors viewed the practice as unacceptable (and thus—if not unorthodox—then at least "heterodox").[65] Witnesses to women's preaching[66] include the mention of Philip's daughters;[67] Helena, the companion of Simon Magus;[68] a Carpocratian teacher named Marcellina who taught in Rome in the mid-second century;[69] an unnamed Marcosian prophetess from the same time;[70] the many visions or "Revelations" of Philumena, who was a prophetess affiliated with Apelles;[71] Flora, to whom Ptolemy wrote and was said to uphold "the apostolic tradition"; Thecla from the apocryphal *Acts of Paul*, who was said to have taught many; the so-called Montanist prophetesses Priscilla, Maximilla, and Quintilla, whose teachings survives in fragments;[72] the visions of Perpetua; and Tertullian's report about a woman who frequently prophesied during the liturgy in Carthage.[73]

64. See primary sources in Gulácsi, *Mani's Pictures*.

65. The *Apostolic Constitutions*, 3.1.6, stating that widows cannot teach because the role is forbidden for all women, which implies that some widows were teaching.

66. For primary sources, see the studies of Kraemer and D'Angelo, *Women and Christian Origins*; and Miller, *Women in Early Christianity*.

67. Mentioned above with Papias; see Eusebius, *Hist. eccl.* 3.39.1.

68. Epiphanius, *Panarion* 21 (and the helpful notes on earlier primary sources in Williams, *Panarion of Epiphanius of Salamis*, 61ff.)

69. Irenaeus, *Haer.* 1.25.6 (and elsewhere).

70. Irenaeus, *Haer* 1.14–20 (and elsewhere).

71. Tertullian, *Praescr.* 30 (and elsewhere).

72. Tabbernee, *Montanist Inscriptions and Testimonia*.

73. *De anima* 9.4, "We have now amongst us a sister whose lot it has been to be favoured with sundry gifts of revelation, which she experiences in the Spirit by ecstatic vision amidst the sacred rites of the Lord's day in the church: she converses with angels, and sometimes even with the Lord; she both sees and hears mysterious communications; some men's hearts she understands, and to them who are in need she distributes remedies. Whether it be in the reading of Scriptures, or in the chanting of psalms, or in the preaching of sermons, or in the offering up of prayers, in all these religious services matter and opportunity are afforded to her of seeing visions (*Est hodie soror apud nos reuelationum charismata sortita, quas in ecclesia inter dominica sollemnia per ecstasin in spiritu patitur; conuersatur cum angelis, aliquando etiam cum domino, et uidet et audit sacramenta et quorundam corda dinoscit et medicinas desiderantibus sumit.*

There are two other bodies of texts that are often not considered for our subject matter but which could serve as sources for pre-Nicene preaching. The first is the many surviving martyrdoms, which were often designed to be read in the liturgy and often the subject of sermons.[74] In fact, the whole concept of martyrdom and public witness could be considered in our understanding of early Christian proclamation. Other texts that could be considered are fourth- and fifth-century sermons. While the well-known collections of preachers like Chrysostom and Augustine obviously reflect later developments and concerns, they nevertheless must have been indebted to earlier models of preaching.[75]

Now that we have surveyed the surviving Christian homilies and sources that inform our understanding about early Christian preaching in the pre-Nicene era, I would like to take a step back and see the proverbial forest through the homiletical trees. In my final section, I will briefly list some of the characteristics found in early Christian preaching.

Characteristics (or "Significance") of Preaching in Pre-Nicene Christianity

The first characteristic of early Christian sermons is that there was no single characteristic (or form, style, or method) applicable to all early Christian sermons. Preaching was a diverse phenomenon in the earliest

---

Iamuero prout scripturae leguntur aut psalmi canuntur aut allocutiones proferuntur aut petitiones delegantur, ita inde materiae uisionibus subministrantur)."

74. E.g., *The Passion of Perpetua and Felicity*, *The Martyrdom of Barsauma of Nisibis*, and *The Martyrdom of Habib the Deacon*.

75. In addition to the well-known homiliticians, many other sources could be consulted, such as the many sermons attributed to Hippolytus, mentioned above, but of uncertain date and origin. Also, as with Irenaeus and others, the many "teachers" of the fourth century also left behind important examples for early Christian preaching, such as Athanasisus (see Kannengiesser, "Homiletical Festal Letters," 73–100). There are even examples like the anonymous *Sermo de passio sanctorum Donati et Advocati*, and the partly recovered sermon by Parmenian of Carthage (see Wilhite, *True Church*, which are (chronologically) not pre-Nicene, but nevertheless they do arise from the "Donatists" who fell outside the orbit of the Constantine and the council of 325 and so are also (technically) non-Nicene. Along these same lines, once could consider the (Pseudo-) *Clementine Homilies*, which are not "homilies" *per se*, but preserve a narrative (the *Homilies* date to the early fourth century, while the *Recognitions* belong to the late fourth century and are only preserved in the Latin translation by Rufinus c. 407); while there are several homilies or speeches found in the narrative, their dating and dubious origin offer little to no help to the current discussion.

centuries. All of the characteristics that follow, therefore, should be understood along the lines of Wittgenstein's notion of family resemblance, and not as essential elements that mark every ancient sermon. Some sermons were unscripted, while others appear to have a very formal and rhetorically polished intentionality to them. Some sermons were topical, while others offer an almost word-by-word exegesis of the scriptural passage.

Therefore, when looking back to early Christian preaching, we should expect diverse concerns and expressions to arise in places as diverse as Rome, Carthage, Alexandria, and Antioch. When Ambrose returned from Palestine teaching the Greek style of singing he had learned, the Christians in Milan enjoyed its exuberance and emotion.[76] A similar difference is found in preaching when Egeria traveled from the far west of the empire to Jerusalem: she reports in her diary some of the differences between the liturgy, such as how during the reading of Scripture and preaching, "it is astonishing how much emotion and groaning there is from all the people. There is no one young or old, who on this day does not sob more than can be imagined . . . because the Lord suffered all this for us."[77] When looking for common characteristics of early preaching, we should also expect that writers as diverse as Novatian of Rome, Gregory of Neocaesarea (Thaumaturgus, "the Wonderworker"), and Ephraem the Syrian would likely have diverse homiletical concerns and expressions reflecting their diverse contexts and occasions.

Even though ancient scholars acknowledge the diversity of forms that the sermons could take, they still note some common traits that are present. In his *1 Apology* (written around AD 155),[78] Justin Martyr reports that on every Sunday "the memoirs of the apostles or the writings of the prophets are read, for as long as there is time. Then, when the reader has stopped, the president, in an address, makes admonition and invitation of the imitation of their good things."[79] Similarly, in his *Apology*

---

76. Augustine, *Confessions* 7.15.

77. *Pilgrimage*, 37 (Gingras, 112). This passage is on Good Friday, which seems to evoke exceptional levels of emotion. However, there are hints that similar displays of pathos were common responses; e.g., *Pilgrimage*, 34.

78. For the debate over the number, order, and genre of Justin's apologies, see Thorsteinsson "Literary Genre and Purpose," 91–114. Here we have used the text and translation from Minns and Parvis, *Justin, Philosopher, and Martyr*; Marcovich, *Iustini Martyris Apologiae pro Christianis*; and Munier, *Apologie pour les Chrétiens*.

79. *1 Apology* 67.4–5 (Minns and Parvis, *Justin, Philosopher, and Martyr*, 258–61).

(written after AD 196), Tertullian explains, "We meet to call one another to remembrance of the Scripture, if the aspect of affairs requires us either to be forewarned or to be reminded of anything."[80] In other words, the reading of the Scriptures was followed by some sort of teaching or exhortation. In addition to the Sunday sermon, some sources speak of daily gatherings for Scripture reading and "instruction."[81] There often seems to be allowance for more than one person to preach, which may be attested to as early as the *Didache*,[82] and in later centuries it became normal for any number of presbyters to preach, followed by the bishop's homily.[83]

One widespread characteristic found in the surviving homilies involves the use of classical rhetoric. On the one hand, we find that the widespread disdain for sophistry prompted most church leaders to use the *sermo humilis*, or common and unadorned style of speech, for their homilies.[84] On the other hand, virtually all of the surviving sermonic material owe a big debt to the classical rhetoricians, such as Aristotle, Cicero, and Quintilian.[85] Some of the most fruitful studies of early Christian writings in general and preaching in particular have analyzed these surviving sources in light of rhetorical form, structure, and device.[86]

---

80. *Apol.* 39.3 (Souter 111–13; CCL) *Coimus ad litterarum divinarum commemorationem, si quid praesentium temporum qualitas aut praemonere cogit aut recognoscere*).

81. *Ap. Trad.* 41.2; Cyprian, *Ep.* 39.4.1; and Pamphilius, *Apologia pro Origene* 9.

82. Preaching does not seem to be limited to one person or office, for after mentioning the preaching (in 4.2) the next line reads, "Moreover, you shall seek out daily the presence of the saints, so that you may find support in their words," *Didache* 4.2 (Holmes 350–51: ἐκζητήσεις δὲ καθ' ἡμέραν τὰ πρόσωπα τῶν ἁγίων, ἵνα ἐπαναπαῇς τοῖς λόγοις αὐτῶν).

83. *Life of Polycarp* 22 (for its late dating, see the compelling argument of Moss, "On the Dating of Polycarp, 539–74). Also, see *Const. Apost.* 2.4.26, where the elders also teach: "Let the presbyters be esteemed by you to represent us the apostles, and let them be the teachers of divine knowledge; since our Lord, when He sent us, said, "Go ye, and make disciples of all nations, baptizing them in the name of the Father, and of the Son, and of the Holy Ghost: teaching them to observe all things whatsoever I have commanded you."" (ANF 7:410). Also, see 2.7.57, "Let the presbyters one by one, not all together, exhort the people, and the bishop in the last place, as being the commander." (ANF 7:421). Also, see Egeria, *Pilgrimage*.

84. See bibliography in Auerbach, *Literary Language*, 25–66 (= chapter one, "Sermo Humilis"); and MacMullen, "Note on *Sermo humilis*," 108–12.

85. Even the *sermo humilis* is a specific rhetorical style taught in the classical schools.

86. The bibliography is now enormous. Many such studies can be found in Holmes's notes and bibliography (see *Apostolic Fathers*, 2007). Paul Foster has studied several early sources in this light; Geoffrey D. Dunn has furthered Tertullian studies using

When Augustine later claims that preachers should appeal to their audience aesthetically, what he calls "the art of pleasing," he insists that this is so only to the extent that it assists in persuading the audience to accept the truth ("to turn the mind").[87] In making such a claim about the rhetorical style of the Christian sermon, Augustine does not think he is saying something new, but rather relaying the normal practice of all trained homiliticians.[88]

Much could be said about the role of rhetoric in early Christian preaching, but for now I will limit myself to one major observation. The rhetorician, including the early Christian homilitician, must tailor the speech to the occasion. Early Christian preaching (and writing) was very occasional, and many of the surviving sermons (and writings derived from sermons) exist today precisely because of their effectiveness in addressing concrete concerns. If the community was threatened with false teaching, the Christian preacher could unleash all of the rhetorical devices available to discredit said teaching, which often even included attacks on the false teacher. Tertullian, in his introduction to a detailed review of the Scriptures in opposition to Marcion's abuse of them, opens with a ruthless *ad hominem* attack. In order to discredit Marcion, Tertullian first discredits his homeland, Pontus on the Black Sea.

> Even its situation would prevent you from reckoning Pontus hospitable: as though ashamed of its own barbarism it has set itself at a distance from our more civilized waters. Strange tribes inhabit it—if indeed living in a wagon can be called inhabiting.... Their sexual activity is promiscuous, and for the most part unhidden even when they hide it: they advertise it by hanging a quiver on the yoke of the wagon, so that none may inadvertently break in.... They carve up their fathers' corpses along with mutton, to gulp down at banquets. There is sternness also in the climate.... Rivers are not rivers, only ice: mountains are piled high up with snow: all is torpid, everything stark.... The only thing warm there is Savagery.... Even so, the most

---

rhetorical criticism; and Margaret M. Mitchell has especially focused on Chrysostom's rhetoric (in light of earlier Christian use of rhetoric, following the work of Hans Dieter Betz on Paul). Many others could be named: e.g., Melton, "Preaching and Melito's Use of Greco-Roman Rhetoric," 460–80. For secondary literature on rhetoric and early Christian preaching, see Mayer, "Homiletics," 569–71.

87. *On Christian Doctrine* 4.13.29.

88. His statement is adapted from Cicero, whom—he assumes—is known by all educated individuals.

barbarous and melancholy thing about Pontus is that Marcion was born there.[89]

This invective against Pontus ensures that none of Tertullian's audience would give credence to someone from such a barbaric region—an argument full of logical fallacies, to be sure, but one that was no doubt persuasive nonetheless.[90] This, of course, is not to say that early Christian preaching lacked substance: works like Irenaeus's *Demonstration of Apostolic Preaching* is equally occasional, arising from "Gnostic" challengers to the gospel. And yet this work can display both a passionate concern to disprove opponents as well as a careful study of the Scriptures.

The worst example of this occasional and polemical preaching is the *Adversus Judaeos* tradition. In the complex "parting of the ways"[91] between synagogue and church, numerous disputes arose. The anti-Semitism found in these texts is obviously a disgrace that cannot be swept under the rug, because one of the responsibilities we have when looking at Christian history is to admit to and learn from the sins of the past. While I in no way want to downplay the ugliness and harmfulness of this tradition, I do think we can at least understand the anti-Semitic rhetoric better when we place it within the broader context of early Christian polemical preaching and writing, which often utilized highly charged and—to put it mildly—uncharitable language, whether the opponents were Marcionites, "Gnostics," or Jews.

---

89. *Marc.* 1.1.3–4: *Pontus, qui dicitur Euxinus, natura negatur, nomine illuditur. Ceterum hospitalem Pontum nec de situ aestimes; ita ab humanioribus fretis nostris quasi quodam barbariae suae pudore secessit. Gentes ferocissimae inhabitant; si tamen habitatur in plaustro. Sedes incerta, vita cruda, libido promiscua et plurimum nuda, etiam cum abscondunt, suspensis de iugo pharetris indicibus, ne temere qui intercedat. Ita nec armis suis erubescunt. Parentum cadavera cum pecudibus caesa convivio convorant. Qui non ita decesserint ut escatiles fuerint, maledicta mors est. ...Duritia de caelo quoque. Dies nunquam patens, sol nunquam libens, unus aër nebula, totus annus hibernum, omne quod flaverit aquilo est. Liquores ignibus redeunt, amnes glacie negantur montes pruina exaggerantur. Omnia torpent, omnia rigent; nihil illic nisi feritas calet . . . Sed nihil tam barbarum ac triste apud Pontum quam quod illic Marcion natus est.* Text and translation from Evans, *Tertullian Adversus Marcionem*, 3–5 (slightly modified).

90. While Tertullian's *Against Marcion* is unlikely to derive from sermonic material, it is a text devoted to exegeting the Scriptures. For a similar tactic against a certain Caanite teacher from what may have originally been oral address to his church, see *On Baptism* 1.

91. The secondary literature on the "parting of the ways" is now colossal; for an introduction and bibliography, see Nicklas, *Jews and Christians?*; Buell, *Why This New Race*; and Boyarin, *Border Lines*.

When examining the anti-Jewish rhetoric of the early church, we discover one other characteristic of ancient Christian preaching that emerges: the priority of the Old Testament in many of the early Christian sermons. For example, Melito's Easter sermon is notorious for its anti-Jewish rhetoric (which I do not at all wish to defend or deny), but it is worth noting that this is, at least in part, because of his concern to claim the "Old Testament," which was still the normal source for teaching and preaching in the second and third centuries.[92] Of the over two hundred surviving sermons by Origen, only thirty-nine focus on New Testament texts.[93] The whole *Adversus Judaeos* tradition, which includes texts like *The Epistle of Barnabas*, Justin's *Dialogue with Trypho*, and others,[94] can be understood as a battle over who could claim to be the legitimate heirs to Israel and whose interpretation of Israel's Scriptures were valid.

Returning to Irenaeus, who incidentally knew Hebrew (he cites the Hebrew of Gen 1:1 in *Dem.* 43), most of his work (both *Dem.* and *Adv. haer.*) is actually devoted to a Christian and Christocentric reading of the Old Testament. Irenaeus runs through salvation history, including the eschatological future to come, offering numerous proofs from the "Old Testament." After completing this salvation narrative, Irenaeus concludes,

> This, beloved, is the preaching of the truth, and this is the manner of our redemption, and this is the way of life, which the prophets proclaimed, and Christ established, and the apostles delivered, and the Church in all the world hands on to her children. This must we keep with all certainty, with a sound will and pleasing to God, with good works and right-willed disposition.[95]

Early Christians like Irenaeus were concerned with what could be called a "canonical" approach, preaching from the whole canon of Scripture.

The Christian reading of the Old Testament brings us to another characteristic of early preaching, and one that is widely misunderstood:

---

92. See Stewart-Sykes, "Domestic Origin," 120, for the sources and secondary literature. Also cf. Luke 24:14–15, 27.

93. *Homilies on Luke* (text in Crouzel, Fournier, Périchon 1962, SF 87; trans. in Lienhard 1996, FC 94). For his non-extant sermons, see Jerome, *Letter* 33, to Paula, who also lists sermons on Deuteronomy, Job, Proverbs, Ecclesiastes, Matthew, Acts, 2 Corinthians, Thessalonians, Galatians, Titus, Hebrews, as well as topical homilies on Easter, peace, fasting, and monogamy.

94. Other important texts include Tertullian, *Adversus Judaeos*; Cyprian, *Ad Quirinum*; Origen, *Contra Celsum*, etc.

95. *Dem.* 98 (MacKenzie 28).

the use of allegory. Recent studies have been able to show that the distinction between allegory and typology (and with that, the alleged differences between the Alexandrian and Antiochene "schools") is a false construct, or at least, an exaggeration of modern scholarship.[96] While there is not enough time to review the discussion on patristic exegesis, it is important to point out that the early Christian spokespersons were eager to find, in addition to the literal significance, the moral and spiritual meanings of any given text.

Because a number of recent studies have revisited early Christian hermeneutics in a more favorable light, a veritable movement is emerging among some biblical scholars that seeks to revisit and retrieve the best of pre-critical exegesis.[97] (This is being popularized in various ways, such as the series edited by Thomas Oden entitled *The Ancient Christian Commentary on Scripture*). While it is true that ancient exegetes often fall short of our modern critical standards and often do misappropriate texts, their approach has rightly anticipated some important contemporary conclusions about hermeneutics.

For one thing, the notion of authorial intent is all but dead in contemporary literary studies.[98] Likewise, it is now recognized that the notion of a text having only one meaning is a modern myth. Texts work at various levels and offer a variety of meanings. Origen's claim that the Scriptures contain truths corresponding to our flesh, soul, and spirit does offer some interesting possibilities. Although he is not always consistent in his application of this framework,[99] his tripartite approach gives him the ability to analyze any given passage in light of its historical,[100] ethi-

---

96. For example, when Paul offers typological reading of Old Testament passages (e.g., Gal 4:21–31), he calls it an "allegory (ἀλληγορούμενα)" (4:24). For further discussion, see Martens, "Revisiting the Allegory," 283–317; and Mitchell, "Christian Martyrdom," 177–206.

97. Important studies include Steinmetz, "Superiority of Pre-Critical Exegesis," 27–38; Simonneti, *Biblical Interpretation*; Young, *Biblical Exegesis*; Heine, *Reading the Old Testament*; Martens, *Origen and Scripture*. Also, see the influential study by de Lubac, *Histoire et Esprit*.

98. Following the seminal essay by Wimsatt and Beardsley, "Intentional Fallacy," 468–88.

99. Lienhard, "Origen as Homilist," 47, notes that even though Origen famously speaks of the flesh, soul, and spirit of scripture (*De princ.* 4.2.4) he most commonly preaches in terms of the flesh and the spirit.

100. Origen, as we have mentioned previously, is often maligned or at least misunderstood for his use of allegory. Reading Origen—especially Origen's sermons—will show that he in no way ignores or denies the history. Instead of rejecting the historical

cal, and theological content. Moreover, Origen's view is novel only to the extent that he systematizes what earlier writers had long practiced *ad hoc*.[101] Origen and other early Christian interpreters have also anticipated the maxim espoused by all our homiletics professors: *after you tell your congregation everything they never want to know about the Hittites and nothing more, your congregation is going to look at you and ask, So what?!*[102]

While we may not agree with early Christian interpretations of passages like the food laws about certain meats—which in *Barnabas* become not prohibited menu items, but blacklisted sexual deviants[103]—we should at least credit the early Christians for preaching these texts at all. To ignore these texts, which is widely done today, is functional Marcionism. The early Christians, on the other hand, could not return to the letter of the Law (since that kills); so instead, they found moral meaning in Israel's ancient Scriptures.

---

meaning, he wants to affirm the additional meanings of the text. See the studies of de Lubac, Lienhard, Heine, and Martens cited.

101. Origen's predecessor, Clement of Alexandria, explains the higher meaning to be found in the text: "And as we are clearly aware that the Saviour teaches His people nothing in a merely human way, but everything by a divine and mystical wisdom, we must not understand His words literally (σαρκίνως), but with due inquiry and intelligence we must search out and master their hidden meaning" (*Quis div. salv.* 5; LCL 92:280–83: δεῖ δὲ σαφῶς εἰδότας ὡς οὐδὲν ἀνθρωπίνως ὁ σωτήρ, ἀλλὰ πάντα θείᾳ σοφίᾳ καὶ μυστικῇ διδάσκει τοὺς ἑαυτοῦ, μὴ σαρκίνως ἀκροᾶσθαι τῶν λεγομένων, ἀλλὰ τὸν ἐν αὐτοῖς κεκρυμμένον νοῦν μετὰ τῆς ἀξίας ζητήσεως καὶ συνέσεως ἐρευνᾶν καὶ καταμανθάνειν). It seems that Origen has simply expanded upon the distinction between the "fleshly" and "spiritual" meanings found in Justin, *Dialogue with Trypho*. Justin's explicit distinction, moreover, can arguably be found in earlier texts (cf. the parallels with *Barn.* 6.1–3 and 1 Cor 9:6–11). The "spiritual meaning" often can be moral, doctrinal, or both.

102. Lienhard, "Origen as Homilist," 42–43, notes how important it was for Origen that the congregation pray for his preaching so that he could rightly interpret the text for the church (citing *Homily on Exodus* 9.2, *Homily on Genesis* 12.1, and *Homily on Jeremiah* 19.14). Lienhard also shows ("Origen as Homilist," 48–49) how Origen's three-fold reading of the Scriptures shifted over time, with age, and with the change from theory to practice: that is, whereas his early work (*De princ.*) had the three-fold schema such that the theological, "spiritual," or cosmological was the highest meaning of the text, in his sermons and actual practice of interpreting scripture, the order was actually rearranged so that the fleshly or literal meaning was the entry point; the soul or second level became the theological and/or cosmological point; and then the third and final level, called the "spiritual" if you insist on rigid consistency, was the moral meaning applied to the life of the believer.

103. *Barn.* 10.

This focus on the moral meaning of a text is another central focus and characteristic of most early sermons. Tertullian described the Sunday sermon primarily in these terms, saying,

> There too are pronounced exhortations, corrections, and godly judgments. For our judgment too is delivered with great weight, as among those who are sure that they are acting under the eye of God, and there is the greatest anticipation of the future judgment, if any one has so sinned, as to be banished from the communion of prayer and assembly and all holy fellowship.[104]

Most descriptions of the sermon emphasize this moral center.[105]

The moralism of early Christian preaching can be seen as a negative because it can be understood as "teaching works righteousness." However, I would argue that this moralism should be seen as a positive: because ancient preachers were not plagued by the Protestant/Catholic debates, they could emphasize the moral message undeniably present in the Scriptures. This is especially a positive for preaching, which is usually not the place for endless caveats about the *ordo salutis*. For example, the earliest surviving Christian homily, the text known as *2 Clement*, repeatedly calls for repentance from sin[106]—so much so that the text has been charged with "teaching works righteousness."[107] Statements on how Christians should "pay [God] what is due," along with the call for Christians to "repay God," admittedly sound like the kinds of works righteousness feared by later Protestants.[108]

However, upon closer inspection, this is not works righteousness at all.[109] Those passages go on to state that what is "paid" is "repentance...

---

104. *Apol.* 39.4 (Souter 111–13; CCL: *ibidem etiam exhortationes, castigationes et censura divina. Nam et iudicatur magno cum pondere, ut apud certos de dei conspectu, summumque futuri iudicii praeiudicium est, si quis ita deliquerit, ut a communicatione orationis et conventus et omnis sancti commercii relegetur*).

105. E.g., throughout the *Didasc. Apost.* and the *Const. eccl. Apost.*; cf. *Const. Apost.* 2.3.6, "the bishop, who is set in the Church, who is obliged by his preaching to testify and vehemently to forewarn concerning that judgment" (ANF 7:398).

106. *2 Clem.* 8–11, 13, 16–17.

107. Torrance, *Doctrine of Grace*.

108. *2 Clem.* 9.7 and 15.2.

109. See Parvis, "2 Clement," 270. For a comprehensive study on this issue for the texts contemporary with *2 Clem.*, see Arnold, *Justification in the Second Century*. For early, more general Christian writings, see Oden, *Justification Reader*; as well as discussion in Williams, *Evangelicals and Tradition*.

faith and love."[110] And even these acts are stipulated to be possible only because God "has shown us such mercy."[111] In short, although early Christian preachers may not always explicate their assumptions about grace and faith when speaking about works of righteousness and their rewards, they can hardly be blamed when the New Testament authors on the whole did the same.[112] The moral call to repentance is a theological call to imitate Christ and thereby participate in Christ's union with God.

110. *2 Clem.* 9.8 and 15.2.

111. *2 Clem.* 3.1; cf. 1.4–8.

112. Examples include the following verses (using the NRSV with emphasis added). "For the Son of Man is to come with his angels in the glory of his Father, and then he will *repay* everyone *for what has been done*" (Matt 16:27). "That they should repent and turn to God and *do deeds* consistent with repentance" (Acts 26:20b). "For *he will repay according to each one's deeds*: to those who by patiently *doing good* seek for glory and honor and immortality, he will give eternal life; while for those who are self-seeking and who obey not the truth but wickedness, there will be wrath and fury" (Rom 2:6–8). "The work of each builder will become visible, for the Day will disclose it, because it will be revealed with fire, and the fire will test *what sort of work each has done*" (1 Cor 3:13). "Do you not know that in a race the runners all compete, but only one receives the prize? Run in such a way *that you may win it*" (1 Cor 9:24). "For all of us must appear before the judgment seat of Christ, so that each may receive *recompense for what has been done* in the body, whether good or evil" (2 Cor 5:10). "*Work out your own salvation* with fear and trembling; for it is God who is at work in you, enabling you both to will and to work for his good pleasure" (Phil 2:12b–13). "Knowing that *whatever good we do, we will receive the same* again from the Lord, whether we are slaves or free" (Eph 6:8). "For the wrongdoer *will be paid back for whatever wrong has been done*, and there is no partiality" (Col 3:25). "Alexander the coppersmith did me great harm; the Lord *will pay him back for his deeds*" (2 Tim 4:14). "And without faith it is impossible to please God, for whoever would approach him must believe that he exists *and that he rewards* those who seek him" (Heb 11:6). "like living stones, let yourselves be built into a spiritual house, to be a holy priesthood, to *offer spiritual sacrifices acceptable* to God through Jesus Christ" (1 Pet 2:5). "And when the chief shepherd appears, *you will win the crown of glory* that never fades away. . . . Humble yourselves therefore under the mighty hand of God, so that he may exalt you in due time. . . . And after you have suffered for a little while, the God of all grace, who has called you to his eternal glory in Christ, will himself restore, support, strengthen, and establish you" (1 Pet 5:4, 6, 10). "Many deceivers have gone out into the world, those who do not confess that Jesus Christ has come in the flesh; any such person is the deceiver and the antichrist! Be on your guard, so that you do not lose what we have worked for, but *may receive a full reward*" (2 John 7–8). "Do not fear what you are about to suffer. Beware, the devil is about to throw some of you into prison so *that you may be tested*, and for ten days you will have affliction. Be faithful until death, and I *will give you the crown of life*" (Rev 2:10). "The nations raged, but your wrath has come, and the time for judging the dead, for *rewarding* your servants, the prophets and saints and all who fear" (Rev 11:18). "See, I am coming soon; my *reward* is with me, *to repay according to everyone's work.*" (Rev 22:12).

In other words, the early Christian teaching on *theosis*, or deification, is—in large part—a call to become godlike and morally godly (aka, "divine"). In his *Demonstration of Apostolic Preaching*, Irenaeus insists, "Purity of the flesh is the restraining abstinence from all shameful things and all unrighteous deeds, and purity of the soul is *the keeping [of] faith* towards God entire."[113]

Another positive that I would point to in early Christian "moral" and "theological" interpretation of the Scriptures is the attention paid to the spiritual state of the interpreter—that is, the preacher. In order to hear the spiritual meaning of the text, the expositor's own spiritual state must be healthy. In texts like the *Epistle of Barnabas* and throughout Origen's oeuvre, the insistence on prayer and fasting is clarified because only a Spirit-filled believer can attain and proclaim God's message. This is so much the case that one of the earliest titles for the third person of the Trinity was "the prophetic Spirit" because the Spirit, or "Breath," of God was the one who filled the voice of the Christian preacher, enabling him or her to speak God's Word.[114]

In addition to the moral meaning, the other aspect of a spiritual or "allegorical" reading of the Scriptures involves an emphasis on the theological meaning. What does the text say about God? Here it will come as no surprise when I point out how early preachers interpreted their Old Testament Christocentrically. I would, however, press this subject further

---

113. *Dem.* 2 (MacKenzie 1; emph. added). Similarly, see Pseudo-Hippolytus, *On the Holy Theophany* 8, "Wherefore I preach to this effect: Come, all ye kindreds of the nations, to the immortality of the baptism. I bring good tidings of life to you who tarry in the darkness of ignorance. Come into liberty from slavery, into a kingdom from tyranny, into incorruption from corruption. And how, saith one, shall we come? How? By water and the Holy Ghost. This is the water in conjunction with the Spirit, by which paradise is watered, by which the earth is enriched, by which plants grow, by which animals multiply, and (to sum up the whole in a single word) by which man is begotten again and endued with life, in which also Christ was baptized, and in which the Spirit descended in the form of a dove" (ANF 5:237); and again (in *On the Holy Theophany* 10), "For he who comes down in faith to the laver of regeneration, and renounces the devil, and joins himself to Christ; who denies the enemy, and makes the confession that Christ is God; who puts off the bondage, and puts on the adoption—he comes up from the baptism brilliant as the sun, flashing forth the beams of righteousness, and, which is indeed the chief thing, he returns a son of God and joint-heir with Christ. To Him be the glory and the power, together with His most holy, and good, and quickening Spirit, now and ever, and to all the ages of the ages. Amen." (ANF 5:237).

114. This can be clearly seen in writers like Justin Martyr, Irenaeus, and Tertullian. See Wilhite, "Personal/Substantial Spirit of Prophecy," and Wilhite, "Tertullian," 45–71.

than is often acknowledged. Early Christians not only found Christ in the Old Testament by way of prophecy, types, and foreshadowing, but they also believed Jesus to be the God of Israel. Many of them (if not most) took the earliest Christian confession, "Jesus is Lord," to its most radical extent: Jesus is the LORD (all caps in our translations) of the Old Testament.

In other words, whereas most modern Christian readers of the Old Testament (both practitioners and academics) assume that the primary person encountered in the God of the Old Testament is the Father, most early Christians assumed that the primary person encountered in the YHWH of Israel was the Son—Jesus pre-incarnate. (This is a point on which I am elaborating in a forthcoming book co-authored with New Testament scholar Adam Winn, and so I will not go into great length here to illustrate it from the sources.)

But one more quote from Irenaeus's *Demonstration of Apostolic Preaching* is informative. When discussing the scene from Gen 18 during which three "men" visit Abraham, Irenaeus insists, "It was not the Father of all, who is not seen by the world, the Maker of all who said: *Heaven is my throne* . . . . It was not He that came and stood in a very small space and spake with Abraham; but the Word of God, who was ever with mankind."[115] Irenaeus then adds, "He it is who spake with Moses in the bush. . . . He it is who came forth and came down for the deliverance of the oppressed, bringing us out from the power of the Egyptians."[116] In other words, whenever Christians read the Old Testament, the primary *persona* they encounter there is the pre-incarnate Christ. This means that whether preaching from the Old or New Testament, early Christians believed they were hearing the words of the Word Himself.

This brings us to our last characteristic of early Christian preaching, which has to do with the nature of preaching itself. Preaching for many early Christians was sacramental.[117] Let me point out to you that we have thus far reviewed the major ingredients for a sacrament in this list of characteristics: Early Christian preaching was occasional, contextual, rhetorically localized, and in a word embodied. Along with this concrete expression, this outward and visible medium, the concern is

---

115. *Dem.* 44 (MacKenzie 14).

116. *Dem.* 44 (MacKenzie 14).

117. I came to this conclusion before learning about the publication of Hans Boersma's recent studies, which I have not had time to incorporate into this essay: Boersma, *Sacramental Preaching*.

with the spiritual meaning of the text as understood in allegorical, moral, and/or theological terms—one could say the inward and invisible grace. Placed by these two factors—that is, the outward-visible and the inward-invisible,[118] along with the role of the Holy Spirit in making the moment sacred (because, as we said, only a Spirit-filled believer can truly proclaim God's Word)—the resulting view involves seeing the act of preaching as one that manifests God's real presence.

A few statements from early Christian texts illustrate this early understanding of preaching. In the *Didache* we read, "My child, remember night and day the one who preaches God's word to you, and honor him as though he were the Lord. For wherever the Lord's nature is preached, there the Lord is."[119] A few decades later, Ignatius writes to the Ephesians and mentions the "mysteries to be loudly proclaimed" ("μυστήρια," the Greek word for "sacrament," and "κραυγῆς," a Greek word for "proclamation").[120] Ignatius then outlines the content of true Christian preaching, and closes his message by stating how the Christians should "obey the bishop and council of elders with an undisturbed mind, breaking one bread, which is the medicine of immortality, the antidote we take in order not to die but to live forever in Jesus Christ."[121] Later, Tertullian describes the preaching of the Scriptures as a "feeding": "In any case we feed our belief on holy words, we raise our hope, we strengthen our confidence, we clinch the teaching none the less by driving home precepts."[122]

A similar concept is at work in the *Didascalia Apostolorum*: the bishop is advised to "be assiduous in his teaching and constant in reading

118. Cf. Ignatius, *Ep. Poly.* 2.2.

119. *Did.* 4.1 (Holmes 348–51: Τέκνον μου, τοῦ λαλοῦντός σοι τὸν λόγον τοῦ θεοῦ μνησθήσῃ νυκτὸς καὶ ἡμέρας, τιμήσεις δὲ αὐτὸν ὡς κύριον. ὅθεν γὰρ ἡ κυριότης λαλεῖται, ἐκεῖ κύριός ἐστιν.) Note that ἡ κυριότης, (i.e., dominion or lordship), is a term also used in Eph 1:21; Col 1:16; 2 Pet 2:10; and Jude 1:8.

120. *Ep. Eph.* 19.1 (Holmes 196–97).

121. *Ep.Eph.* 20.2 (Holmes 198–99): τὸ ὑπακούειν ὑμᾶς τῷ ἐπισκόπῳ καὶ τῷ πρεσβυτερίῳ ἀπερισπάστῳ διανοίᾳ, ἕνα ἄρτον κλῶντες, ὅ ἐστιν φάρμακον ἀθανασίας, ἀντίδοτος τοῦ μὴ ἀποθανεῖν ἀλλὰ ζῆν ἐν Ἰησοῦ Χριστῷ διὰ παντός). The bishop and elders are to be "obeyed" because (and only because?) they are restating the commands and moral precepts of the Gospel via preaching. While this statement is always understood to refer to two different acts (preaching and the Eucharist), I wonder if the "bread" that is broken is in fact the Word of God (cf. Matt 4:4) just as is the "medicine of immortality" (cf. Matt 8:8b and Ign., *Ep. Poly.* 2.1–2).

122. *Apol.* 39.3 (Souter 111–13; CCL: *Certe fidem sanctis vocibus pascimus, spem erigimus, fiduciam figimus, disciplinam praeceptorum nihilominus inculcationibus densamus*).

the divine Scriptures with diligence, that he may interpret and expound the Scriptures fittingly. And let him compare the Law and the Prophets with the Gospel, so that the sayings of the Law and the Prophets may be in accord with the Gospel"; and then the text adds (also in 4.2.5), "Be diligent therefore and attentive to the word, O bishop, so that, if thou canst, thou explain every saying: that with much doctrine thou mayest abundantly nourish and give drink to thy people."[123] In other words, the act of preaching itself was a kind of sacred food and drink or sacrament, and the act of expositing the words of the Scriptures manifested the real presence of the Word of God.

Conclusion

In conclusion, there is likely much that can be learned about early Christian preaching by looking further into these characteristics which I have only briefly listed here. In sum, I think that the significance of pre-Nicene Christian preaching is found in that which is signified—the embodiment of, emphasis on, and real presence-ing (or "presenting") of the Lord Jesus Christ. Through the preacher proclaiming His saving acts and divine character, the audience encounters the transforming and deifying Spirit of God. We began by citing Constantine's claim that "A bad expositor (κακὸς ἑρμηνεὺς) is in very truth the image and representation of the devil." What this quote assumes is that the opposite is also the case: a good expositor is in the image and likeness of Christ.

Bibliography

Armstrong, Jonathan J. *The Role of the Rule of Faith in the Formation of the New Testament Canon According to Eusebius of Caesarea.* Lewiston, NY: Edwin Mellon, 2014.

Arnold, Brian J. *Justification in the Second Century.* Berlin: De Gruyter, 2017.

Auerbach, Eric. *Literary Language and Its Public: In Late Latin Antiquity and in the Middle Ages.* Translated by Ralph Manheim. Princeton: Princeton University Press, 1993 (1958 Germ. orig.).

---

123. *Didasc. Apost.* 4.2.5 (pp.12–13); cf. *Const. eccl. Apost.* 12, where "Thomas" refers to the one "who speaketh to thee the word of God and is to thee the cause of life." There are still other roles stipulated for the bishop, such as judging the confession of sins (*Didasc. Apost.* 5.2.7–5.2.11). Also, see *Const. Apost.* 2.4.26, which states, "The bishop, he is the minister of the word, the keeper of knowledge, the mediator between God and you in the several parts of your divine worship. He is the teacher of piety" (ANF 7:410).

Baldovin, John F. "Hippolytus and the Apostolic Tradition: Recent Research and Commentary." *Theological Studies* 64 (2003) 520–42.

Barnes, Timothy David. *Tertullian: An Historical and Literary Study*. Rev. ed. Oxford: Clarendon Press, 1985.

Bauer, Walter. *Der Wortgottesdienst der ältesten Christen*. Tubingen: Mohr, 1930.

———. *Orthodoxy and Heresy in Earliest Christianity*. Edited by Robert A. Kraft and Gerhard Kroedel. Philadelphia: Fortress, [1934]1979.

Bobertz, Charles A. "The Historical Context of Cyprian's *De Unitate*." *Journal of Theological Studies* 5 (1990) 107–11.

Boersma, Hans. *Sacramental Preaching: Sermons on the Hidden Presence of Christ*. Grand Rapids, MI: Baker, 2016.

———. *Scripture as Real Presence: Sacramental Preaching in the Early Church*. Grand Rapids, MI: Baker, 2017.

Boyarin, Daniel. *Border Lines: The Partition of Judaeo-Christianity*. Philadelphia: University of Pennsylvania Press, 2004.

Bray, Gerald L. *Biblical Interpretation: Past & Present*. Downers Grove, IL: IVP Academic, 1996.

Brent, Allen. *Hippolytus and the Roman Church in the Third Century*. Leiden: Brill, 1995.

Buell, Denise Kimber. *Why This New Race: Ethnic Reasoning in Early Christianity*. New York: Columbia University Press, 2005.

Bultmann, Rudolf. *Theologie des Neuen Testaments*. Tübingen: Mohr Siebeck, 1953.

Burghardt, Walter J., and David G. Hunter. *Preaching in the Patristic Age: Studies in Honor of Walter J. Burghardt, S.J.* New York: Paulist, 1989.

Buttersworth, G. W. *Clement of Alexandria: The Exhortation to the Greeks. The Rich Man's Salvation. To the Newly Baptized*. LCL 92. Harvard: Harvard University Press, 1919.

Cerrato, J. A. *Hippolytus between East and West: The Commentaries and the Provenance of the Corpus*. New York: Oxford University Press, 2002.

Clarke, G.W. *The Letters of Cyprian of Carthage*. 4 vols. Ancient Christian Writers 43, 44, 46, 47. New York: Newman Press, 1984–89.

Cohink, Lynn H. *The Peri Pascha Attributed to Melito of Sardis*. Providence, RI: Brown Judaic Studies, 2000.

Congdon, David W. "Is There a Kerygma in This Text? A Review Article." *Journal of Theological Interpretation* 9 (2015) 299–311.

———. "Kerygma and Community: A Response to R. W. L. Moberly's Revisiting of Bultmann." *Journal of Theological Interpretation* 8 (2014) 1–21, 10–11.

Cothenet, Édouard. "Les Prophètes Chrétiens comme exégètes charismatiques de l'écriture." In *Prophetic Vocation in the New Testament and Today*, edited by J. Panagopoulos, 77–107. Leiden: Brill, 1977.

Cunningham, Mary B., and Pauline Allen. *Preacher and Audience: Studies in Early Christian and Byzantine Homiletics*. Leiden: Brill, 1998.

de Lubac, Henri. *Histoire et Esprit: L'intelligence de l'Ecriture d'après Origène*. Paris: Aubier, 1950.

Dunn-Wilson, David. *A Mirror for the Church: Preaching in the First Five Centuries*. Grand Rapids, MI: Eerdmans, 2005.

Edsall, Benjamin A. "Kerygma, Catechesis and Other Things We Used to Find: Twentieth-Century Research on Early Christian Teaching since Alfred Seeberg (1903)." *Currents in Biblical Research* 10 (2012) 410–41.

Edwards Jr., O. C. *A History of Preaching*. 2 vols. Nashville: Abingdon, 2004.

Evans, Ernest. *Tertullian Adversus Marcionem*. Oxford: Oxford University Press, 1972.

Fitzmyer, Joseph A. "Preaching in the Apostolic and Subapostolic Age." In *Preaching in the Patristic Age: Studies in Honor of Walter J. Burghardt*, edited by David G. Hunter, 19–35. New York: Paulist, 1989.

Forbes, Christopher. *Prophecy and Inspired Speech in Early Christianity and Its Hellenistic Environment*. Peabody, MA: Hendrickson, 1997.

Gibson, Michael D. "Does Jesus Have a Say in the Kerygma? A Critical Remembrance of Bultmann." *Scottish Journal of Theology* 58 (2005) 83–103.

Gulácsi, Zsuzsanna. *Mani's Pictures: The Didactic Images of the Manichaeans from Sasanian Mesopotamia to Uygur Central Asia and Tang-Ming China*. Leiden: Brill, 2015.

Harrington, Daniel J. "The Reception of Walter Bauer's *Orthodoxy and Heresy in Earliest Christianity* during the Last Decade." *Harvard Theological Review* 73 (1980) 289–98.

Harrower, Scott, and Michael Bird, eds. *Second Century Christianity: A Comprehensive Guide to Its Sources*. (n.p.).

Heine, Ronald E. *Reading the Old Testament with the Ancient Church: Exploring the Formation of Early Christian Thought*. Grand Rapids, MI: Baker, 2007.

Hills, Julian. *Tradition and Composition in the* Epistula Apostolorum. Minneapolis: Fortress, 1990.

Kannengiesser, Charles. "The Homiletical Festal Letters of Athanasius." In *Preaching in the Patristic Age: Studies in Honor of Walter J. Burghardt*, edited by David G. Hunter, 73–100. New York: Paulist, 1989.

Knopf, R. "Die Anognose zum zweiten Clemensbrief," *Zeitschrift für die neutestamentliche Wissenschaft* 3 (1902).

Kraemer, Ross Shepard, and Mary Rose D'Angelo. *Women and Christian Origins*. Oxford: Oxford University Press, 1999.

Lawson, R. P., trans. *The Song of Songs: Commentary and Homilies*. Westminster, MD: Newman, 1957.

Lemcio, Eugene E. "The Unifying Kerygma of the New Testament I and II." *Journal for the Study of the New Testament* 33 and 38 (1988, 1990) 3–17, 3–11.

Lienhard, Joseph T. "Origen as Homilist." In *Preaching in the Patristic Age: Studies in Honor of Walter J. Burghardt*, edited by David G. Hunter, 36–52. New York: Paulist, 1989.

Lieu, Judith. "Melito of Sardis." *Expository Times* 110 (1998).

Lightfoot, J. B. *Apostolic Fathers*. New York: Macmillan, 1890.

Lindemann, Andreas. *Die Clemensbriefe*. HNT 17. Tübingen: Mohr Siebeck, 1992.

MacKenzie, Iain M. *Irenaeus's Demonstration of the Apostolic Preaching: A Theological Commentary and Translation*. Aldershot: Ashgate, 2002.

MacMullen, Ramsay. "A Note on *Sermo humilis*." *Journal of Theological Studies* 17 (1966) 108–12.

Marcovich, Miroslav. *Iustini Martyris Apologiae pro Christianis*. Berlin: Walter de Gruyter, 1994.

Markschies, Christoph. *Valentinus Gnosticus?* Tubingen: Mohr Siebeck, 1992.

Martens, Peter W. *Origen and Scripture: The Contours of the Exegetical Life*. Oxford: Oxford University Press, 2012.

———. "Revisiting the Allegory/Typology Distinction: The Case of Origen." *Journal of Early Christian Studies* 16 (2008) 283–317.
Melton Jr., Frankie J. "Preaching and Melito's Use of Greco-Roman Rhetoric." *Bibliotheca Sacra* 167 (2010) 460–80.
Meyer, Marvin W. "Introduction to *The Letter of Peter to Philip*." In *Nag Hammadi Codex VII*, edited by Birger A. Pearson, 231. Nag Hammadi and Manichaean Studies 30. Leiden: Brill, 1995.
Mayer, Wendy. "Homiletics." In *The Oxford Handbook of Early Christian Studies*, edited by Susan Ashbrook Harvey and David G. Hunter, 565–83. Oxford: Oxford University Press, 2008.
Miller, Patricia Cox. *Women in Early Christianity: Translations from Greek Texts*. Washington, DC: Catholic University of America Press, 2005.
Minns, Denis, and Paul Parvis, eds., trans. *Justin, Philosopher, and Martyr: Apologies*. Oxford: Oxford University Press, 2009.
Mitchell, Margaret M. "Christian Martyrdom and the 'Dialect of the Holy Scriptures': The Literal, the Allegorical, the Martyrological." *Biblical Interpretation* 17 (2009) 177–206.
Moss, Candida. "On the Dating of Polycarp: Rethinking the Place of the *Martyrdom of Polycarp* in the History of Christianity." *Early Christianity* 1 (2010) 539–74.
Mühlenberg, E., and J. van Oort, eds. *Predigt in der Alten Kirche*. Kampen: Kok Pharos, 1994.
Munier, Charles. *Apologie pour les Chrétiens*. SC 507. Paris: Éditions de Cerf, 2006.
Nautin, Pierre. *Le Dossier d'Hippolyte et de Méliton dans les florilèges dogmatiques et chez les historiens modernes*. Paris: Cerf, 1953.
———. *Origène: Sa vie et son oeuvre*. Paris: Beauchesne, 1977.
Nicklas, Tobias. *Jews and Christians?: Second-Century "Christian" Perspectives on the "Parting of the Ways"*. Tübingen: Mohr Siebeck, 2014.
Oden, Thomas C. *The Justification Reader*. Grand Rapids, MI: Eerdmans, 2002.
Olivar, Alexander. "Reflections on Problems Raised by Early Christian Preaching." Translated by Joseph Munitiz. In *Preacher and Audience: Studies in Early Christian and Byzantine Homiletics*, edited by Mary B. Cunningham and Pauline Allen, (21–32). Leiden: Brill, 1998.
Parvis, Paul. "2 Clement and the Meaning of the Christian Homily." *Expository Times* 117 (2006) 265–70.
Perrone, Lorenzo, Marina Molin Pradel, Emanuela Prinzivalli, and Antonio Cacciari. *Die neuen Psalmenhomilien: eine kritische Edition des Codex monacensis graecus 314*. Berlin: De Gruyter, 2015.
Quasten, Johannes. *Patrology*. Westminister, MD: Newman, 1950.
Salzmann, Jorg Christian. *Lehren und Ermahnen: zur Geschichte des christlichen Wortgottesdienstes in der ersten drei Jahrhunderten*. WUNT 2.59. Tubingen: Mohr Siebeck, 1994.
Scheck, Thomas P., and Christopher A. Hall, trans. *Homilies on Numbers*. Downers Grove, IL: IVP Academic, 2009.
———, trans. *Origen: Homilies 1–14 on Ezekiel*. New York: Newman, 2010.
Simonneti, Manlio. *Biblical Interpretation in the Early Church: A Historical Introduction to Patristic Exegesis*. Edinburgh: Continuum, 1994.
Steinmetz, David C. "The Superiority of Pre-Critical Exegesis." *Theology Today* 37 (1980) 27–38.

Stewart-Sykes, Alistair. *The Apostolic Church Order: The Greek Text with Introduction, Translation and Annotation*. Early Christian Studies 10. Strathfield: St. Paul's Publications, 2006.

———. "The Domestic Origin of the Liturgy of the Word." *Studia Patristica* 40 (2006) 115–20.

———. *From Prophecy to Preaching: A Search for the Origins of the Christian Homily*. Leiden: Brill, 2001.

———. "Hermas the Prophet and Hippolytus the Preacher: The Roman Homily and Its Social Context." In *Preacher and Audience: Studies in Early Christian and Byzantine Homiletics*, edited by Mary B. Cunningham and Pauline Allen, 33–63. Leiden: Brill, 1998.

———. *The Lamb's High Feast: Melito, Peri Pascha and the Quartodeciman Paschal Liturgy at Sardis*. Supplements to Vigiliae Christianae. Leiden: Brill, 1998.

Tabbernee, William. *Montanist Inscriptions and Testimonia: Epigraphic Sources Illustrating the History of Montanism*. Macon, GA: Mercer University Press, 1997.

Thorsteinsson, Runar M. "The Literary Genre and Purpose of Justin's Second Apology: A Critical Review with Insights from Ancient Epistolography." *Harvard Theological Review* 105 (2012) 91–114.

Torrance, Thomas F. *The Doctrine of Grace in the Apostolic Fathers*. Eugene, OR: Wipf and Stock, 1996 (orig. 1959).

Tuckett, C. M. *2 Clement: Introduction, Text, and Commentary*. Oxford: Oxford University Press, 2012.

Wilhite, David. *Ancient African Christianity*. London: Routledge, 2017.

———. *The Gospel According to Heretics: Discovering Orthodoxy through Early Christological Conflicts*. Grand Rapids, MI: Baker, 2015.

———. "The Personal/Substantial Spirit of Prophecy: Irenaeus's Use of Paul Against the Heresies." In *Irenaeus and Paul*, edited by Todd Still and David Wilhite. London: T. & T. Clark, forthcoming 2019.

———. "Tertullian and the Spirit of Prophecy." In *Tertullian and Paul*, edited by Todd Still and Wilhite, 45–71. London: T. & T. Clark, 2013.

———. *The True Church: Retrieving a North African Sermon on the Song of Songs*. New Haven: ICCS, 2017.

Wilken, Robert L. "Diversity and Unity in Early Christianity." *Second Century* 1 (1981) 101–10.

Williams, D. H. *Evangelicals and Tradition: The Formative Influence of the Early Church*. Grand Rapids, MI: Baker, 2005.

Williams, Frank, trans. *The Panarion of Epiphanius of Salamis, Book I (Sects 1–46)*. Leiden: Brill, 2009.

———. *The Panarion of Epiphanius of Salamis: Books II and III. De Fide*. Leiden: Brill, 2013.

Wimsatt, W. K., and M. C. Beardsley. "The Intentional Fallacy." *The Sewanee Review* 54 (1946) 468–88.

Witherington, Ben. *The New Testament Story*. Grand Rapids, MI: Eerdmans, 2004.

Young, Frances. *Biblical Exegesis and the Formation of Christian Culture*. Cambridge: Cambridge University Press, 1997.

Chapter Five

Preaching from Augustine to Aquinas

PAUL SCOTT WILSON

Augustine (AD 354-430)

IN TERMS OF PREACHING, Augustine is the most important person of this period. He wrote his preaching volume entitled *On Christian Doctrine* in two stages. He wrote the first three books in AD 397 when he was forty-two, just after he became the bishop, with the accompanying responsibility to teach preaching. He pioneered sound principles for biblical interpretation and what classical rhetoric calls "discovery" of what to say. Late in life, Augustine wrote Book IV on "teaching" (4:0), and some scholars mistakenly only refer to it as "homiletics." The whole book is the first and only major one on homiletics through much of the Middle Ages.

Born near Carthage, North Africa, in AD 354, Augustine tells in his autobiography, *Confessions*, about his wild student living followed by a career teaching rhetoric, eventually at the imperial court in Milan in Italy. Christianity became the sole official religion of the Roman Empire six years before he was baptized by Ambrose at Easter in AD 386 at the age of thirty-one. Five years later, in spite of what he called his "protests and weeping," he was ordained while visiting Hippo, and four years afterward at forty-one, became Bishop of Hippo. He addressed the Council of Hippo in AD 393, which finalized the scriptural canon. He wrote *The*

City of God in response to the Visigoths sacking Rome in AD 410. Twenty years later, he died at age seventy-six during the first year of a siege of Hippo by the Germanic Vandals as the Roman Empire was falling.

His ideas on preaching, divine grace, and salvation were foundational for the Protestant Reformers. Of his several hundred sermons that survive, many were transcribed by stenographers and students who sat at the front of the sanctuary. Many sermons are exegetical, while several others are doctrinal with no specific biblical text. We may highlight four aspects of his homiletic[1] that became or were already standard:

1) He followed Irenaeus (AD 130–202) in upholding "the rule of faith," which states that the Scriptures mean what the bishops commonly affirm in their preaching and practice. If in doubt, the interpretation of "the greater number of catholic Churches" is preferred.[2]

2) Some subject matters in Scripture are meant to be taken literally ("openly"), including "all those teachings which involve faith, the mores of living, and ... hope and charity." Literal texts illuminate "obscure" ("figurative," "allegorical," or "prophetic") texts.[3] In other words, the Scriptures interprets the Scriptures.

3) Augustine defends the literal meaning. Origen, in the previous century, said that some texts could not be literally true: the Garden of Eden, Noah, Jesus' temptation from a height so great that He could see all the kingdoms of the world, including India.[4] Of the different order of Jesus' temptations in Matthew and Luke, Augustine says, "It is, however, a matter of no real consequence, provided it be clear that all these incidents did take place."[5] Concerning different versions of the miracle of five loaves, "The truth is, that the one has reported simply a part, and the other given the whole."[6]

4) He reinforces early church understandings of the Scriptures: the Old Testament is revealed in the New; the New Testament is disguised

---

1. I have explored Augustine's homiletic previously, especially in my *Concise History of Preaching*, 59–66; and *God Sense*, 41–45, and I draw on some of that work in what follows.
2. Robertson, *On Christian Doctrine*, 2.8. All citations are from this edition.
3. Robertson, *On Christian Doctrine*, 2.9.
4. Origen, *On First Principles*, 4:15, 384.
5. Augustine, *Harmony of the Gospels*, 120.
6. Augustine, *Harmony of the Gospels*, 149.

in the Old; the Old Testament references to God are frequently assigned to Jesus; the Old Testament is prophetic of Christ, but it also relates historical events that actually happened.

These are six of Augustine's innovations for preaching:

1) He borrows from what Cicero said about public speaking and applies it to preaching. Thus, the purpose of preaching is to teach, delight, and "move" or persuade. Teaching is essential, and delighting and persuading may naturally follow.[7] The preacher "should not consider the eloquence of his teaching, but the clarity of it."[8] Sermons should not be prepared word for word and memorized, for that can mar effective communication.[9]

2) Augustine promotes the three ancient styles of speaking: the subdued or plain style is for teaching; the moderate or middle style is for delighting—it is the most carefully crafted and enjoyable to listen to, as it is today in narrative or imagistic speech; and the grand style is for persuading or emotionally moving the audience.[10] In Cicero, these are separate kinds of speech, but Augustine encourages all three types of speech in any one sermon to provide variety and prevent boredom.[11]

3) The primary principle for interpretation of a figurative passage is the rule of love, which he defines as "the motion of the soul toward the enjoyment of God for His own sake, and the enjoyment of one's self and of one's neighbor for the sake of God."[12] Without love, one cannot understand the Scriptures.[13]

4) He refuses to teach his students rhetoric, but instead instructs them to imitate the Bible: "If it is useful, it is found here."[14]

---

7. Origen, 4:12ff.
8. Origen, 4:9.
9. Origen, 4:10.
10. Origen, 4:19–20.
11. Cicero, *Orator*, section 69.
12. Robertson, *On Christian Doctrine*, 3:10:16.
13. Robertson, *On Christian Doctrine*, 1:36.
14. Robertson, *On Christian Doctrine*, 2.42.

5) Augustine preserves the grand style in preaching. It is impassioned, fast-paced speech[15] that moves people to tears or change their lives through an encounter with the truth.[16] It primarily addresses pathos or emotion in rhetorical terms. It can use all of the "ornaments" of language such as imagery and rhetoric, but it does not need them.[17]

6) Augustine gives early support for what I, as well as others, call proclamation (in contrast to teaching in preaching)—that is, impassioned declaration of the good news to the people. African American celebration, which may come as an emotional climax to a sermon, often employs various forms of proclamation. Melito of Sardis's homily from AD 170, "On the Passover," includes several early examples of celebration. Augustine mentions something similar. He says, "It must be admitted that our [biblical] authors are lacking that rhetorical ornament which consists of rhyming closings."[18] He suggests the biblical writers could be easily reworked to provide what is needed.

The following Christmas sermon by Augustine vividly describes its true celebration. Christmas was first celebrated only around AD 313, after Constantine became a Christian. Note the balanced phrasing of what Augustine called "contraries" in his impassioned witness:

> My mouth will speak the praise of the Lord. . . . He is . . . the Word God before all time, the Word made flesh at a suitable time. Maker of the sun, he is made under the sun. Disposer of all ages in the bosom of the Father, He consecrates this day in the womb of His mother; in Him He remains, from her He goes forth. Creator of heaven and earth, He was born on earth under heaven. Unspeakably wise, He is wisely speechless; filling the world, He lies in a manger; Ruler of the stars, He nurses at His mother's bosom. He is both great in the nature of God and small in the form of a servant, but so that His greatness is not diminished by His smallness, nor His smallness overwhelmed by His greatness. For He did not desert His divine works when He took to Himself human members. Nor did He cease *to reach from end to end mightily, and to order all things sweetly,* [c.f. Wisdom 8:1] when, having put on the infirmity of the flesh, He was received into the Virgin's womb, not confined therein. . . . [T]he Word

---

15. Robertson, *On Christian Doctrine*, 4:17:34
16. Robertson, *On Christian Doctrine*, 4:20:41–42.
17. Robertson, *On Christian Doctrine*, 4:20:42.
18. Robertson, *On Christian Doctrine*, 4:20:41.

of God, through which all things have been made . . . is not hemmed in by space, nor extended by time, nor varied by long and short pauses, nor composed by sounds, nor terminated by silence; how much more could this Word, this great Word . . . go forth to reveal Itself to the eyes of men, and, on the other hand, illuminate the minds of the angels! And appear on earth, and, on the other hand, transcend the heavens! And be made man, and, on the other hand, make men![19]

Early Church Hermeneutics: Multiple Meanings of the Scriptures

A brilliant insight of the early church is a) that the Scriptures have many possible legitimate meanings; and b) that theological lenses are needed to read it. Philo the Jew identifies two senses in Jewish Scriptures, the literal concerning the letters of the text and the spiritual concerning the real meaning, "the invisible intention latent in the text."[20] Origen spoke of three senses (flesh, moral, and spirit): when the flesh sense of a text has trouble, it is a divine signal to go to the spiritual meaning.[21] Augustine speaks of four senses of Scripture, two of which are not in Origen.[22] The literal cannot be the only sense of Noah: "For what right-minded man will contend that books so religiously preserved during thousands of years, and transmitted by so orderly a succession, were written without an object, or that only the bare historical facts are to be considered when we read them?"[23]

The early church fathers understood that God intends various meanings and gives instruction on reading texts. They cite various textual supports: First Corinthians 2:7 (NRSV) says, "But we speak God's wisdom, secret and hidden, which God decreed before the ages for our glory." Paul says we are "ministers of a new covenant, not of letter but of spirit, for the letter kills, but the Spirit gives life" (2 Cor 3:6). Not everyone was meant

---

19. Augustine, "Sermon 5," 85–87.
20. Philo, *Contemplative Life*, 236–7.
21. Origen, *On First Principles*, 4:11.
22. To the literal (historical) and allegorical he adds the analogical (demonstrating the congruence of Old and New Testaments) and the etiological (giving the causes of things said and done). See Preus, *From Shadow to Promise*, 21, n. 26. See also Evans, *Language and Logic*, 114–15.
23. Augustine, *City of God*, 307.

to unlock the secret meanings of Scripture, however, says Origen, as Isa 6:9 states, "Go and say to this people: 'Keep listening but do not comprehend; keep looking, but do not understand.'" The senses were God's way of providing a key to unlock what literary critic Northrop Frye called the Bible, namely *The Great Code*.[24]

The number and names of the various senses of the Scriptures varied in the early church, but the standard exegetical model became known as the fourfold method or *quadriga*. (These four were not Augustine's four). It was provided by John Cassian, John Chrysostom's deacon, who brought it back with him from the East when Chrysostom was banished by the Empress to the Black Sea. Cassian included it in his *Conferences*, a book that Benedict made required reading for the *Benedictine Rule* (c. AD 529), which guided monastic life in the West.[25]

Cassian believes that the Bible warrants three senses beyond the literal, as in the Trinity itself. In 1 Cor 13:13, which mentions "faith, hope and love, and the greatest of these is love," faith is the allegorical or Christ-meaning of the text (not necessarily the "wild" interpretation often associated with allegory); hope is the anagogical or eschatological meaning; and love is the moral meaning—what we do in relation to our neighbors and God. The moral meaning or sense was primary because it was readily understood, even by simple, uneducated people, and gave them a way of bettering themselves before God.

Reason and the Early Middle Ages

Petrarch called the period from the time of Augustine to AD 800 the Dark Ages because so much that was good in the Roman Empire had been lost: knowledge, culture, agriculture, and trade. Mass migrations occurred mainly from the north. The period was marked by great suffering. Plagues and wars caused a decline of population estimated to have exceeded 50 percent.

---

24. Frye, *Great Code*.

25. Cassian offers a famous example of the four meanings of "Jerusalem" as it is found in various places in the Scriptures: literally, it is the actual city. The allegorical sense is the Christ sense and in this case, Jerusalem is the church, the body of Christ. The prophetic sense (eschatological, anagogic) concerns the last things, Jerusalem is the heavenly city of God. The moral sense applies to practical living and saving the soul. See Preus, *From Shadow to Promise*, 21–22.

In AD 800, the coronation of Charlemagne as Emperor of Rome began a century of the Carolingian renaissance, in which the culture was revived and Europe united. Monasteries became centers of higher education. These schools did not compare with what was available in the Muslim world, which preserved the works of ancient Greece, including math and science. The Christians, during the Crusades from 1095 to 1291, used preaching to recruit and encourage traveling soldiers from improvised pulpits on the roadsides. Various traveling preaching orders like the Franciscans and the more scholarly Dominicans were established. The rediscovery of Aristotle in the West led to the founding of universities, including those in Bologna (1088), Paris (c. 1150), and Oxford (1167). Handbooks on preaching flourished. With the rise of scholasticism, a tradition of university sermons began.

Newly rediscovered Aristotelian principles of reason, empirical knowledge, evidence, and data were brought to bear on the early church's past, with much opposition. Anselm of Canterbury (1033–1109) used reason to reinforce matters that were already decided by the Scriptures and faith. God, he argued, is "that than which a greater cannot be thought." Peter Abelard (1079–1142) upset many with his *Sic et Non* (Yes and No), in which he argued that there were contradictions amongst the early church fathers. They did not all agree, even though up to that time the fathers served as simple, self-evident "proofs" of church doctrine. Peter Lombard (d. 1160) systematically organized theology under the four headings: God, Created Beings, Salvation, and the Last Things. His *Four Books of Sentences* served as the standard theological textbook until the Reformation. Three-point sermons were already a norm by the twelve hundreds when Robert of Basevorn observed, with surprising humor, "Only three statements, or the equivalent of three, are used in the theme—either from respect for the Trinity, or because a threefold cord is not easily broken [Ecc 4:12], or because this method is mostly followed by Bernard [of Clairvaux], or, as I think more likely, because it is more convenient for the set time of the sermon."[26]

Anselm of Canterbury (1033–1109)

"Anselm concerns himself with other important, and often interrelated, aspects of the Christian faith, developing the arguments through

---

26. Robert of Basevorn, *Form of Preaching*, 138.

reasoning, rather than through explicit reliance on Scriptural or patristic authority in the course of argumentation."[27] His *Monologium* is based on individual meditations on the Being of God, and his argument is not based on Scripture but reason. Anselm puts it this way in the Proslogion's Prologue (v. 1, 93): "that God truly is, and that he is the supreme good needing no other, and that he is what all things need so that they are and so that they are well, and whatever else we believe about the divine substance."

Anselm does cite the Scriptures at certain points in his work, as well as "what we believe" (*quod credimus*), but attention to his texts indicates that he does not rely on scriptural or doctrinal authority directly to resolve problems or provide starting points for his reasoning. In some cases, he has the student or his own questioning voice (as in *Proslogion*, chapter 8) bring up scriptural passages of truths of Christian doctrine in order to raise problems that require a rational resolution. In other cases (as in *De Concordia*; Book 1, chapter 5), he does use scriptural passages as starting points for arguments, but for erroneous arguments that he then criticizes.

In yet other cases, Anselm brings up the Scriptures precisely to explain how certain passages or expressions should be rightly understood (as in the *De Casu Diaboli*, explaining the issue of God causing evil should be understood). Lastly, Anselm cites the Scriptures after the course of his argument in order to reconnect the rational argumentation with Christian revelation (as in Proslogion, chapter 16, where Anselm's previous reasoning culminates in God "inhabiting" an "inaccessible light").[28]

Thomas Aquinas (c. 1225–1274)

When Thomas Aquinas (c. 1225–1274), our final figure, joined the Dominican Order of Preachers in 1243, the scholastic movement was already underway. He was ordained and appointed professor at the University of Paris, where he taught preaching, commentary on Lombard's *Sentences*, and theological debate. In his famous *Summa Theologiae*, he reconciled Aristotelian philosophy with Christian thought and helped legitimize the

---

27. Sadler, "Anselm of Canterbury (1033–1109)."

28. For discussion of Anselm and Scripture, cf. Barth, 1960, Tonini, 1970, and Henry, 1962. Anselm's formula *fides quaerens intellectum*, God, "a being than which nothing greater can be conceived," Proslogium,

study of Aristotle by Christians. He argued that rational science confirms revelation but is separate from it and the supernatural. Reason on its own could not lead to truth. He moves, as did his theology classes and many sermons, from questions to arguments against his position to arguments for it. It was the classic mode of medieval disputation.

Aquinas's one hundred and fifty biblical sermons come to us mainly in point form, with numerous elaborate divisions and subdivisions in the medieval tradition of "prepared sermons." We know that his preaching was powerful, though it is hard to see from the records why this would be so: In Naples and Rome he repeatedly moved people to tears and had to pause to allow congregations to weep. Most popular sermons of his time were not appealing to reason but to emotion, blind obedience, visions, allegories, and moralistic and fantastic stories (*exempla*).

His homiletical method, perhaps too simply stated, is this: start with a verse from the Scriptures and make a number of main points (headings) from it, or find verses from other texts that are similar to the first one and make the number of points they will support. He makes numerous subpoints and treats each in turn, developing the idea clearly before going on to proof texts, and he shapes the whole by his doctrinal understanding.

On the first Sunday in Advent he preaches on the text, "For salvation is nearer to us now than when we first became believers; the night is far gone, the day is near" (Rom 13:11–12). He opens without an introduction:

Point I: "This word *Day* is to be taken in a four-fold sense—[a.] The day of mercy is the birth-day of the Lord [the literal sense]. [b.] The day of grace is the time of grace [or salvation, the allegorical sense]. [c.] the day of justice is the day of judgement [the moral sense]. [d.] the day of glory is the day of eternity [the anagogical or eschatological sense]."

Point II and its subpoints concern what listeners are exhorted to do, again based on the four senses: *mercy* is to be celebrated and honored; *grace* is to be received; *judgement* is to be feared; and *glory* is to be attained.

Point III identifies in turn the virtues appropriate to mercy, grace, judgment, and glory.

In Point IV, he returns to Romans to demonstrate in turn how Paul extols these virtues.[29]

---

29. Ashley, *Ninety-Nine Homilies*, 3–5.

Aquinas is one of the foremost pioneers of elaborate, reasoned point-form sermons. He also expanded the understanding of the literal sense so that it became what it was for the Reformers, a double literal sense. He said that the literal "words signify things," that is, historical events. But he adds, "What is special here [in the Bible] is that the things meant by the words [i.e., the events] also themselves mean something . . . the spiritual sense."[30] For Aquinas, the literal sense includes the intended spiritual or theological meanings: "The literal sense is that which the author intends, and the author of Holy Scripture is God who comprehends everything all at once in his understanding."[31] In other words, it is a double literal sense. Fifty years later, Nicholas of Lyra (c. 1270-1349), would claim this second literal sense to be "just as literal as the first."[32]

Three Keys to Fourfold Exegesis

Three of the early church doctrinal understandings provide a key to the multiple senses, which involve their doctrines of plenary or verbal inspiration of the Scriptures, the unity of the Scriptures, and the doctrine of the fall.

(1) *Plenary or Verbal Inspiration of the Scriptures*—Our ancient ancestors typically understood the Scriptures to be completely inspired, word for word, and the multiple senses are a gift God provides as a means of unlocking biblical truth. We must nonetheless be careful not to read rationalist theories of verbal inspiration back into the early church, for their exegesis and interpretation, like that of the Jewish tradition, was rich, flexible, and imaginative. In their understanding, the Scriptures descended from heaven and were transcribed as the dictation of God by humans whose own contributions were not recognized. God spoke in a code that could be understood properly only by those who had the appropriate knowledge and spiritual insight. The Bible itself testifies to its own rich potential and gives license for its own spiritual mining: "All Scripture is inspired by God and is useful for teaching, for reproof, for correction, and for training in righteousness" (2 Tim 3:16 NKJV).

---

30. Aquinas, *Summa Theologia*, 1a.1, 10, 38–39.
31. Aquinas, *Summa Theologia*, 1a.1, 10, 39.
32. Nicholas of Lyra, *Prologus secundus de intentione auctoris et modo procedendi* (fol. 4ra B). Cited by Preus, *From Shadow to Promise*, 68.

Today, when we encounter contradictions or apparent conflicting statements in a biblical text or it fails in other ways to make obvious sense, we look for some historical or cultural information to provide an explanation, or to the hand of a biblical editor who may have altered the text. The ancients used such textual conflict as a signal to look for higher spiritual meanings.

Origen cites Isa 6:9–10 to prove that everyone is not intended to understand the Scriptures (*On First Principles*, Book IV): "Go and say to this people: 'Keep listening, but do not comprehend; keep looking, but do not understand.' Make the mind of this people dull, and stop their ears, and shut their eyes, so that they may not look with their eyes, and listen with their ears, and comprehend with their minds, and turn and be healed." In short, God conceals truth from those not suited for it and discloses it only to those who are chosen. The goal of human life is spiritual growth and development, and the goal of studying the Bible similarly is to move beyond the literal sense of scriptural words in order to arrive at the higher spiritual meaning God intended.

(2) *Unity of the Scriptures*—From the time of the early church, people understood the Scriptures form a unity[33] in that it testifies to one God and the unity of God's will and actions. God is not whimsical and unpredictable, acting this way in one moment and that way in another. Nor is there one God of wrath in the Old Testament and another God of love in Paul, as Marcion claimed. Rather, God has a unified will and purpose for humanity and acts toward humans in ways that are consistent with it. The Scriptures testify to this unity in various ways, not least through affirming that God cannot speak deceitfully or lie (2 Sam 7:28; John 17:17; Heb 6:18). The multiple senses are remarkable hermeneutical instruments that provide the early church with a way to understand the Hebrew Scriptures in the light of Christ and thereby preserve the Old Testament for Christian life and faith, defend the Scriptures from attack, and defend monotheism in spite of differences between the Old and New Testaments. The ongoing life of the community of faith makes a similar testimony. Revelation is often hidden in the Scriptures, yet because the

---

33. This unity of Scripture has been challenged, says Ebeling, first, by the inability of the Scriptures to produce a unified theology of the two Testaments; second, by each Testament having an inner unity; and third, by the fact that outside historical sources are pertinent to the reading of the Bible. See Childs, *Biblical Theology*, 7.

biblical message is consistent and forms a unity, simple meanings in one place can be used to unlock difficult meanings elsewhere (a practice known as the analogy of faith, or its relative, the analogy of the Scriptures).

(3) *The Doctrine of the Fall*—The multiple senses are a means of compensating for what was lost in the fall of man. God's plan is evident in both the natural created order and in the Scriptures, which God dictated word by word for human benefit. Humans cannot fully comprehend what God says because of the fall, and God therefore adapts what is said to our deficient abilities. Some scholars identify this idea as the foundation of all medieval biblical interpretation:[34] God is inerrant, and since God planned everything in nature and the Scriptures, even the means of a decoding standard such as the multiple senses is part of God's intent. The Scriptures make sense, have meaning, and give life. If they fail in this regard, the Scriptures are not at fault; instead, human sin is responsible. Apparent problems in the Scriptures point to deficiencies in understanding and the interpreter's task in making sense of the text as it stands. Through the multiple senses, God restores to humanity a means of comprehending God's saving purposes and growing in spiritual insight.

A text may be read for what it says about the historical event it describes, hence the literal sense; theological doctrine in connection to Christ, hence the allegorical sense; how life is lived, hence the moral (tropological) sense; and the next life, hence the prophetic or soul (anagogical) sense. John Cassian, in his *Conferences,* took the word "Jerusalem" to mean literally, the geographical city; allegorically, the church; morally, the human soul; and prophetically, the heavenly city of God.

True Biblical Interpretation

Interpretation involves the opening up of the words and statements of the Scriptures in order to bring out its single, full, and natural sense. The Church of Rome believes that passages of Scripture have four senses: the literal, the allegorical, the tropological, and the anagogical. An illustration of this can be found in the way the figure of Melchizedek is understood.

---

34. Evans, *Language and Logic,* 1.

He offered bread and wine to Abraham (Gen 14:18). The literal sense is that the king of Salem, with the food that he brought, refreshed the soldiers of Abraham, who were tired after their travels. The allegorical sense is that the priest offers up Christ in the Mass. The tropological sense is that we are exhorted to give to the poor. The anagogical sense is that Christ who is in heaven shall be the bread of life to the faithful.

This pattern of the fourfold meaning of Scripture, however, must be rejected and destroyed. The Scriptures have only one sense, the literal one. An allegory is only a different way of expressing the same meaning. The anagogy and tropology are ways of applying the sense of the passage.

The principal interpreter of the Scriptures is the Holy Spirit, so the one who makes the law is the best and highest interpreter of it. The supreme and absolute means for the interpretation is the Bible itself: "So they read distinctly from the book, in the Law of God; and they gave the sense, and helped them to understand the reading" (Neh 8:8).

There are, however, three subordinate means to help us interpret a passage of Scripture: the analogy of faith, the circumstances of the particular passage, and comparison with other passages.

The analogy of faith is a summary of the Scriptures, drawn from its well-known and clear parts. There are two elements in it. The first is related to faith, explained in the Apostles' Creed. The second concerns charity or love, which is expounded in the Ten Commandments. In 2 Tim 1:13, Paul says, "Hold fast the pattern of sound words which you have heard from me, in faith and love which are in Christ Jesus."

The circumstances of a passage can be clarified by asking the following simple questions: Who is speaking? To whom? On what occasion? At what time? In what place? For what end? What goes before? What follows?

A comparison of different passages involves comparing them with each other so that their meaning may be clearer. "But Saul . . . confounded the Jews who dwelt in Damascus, proving [i.e., by comparing one thing with another] that this Jesus is the Christ" (Acts 9:22).

Comparing different passages may involve two things: The first involves comparing a statement in one context with the other places where it appears in the Scriptures. For example, Isa 6:10 says, "Make the heart of this people dull, and their ears heavy, and shut their eyes; lest they see with their eyes, and hear with their ears, and understand with their heart, and return and be healed." This is repeated six times in the New

Testament (Matt 13:14; Mark 4:12; Luke 8:10; John 12:40; Acts 28:27; Rom 11:8).

When texts are repeated like this, they often contain alterations for various reasons. Examples include the following:

(i) Exegetical: to clarify their exposition, such as the following verse references.

- Ps 78:2 cited in Matt 13:35
- Ps 78:24 cited in John 6:31
- Isa 28:16 cited in Rom 9:33
- Ps 110:1 cited in 1 Cor 15:25
- Ps 116:10 cited in 2 Cor 4:13
- Gen 13:15 cited in Gal 3:16

(ii) Diacritical: to distinguish, indicate or clarify places, times and persons, as in the citation of Mic 5:2 in Matt 2:6.

(iii) To limit the sense of a passage to the original intention and meaning of the Holy Spirit. Examples will be found in these passages:

- Deut 6:13 in Matt 4:10
- Isa 29:13 in Matt 15:8
- Gen 2:24 in Matt 19:5
- Isa 59:20 in Rom 11:26

(iv) For application, so that a type might be related to its fulfillment, the general to the special, and vice-versa. Examples include,

- Jonah 1:17 in Matt 12:40
- Isa 61:1 in Luke 4:18
- Ps 22:18 in John 19:28
- Exod 12:46 in John 19:33
- Ps 69:25 in Acts 1:20

(v) For the sake of brevity, some things may be omitted. Omission may also occur because the words are not appropriate to the matter in hand. One example of this is the use of Zech 9:9 in Matt 21:5.

The second kind of comparison involves comparing one context with another. Again, these may be either similar or different. Places that are similar agree with one another in certain respects, perhaps in their phraseology and manner of speech, or in their sense. Places that agree with respect to *phraseology* include,

- Gen 28:12 and John 1:51
- Gen 3:15 and Rom 16:20
- Gen 8:21 and Eph 5:2

Greek and Hebrew concordances prove very helpful for tracing examples of this kind.

Places that agree in sense are those which have the same meaning. Under this heading we should especially note the comparison of a general principle with a particular illustration of it. For example:

- Prov 28:13 and Ps 32:3, 4
- 2 Sam 15:25 and 1 Pet 5:6

So much for places that are similar. Places that are unlike one another apparently do not agree with one another, either in phraseology or meaning. For example:

- Rom 3:28 and Jas 2:24
- 1 Kgs 9:28 and 2 Chr 8:18
- Acts 7:14 and Gen 46:27
- Acts 7:16 and Gen 48:22
- Zech 11:13 and Matt 27:9

Augustine finds "almost everything" in the Old Testament figurative or allegorical, including the historical,[35] because for him it is about Christ. As he says concerning Noah, "We cannot agree with those who receive the bare history, but reject the allegorical interpretation, nor with those who maintain the figurative and not the historical meaning."[36] Of the fullness of the Ark he says, "But none but a contentious man can

---

35. Augustine, *On Christian Doctrine*, III, 9:14.
36. Augustine, *City of God*, 307.

suppose that there was no prefiguring of the church in so manifold and circumstantial a detail."[37]

Augustine and Calvin on Psalm 3: Examples of Exegesis

Even such a brief survey as the preceding one can help us begin to understand why the advent of modern biblical criticism was so necessary. Still, an additional perspective is needed that provides a glimpse of the kind of biblical criticism—the kind of biblical preaching—that was making its mark at the beginning and end of this period. One example can be cited briefly in comparing, for instance, the interpretations of Augustine and Calvin of Ps 3:1-4. The following extract from Augustine's commentary on Ps 3 demonstrates typical medieval exegesis of the sort that continued until the Reformation era, partly due to Augustine's influence. From the outset of his commentary, Augustine finds justification in a later verse (3:6) for dispensing with the historical sense of the text in favor of a Christological reading, based on the understanding that figures in the Old Testament foreshadow or are types of events in the New Testament. The words of the Psalm are in italics as well as New Testament texts he uses for support:

> *The Psalm of David when he fled from the face of his son Absalom.* The words of this Psalm: *I have fallen asleep and have taken my rest, and I have risen up, because the Lord will uphold me* [P. 3:6], lead us to believe that we must apply them to the Person of Christ. For they are more in keeping with our Lord's passion and resurrection than with the account which history gives of David's flight before the face of his own rebel son [2 Kgs 15:17]. And since it is written of Christ's disciples [in Matt 9:15]: *As long as the bridegroom is with them, the children of the bridegroom do not fast*, it need not surprise us that the disloyal son should be the figure [i.e., the type] of the disloyal disciple who betrayed his Master. From a literal standpoint one may say, it is true, that Christ fled before him when, on the departure of Judas, He withdrew with the rest to the mountain. In a spiritual sense, however, when the Son of God, Power and Wisdom of God as He is, forsook the mind of Judas, the devil straightway took possession of it. *The devil*, so it is written, *entered into his heart* [John 13:2]. One may therefore safely say that Christ fled from his face; not that Christ gave place before the devil, but

37. Augustine, *City of God*, 308.

> that on Christ's departure the devil assumed the mastery. This departure of our Lord, I think, is termed a flight in the Psalm on account of its swiftness; a swiftness also indicated in our Lord's injunction: *That which thou dost, do quickly* [John 13:27]. We even use the expression in ordinary speech: The word has fled, we say, when it refuses to come to mind; and of a great scholar: Nothing escapes him. In the same sense, truth escaped the mind of Judas when it ceased to enlighten him.
>
> Now Absalom, according to some interpreters, signifies in Latin *patris pax*, "peace of his father." It may very well seem puzzling that the name, "peace of his father," can be appropriate, either in the history of Kingdoms [i.e., the Book of Kings] where Absalom is at war with his father, or in the history of the New Testament where Judas is the betrayer of our Lord. But a careful reader will perceive in the first instance that during the struggle there was peace in David's heart towards the son whose death he even bewailed with bitter grief: *Absalom my son!* he cried. *Would to God I might die for thee* [2 Kgs 18:33]. And when the history of the New Testament shows us the great, the truly wonderful forbearance of our Lord, who bore with Judas so long just as though he were upright, and although He was aware of his designs yet admitted him to the feast in which He set before and entrusted to His disciples His own body and blood under a figure [i.e., a type], who finally in the other's very act of betrayal accepted his kiss [Mt. 26:49], we can easily see that Christ showed nothing but peace toward the man who betrayed Him, although the traitor's heart was prey to intentions so criminal. Absalom, then is termed "peace of his father" because his father cherished the peace which his son lacked....
>
> *But Thou, O Lord, takest me up* [v. 4]. Christ speaks to God in His human nature, since God's taking of human nature is the Word made flesh. *My glory*. He even calls God His glory, this Man whom the Word of God has so taken upon Himself that God and He are One....[38]

Plainly for Augustine, the historical dimension of the literal text is almost irrelevant. Not all of the history of criticism, nor indeed of Augustine's criticism, was marred by such interpretation. Much of what was written by the great interpreters of the medieval period can still be read to considerable advantage.

By the time we get to Calvin, the historical level of the text dominates, at least, how his age imagined that history from the chronicles of

---

38. Augustine, "Discourse on Psalm 3," 30-33.

David's life. Calvin uses every opportunity to make links between the psalm and David's life. The grammatical level of the text is also engaged, since Calvin knew Hebrew. Nearly everything he says is set within a theological context, and he uses what opportunities he has to move into sermonic reflection. Note that only at the end of his comments on verse 4 does he make a link to the life of Christ, stating that the Old Testament provided in shadows or figures what the NT states plainly. Here are portions of Calvin's commentary, starting with his commentary on the title:

> *A psalm of David, when he fled from Absalom his Son.*

> How bitter David's sorrow was under the conspiracy of his own household against him, which arose from the treachery of his own son, it is easy for every one of us to conjecture from the feelings of nature. And when, in addition to this, he knew that this disaster was brought upon him by God for his own fault in having defiled another man's wife, and for shedding innocent blood, he might have sunk into despair, and been overwhelmed by anguish, if he had not been encouraged by the promise of God, and thus hoped for life even in death. . . .

> 1. *O Lord, how are my oppressors multiplied! Many rise up against me.*
> 2. *Many say to my soul, There is no help for him in God. Selah.*

> Sacred history teaches that David was not only dethroned, but forsaken by almost all men; so that he had well nigh as many enemies as he had subjects. It is true there accompanied him in his flight a few faithful friends; but he escaped in safety, not so much by their aid and protection as by the hiding-places of the wilderness. . . . It was a mark of uncommon faith, when smitten with so great consternation, to venture freely to make his complaint to God, and, as it were, to pour out his soul into his bosom. And certainly the only remedy for allaying our fears is this, to cast upon him all the cares which trouble us; as, on the other hand, those who have the conviction that they are not the objects of his regard, must be prostrated and overwhelmed by the calamities which befall them.

> 3. *And thou, Jehovah, art a shield for me, my glory,*
>   *and he that exalteth my head.*
> 4. *I have cried to the Lord with my voice, and he heard*
>   *me out of his holy hill. Selah.*

> The copulative *and* should be resolved into the disjunctive particle *but*, because David employs language full of confidence,

in opposition to the hardihood and profane scoffings of his enemies, and testifies that whatsoever they may say, he would nevertheless rely upon the word of God.... But being persuaded that he was not utterly cut off from the favour of God, and that God's choice of him to be king remained unchanged, he encourages himself to hope for a favourable issue to his present trials. And, in the first place, by comparing God to *a shield*, he means that he was defended by his power. Hence also he concludes, that God *was his glory*, because he would be the maintainer and defender of the royal dignity which he had been pleased to confer upon him.

As to the expression, *from the hill of his holiness*, or, which signifies the same thing, *from his holy hill*, it is improperly explained of heaven, as has been done by some. Heaven, I indeed confess, is often called, in other places, God's holy palace; but here David has doubtless a reference to the ark of the covenant, which at that time stood on Mount Sion. And he expressly affirms that he was heard from thence, though he had been compelled to flee into the wilderness. The Sacred History relates, (2 Sam. xv. 24,) that when Abiathar the priest commanded the ark to be carried by the Levites, David would not suffer it. And in this wonderful faith of the holy man appears conspicuous. He knew that the Lord had chosen Sion to be the dwelling place of the ark.... Now, he boasts, that although he was deprived sight of the ark, and notwithstanding the distance to which he was removed from it, God was near to him to listen to his prayers....

Hence the confidence with which he prayed; and this confidence was not without success. In our day, since there is fulfilled in Christ what was formerly shadowed forth by the figures of the law, a much easier way of approach to God is opened up for us, provided we do not knowingly and willingly wander from the way.[39]

Implications

So much of the poetry in the original Latin is lost in translation, but the power of the rhetorical structure using "contraries" comes through even in the English. We can still hear powerful passages that sound remarkably like Augustine in churches such as some black congregations that have strong oral (rhetorical) traditions. This kind of careful structuring

---

39. Calvin, *Commentary on the Book of Psalms*, 27-33.

(including his use of "similarities") can be an excellent way of communicating difficult doctrinal ideas in a lively and interesting manner.

Augustine's emphasis on varying the styles—subdued, temperate, and grand—involving the form, content, and manner of our delivery may be instructive for us. We may resist conscious variance in style, for it may seem like congregational manipulation to us. But for him it was good communication, like giving a gift with the proper wrapping. Our purpose is not to imitate someone else's style, but to find and use our own in order to communicate more effectively.

Augustine's lack of personal reference in his sermons is in direct contrast to Paul, but this particular philosophy is reinforced by Calvin and others. Many preachers have excellent intentions for this: they do not want to draw attention away from the Word. The unintended effect today can be to place the preacher above the struggles of the parishioners.

As Bible interpreters, we would do well if we followed Augustine's "primary principle": keep studying a text until we have found something that contributes to *the rule of love*. Most of the great preachers, and particularly Luther and Wesley, who developed the direction of Augustine's thought, have been attentive to his emphasis on the primacy of God's grace in overcoming our sin. Our messages can be enhanced by remembering that we are supposed to preach grace, founded not on anything we can do on our own, but on God's generous actions of enabling love.

The secular and ecclesiastical leaders of the Carolingian renaissance made efforts to write better Latin, copy and preserve patristic and classical texts, and develop a more legible, classicizing script. They also applied rational ideas to social issues for the first time in centuries, providing a common language and writing style that enabled communication throughout most of Europe.

Conclusion

The limitation of our ancestors is plain: some of the readings they had of texts involved gleaning doctrinal meanings that they hung on the text like ornaments on a Christmas tree, but had little to do with the text as we understand it. Their brilliance was also clear: first, their spiritual senses gave them the ability to understand theological readings, which allowed them to preserve the Old Testament as Christian Scripture; second, the senses allowed them to discover the "God" meanings of texts; and third, the various senses were lenses that preachers could use to discover what to preach.

Today we have historical criticism, literary criticism, and various theologies, which provide many lenses for interpretation: black, feminist, liberation, Min Jung, and so forth. They open important avenues of social understanding. But none of these new lenses focus specifically on what texts say about God. When we say with the Reformers that the Scriptures have only one sense and that is the literal, we forget that they held to a double literal sense. Luther, for example, sought the Christ-meaning, and Calvin sought the reading given by the Holy Spirit.

Today many preachers are so devoted to the historical meaning of a text, or to the moral instruction we may derive from it, they forget to ask what the relationship of their sermons is to the gospel. God is often not the focus of their sermons—human actions are. God's saving actions are not central. We still have a moral sense of the Scriptures, and we still use it nearly every time we apply a text. Most often it is anthropocentric, chiefly regarding what we must do. It is not the higher spiritual sense of the ancients that, in guarded ways, we must recover.

Bibliography

Aquinas, Thomas. *Summa Theologia*. Vol. 1. Edited by Thomas Gilby. London: Eyre & Spottiswoode/New York: McGraw-Hill, 1963.

Ashley, John M., trans. *Ninety-Nine Homilies of S. Thomas Aquinas*. London: Church, 1867.

Augustine. *The City of God*. In *A Select Library of the Nicene and Post-Nicene Fathers of the Christian Church*. Vol. 2. Translated by Marcus Dods, edited by Philip Schaff. Grand Rapids, MI: Eerdmans, 1994.

———. "Discourse on Psalm 3." In vol. I of *St. Augustine on the Psalms* of Ancient Christian Writers, translated by Dame Scholastica Hebgin and Dame Felicitas Corrigan, 30–33. Westminster, MD: Newman, 1960.

———. *The Harmony of the Gospels*. In vol. 6 of *A Select Library of the Nicene and Post-Nicene Fathers of the Christian Church*, translated by S. D. F. Salmond and edited by Philip Schaff. Grand Rapids, MI: Eerdmans, 1991.

———. "Sermon 5." In *Sermons for Christmas and Epiphany*, translated by Thomas Comerford Lawler, 85–87. Westminster, MD: Newman and London: Longmans, Green, 1952. [Benedictines of St. Maur (Paris 1683), #187].

Calvin, John. *Commentary on the Book of Psalms*. Vol. 1. Translated by James Anderson. Grand Rapids, MI: Eerdmans, 1949.

Childs, Brevard. *Biblical Theology of the Old and New Testaments: Theological Reflection on the Christian Bible*. Minneapolis: Fortress, 1993.

Evans, G. R. *The Language and Logic of the Bible: The Earlier Middle Ages*. Cambridge: Cambridge University Press, 1984.

Frye, Northrup. *The Great Code: The Bible & Literature.* Wilmington: Mariner, 2002.

Origen. *On First Principles.* 4:15. Notre Dame: Christian Classics, 2013.

Philo. *The Contemplative Life.* Cited in R. P. C. Hanson's *Allegory and Event: A Study of the Sources and Significance of Origen's Interpretation of Scripture,* 236–7. London: SCM, 1959.

Preus, James Samuel. *From Shadow to Promise: Old Testament Interpretation from Augustine to the Young Luther.* Cambridge, MA: The Belknap Press of Harvard University, 1969.

Robert of Basevorn. *The Form of Preaching.* Translated by Leopold Krul O.S.B., in *Three Medieval Rhetorical Arts,* edited by James J. Murphy. Berkeley: University of California Press, 1971.

Robertson, D. W., Jr., trans. *On Christian Doctrine.* Upper Saddle River, NJ: Prentice Hall, 1958.

Sadler, Greg. "Anselm of Canterbury (1033–1109)." *Internet Encyclopedia of Philosophy.* http://www.iep.utm.edu/anselm/.

Wilson, Paul Scott. *A Concise History of Preaching.* Nashville: Abingdon, 1992.

———. *God Sense: Reading the Bible for Preaching.* Nashville: Abingdon, 2001.

Chapter Six

Preaching and the Reformation

Timothy George

Five hundred years ago this fall, on October 31, 1517, a thirty-three-year-old German professor named Martin Luther called for a public discussion of the sale of indulgences, and all hell broke loose. The tumult that ignited the Protestant Reformation began in a backwater university town of some two thousand inhabitants, "Little Wittenberg," as Luther called it. Wittenberg may have seemed an outpost at "the edge of civilization,"[1] but it did boast a university, one founded in 1502 by princely and imperial but not papal authority.

That one of its professors would call for academic debate on the commercial trade in papal indulgences, long recognized by reform-minded critics as a major abuse in the church, was not surprising and may even have been predictable. After all, as early as the Fourth Lateran Council (1215), traffic in "indiscriminate and excessive indulgences"—the kind Luther's parishioners were running to buy—had been condemned by the church. The Reformation was born in a crisis of preaching and pastoral care. But Luther's act was a spark that ignited a conflagration. One confrontation led to another, and soon Europe was ablaze with edicts, bans, bulls, anathemas, and condemnations.

The 95 Theses had been written in Latin, the common tongue of learned discourse, but they were soon translated, published, and distributed from one end of Europe to the other. Luther became a household

---

1. For the term "on the edge of civilization" (*in termino civilitatis*), see Schilling, *Martin Luther*, 91.

name in a matter of a few months, all the way from the Atlantic to the Baltic, from Lisbon to Lithuania.

At this point, Luther was not calling for the abolition of indulgences. Even the way Pope Leo X had issued them as a funding scheme for the rebuilding of St. Peter's Basilica, thereby draining money from Germany and sending it to Italy, was only a secondary concern for Luther. What really bothered Luther was that indulgences were being *preached*—and being preached in a way that undermined the central teaching of the Scriptures about God's grace and forgiveness.

The Dominican friar Johann Tetzel, who had been appointed as commissioner of indulgences by Albrecht of Magdeberg, was a very skilled and persuasive preacher. He did not invent the little jingle that we associate with his preaching campaign: "When the coin in the coffer rings, the soul from purgatory springs." That had been around for some time, but he certainly used it to good effect. One individual returning from Halle reported to Luther that Tetzel preached that if one bought a certain kind of indulgence, no matter what the sin committed, even if one had violated the Blessed Virgin Mary, a plenary indulgence could be obtained. (Luther mentions this in Thesis 75). Cheap grace on the cheap.

When church officials heard about all of this hubbub down in Rome, they assumed that this was just another monks' quarrel. *Dominicans versus Augustinians. Those monks up in Germany—they are always fussing about something!* They were not entirely wrong, for it was indeed a monks' quarrel, yet it was more than just a competition between orders. Instead, it was a conflict of clashing proclamations. This clash of proclamations stood at the headwaters of the Reformation. To begin with, the Reformation was about preaching and pastoral care.

Not all monks are priests and not all priests are preachers. But Luther was both and had been ever since Johann von Staupitz, his mentor and superior in the Augustinian order, had charged him in that famous conversation under the pear tree in September of 1511 to take up the task of preaching to the monks in the Augustinian monastery in Erfurt. At Staupitz's urging, Luther also proceeded to get a doctorate so he could become a teacher of the Holy Scriptures in the university. He received his doctoral degree from the University of Wittenberg on October 19, 1512.

When Luther became a doctor of theology, he had to take a vow to teach and preach the Holy Scriptures faithfully and purely. He never renounced that vow. In fact, he clung to it tenaciously. Later on, when people came to him and asked, "Who are you to go against fifteen hundred years of church tradition? Are you alone wise? If you have all the truth, who are you?" he would go back to the fact that he had been summoned and called to be a preacher and teacher of the Holy Scriptures. This was not something he had taken unto himself. In fact, he protested against it.

When Staupitz first gave him this charge, Luther replied that he could never do such a thing. It would kill him, he said. Staupitz retorted, "Well, if it does, that is okay, for God has lots of things for clever people like you to do in heaven!" Luther had taken a vow of obedience, so he had to do what he was told. Later on, Luther did renounce his monastic vows. He gave up celibacy when he married Katie von Bora, a runaway nun. He renounced the vow of poverty and became an owner of the Black Cloister in Wittenberg. But Luther never renounced his doctoral vow to teach and preach purely the Holy Scriptures. He had been summoned to this office, as he said again and again, "against my will."

We will never understand preaching in the Reformation, or anything else about the Reformation, until we first learn to take seriously this hesitation, this reluctance, this shrinking from the summons to take up the preaching task. It's biblical, isn't it? Isn't it, Moses? "I can't speak." Isn't it, Jeremiah? "I am just a child, I can't do this." Isn't it, Isaiah? "Woe is me, I'm undone! I have unclean lips, and I live among people of unclean lips." Go get somebody else! It is not as though Luther, Calvin, Zwingli, Bucer, or Cranmer went in one day to a vocational guidance seminar, took the Myers-Briggs test, and all came out ENTJ, so somebody said, "These fellas would make good preachers!" No, there was a hesitance, there was a reluctance. I suggest that this is at the very heart of what Reformation preaching is about.

Reinhold Niebuhr once said he was determined not to be a pretty preacher.[2] Martin Luther was not a pretty preacher either—far from it. He was bombastic and dogmatic, he was vulgar, and he was just plain crude. Sometimes he spoke more about farting than faith. In one of my early books on the Reformation, I was trying to get as close as I could to the original. I quoted Luther where he was struggling with Satan and said, "I messed in my britches," but he didn't say "messed." So I put it in the way Luther said it, and sure enough, my good, pious editor scratched it out and said Luther soiled himself or something like that. But, if you go back and read the footnotes, they are in the original German, so you can get it straight from the horse's mouth. I wouldn't have picked Luther out

---

2. Niebuhr, *Leaves*, 26.

of a lineup of promising preachers, would you? Luther? Why him? Maybe God knew something we didn't know about how to choose preachers.

So how did the Reformation come about? Luther put it this way: "I simply taught, preached, wrote God's Word; otherwise I did nothing. And then, while I slept, or drank Wittenberg beer with my Philip [Melanchthon] and my [Nicolaus von] Amsdorf, the Word so greatly weakened the papacy that never a prince or emperor did such damage to it. I did nothing. The Word did it all."[3] Is that posturing? Is it false humility? Nevertheless, we need to hear what Luther thought he was trying to do. But that is not how we think of the Reformers anymore. Instead, we think of them as revolutionaries out to shake the world and overturn kingdoms like those of Robespierre, Lenin, or Che Guevara.

We think of the Reformation as Act I in a play called *Modernity*, a process that produced people like us: moderns, post-moderns, and people of culture, enlightenment, refinement, and nuance and niceness. The one Reformer we do like, sort of, is Desiderius Erasmus. And who wouldn't love Erasmus? Dear, sweet, moderate, quizzical, enigmatic, skeptical Erasmus. No Wittenberg beer for him—only the finest wine from Cyprus. He ordered a whole case of it when he was in residence in Cambridge working on the Greek New Testament.

Erasmus also wrote a book on preaching. Published the year before he died in 1535, it is called *Ecclesiastes: The Preacher*. This is a wonderful treatise on preaching in the best rhetorical tradition of classical antiquity recovered by humanist scholars of the day—of whom he was the chief. There are lots of good things in Erasmus' treatise on preaching: Aristotle, Quintilian, and so on. You can learn much about the art and technique of preaching by reading Erasmus. But from reading Erasmus's book you wouldn't get the sense that there was anything eternally important, anything eternally at stake in the act of preaching.

One thing that is missing is the sense of struggle—the sermon as a struggle, or conflict. Luther had a word for this, *Anfechtungen*. It is a hard word to translate into English. We often say "temptation," but that is too weak; it doesn't quite do it. It is a word that connotes conflict, combat, struggle, and bouts of dread and despair. Right in the middle of the word *Anfechtung* is the word *Fechter*. A *Fechter* is a fencer or gladiator, someone attacking you, a person coming at you with a sword. And Luther

---

3. Luther, "Second Sermon," 294.

often characterized this struggle in terms of a battle with the Evil One, with the Devil.

Of course, Erasmus did not deny the existence of the Devil, but the Devil in Erasmus is very puny—it's the Devil on Prozac. For Luther, Satan is a raging volcano, which accounts, in part, for the dialectical character of Luther's preaching. There was always this tension, this struggle, going on in the sermon because it went on in the preacher: Law and Gospel. Grace and wrath. God and Satan. Some analysts have even said that Luther had a *Manichean* bent about him. I do think that was a dangerous tendency in Luther, though I don't believe he ever quite gave into it.

There is a verse in the Book of Hebrews that is quite arresting, indeed scary: "It is a fearful thing to fall into the hands of the living God, for our God is a consuming fire" (Heb 10:31; 12:29 KJV). If you are a preacher, that verse ought to make you shudder. Because not only is it a fearful thing to fall into the hands of the living God, it is also a fearful thing to speak on behalf of the living God. That is what preachers do every time they climb into a pulpit, open the Bible, open their mouths, and try to say anything at all that is significant.

"I did not learn my theology all at once," Luther said, "but I had to search deeper for it, where my *Anfechtungen* took me. . . . Not understanding, reading, or speculation, but living, nay, rather dying and being damned makes one a theologian."[4] This is what makes one a preacher, too. Now, how did Luther understand this task of preaching in terms of the God in whom he believed? How did Luther understand preaching theologically? To answer that question, I think we need to take a brief look at preaching before the Reformation.

Hugh Latimer famously described preaching on the eve of the Reformation this way: "Preaching was as rare as strawberries that came but once a year and did not tarry long and were soon gone."[5] Latimer may have been describing accurately the way preaching was carried out in some places, but we know in fact that there was a great hunger for preaching in the centuries leading up to the Reformation. We cannot understand the impact of Reformation preaching without getting a sense of this gaping hunger for the verbal exposition of the Bible in the late medieval period.

---

4. Quoted in George, *Theology of the Reformers*, 61.
5. Quoted in Wabuda, *Preaching During the English Reformation*, 26.

Take Margery Kempe, for example, the amazing mystic English woman from Lynn in England, who prayed,

> Alas! Lord, that, however many clerks Thou hast in this world, Thou wouldst not send me one of them who might fill my soul with Thy word and with reading of Holy Scripture. For all the clerks that preach could not fill it full. For, methinketh, my soul is ever so hungry that, if I had gold enough, I would give every day a noble to have every day a sermon, for Thy word is worth more to me than all the world.[6]

Now, Margery Kempe was certainly a remarkable woman. She had fourteen children in twenty years, she operated her own brewing business, and at the age of forty she undertook an eighteen-month pilgrimage to Jerusalem. Yet, she was not alone in her desire to hear regular sermons from effective preachers.

Mendicant friars, especially the Dominicans and Franciscans, but also the Carthusians and Augustinians, were beggars, yes, but they were also preachers. The mendicants did not remain in cloisters but rather fanned out into the cities, market squares, and universities. They traveled widely throughout Europe preaching on special days, saints' days, feast days, and days of indulgence. The most famous of the mendicant preachers were Bernardino da Siena, a Franciscan, and Girolamo Savonarola, a Dominican. Savonarola called down the wrath of God on the leaders of Florence and was eventually executed in 1498. When Luther traveled to the Diet of Worms in 1521, he carried with him a medallion of Savonarola to remind him that his life could also end in the flames as Savonarola's had.

So these mendicant friars were speaking all over Europe in different ways and venues, to great crowds sometimes. But there was also a rather new institution on the eve of the Reformation: the *Leutpriester*, the people's priest. This institution became popular in the free imperial cities of the Holy Roman Empire. Those citizens who had benefited from the early burgeoning of capitalism, such as the burghers and the guilds, were able to endow preacherships—paid for, not by the church, but by the cities and private donors. The urban *Leutpriester* were expected to preach every Sunday and feast day in the liturgical calendar. Since there were many such days in the course of the year, a great deal of preaching took place.

---

6. Butler-Bowden, *Book of Margery Kempe*, 186.

The two most famous of these *Leutpriester* were Huldrych Zwingli, who became the Reformer of Zurich in 1519, and Johann Geiler von Kaysersberg in Strasbourg, for whom the great pulpit in the cathedral there was built. Geiler would take an hourglass when he entered the pulpit on Sunday and preach a textual sermon for one solid hour. Then, he would turn the hourglass over and preach for another hour on a thematic sermon. He also wrote a treatise on preaching, justifying what he was doing.

What was preaching, in Geiler's opinion? He makes it clear that preaching is not a sacrament. There were, and still are, seven sacraments in the Catholic Church, but the two most directly related to preaching were the Eucharist and penance. While confession was only required once a year in preparation for Communion at Eastertide, more frequent recourse to confession was certainly encouraged. As Eamon Duffy, one of our best Catholic Reformation scholars, has explained, in the liturgy and sacramental mysteries that were its central moments, especially the Eucharist, medieval people found the key to the meaning and purpose of their lives.[7]

For Geiler and other late medieval preachers, preaching was attached to the sacrament of penance. It was intended as an inducement to the confessional. If you know the story of Luther, you will recognize that it was precisely here that he had his greatest struggles in the monastery. At confession, he found himself more and more turned in on himself. He adopted this term that we get from Augustine, *incurvatus in se*, meaning "curved in, twisted like a coiled spring" in on himself. Augustine had said we're twisted and bent down to the earth (maybe reflecting his neo-Platonism a little bit). But Luther intensified that image to signify not just bent down toward the earth but bent down toward, or twisted in, on ourselves. The thing that bothered Luther most about the confessional were the sins he could not remember, the sins he had committed even in his sleep—not just the conscious mind.

Four hundred years before Freud wrote *The Interpretation of Dreams*, Luther realized there was a deeper dimension to the human personality. Sin works its way into the deepest textures of the human soul. So, a deep doctrine of sin needs a deeper doctrine of grace. If you have a light view of sin as something you can overcome by self-improvement, then you don't need such a strong doctrine of grace—you can get by with just a little bit. Luther understood that there was more to it than that.

---

7. Duffy, *Stripping of the Altars*.

In the nineteenth century, Protestant historians began to talk about the Reformation in terms of the formal and material principles. This is not language that the Reformers used, but it was picked up and became a part of the tradition. The formal principle refers to the normative authority of the Holy Scriptures as the determinative rule of Christian life and faith. The material principle refers to the central message of grace and forgiveness as taught in the doctrine of justification by faith alone. These two principles do not encompass everything that the mainline Protestant Reformers wanted to say against a resurgent Catholicism on the one hand and a proliferating sectarianism on the other. But they did entail a number of changes in the worship and preaching of the church.

This cannot be said too strongly: Luther did not intend to start a new church. To the day he died, Luther wanted to be nothing more nor less than a good, faithful, and obedient servant of the one holy catholic and apostolic church. He wanted to call that church to renewal and reform on the basis of the Word of God. But although he did not start a new church, as a result of his insight, a new spirituality and transformation of worship developed that was related to preaching. Let us note two things about this.

First, *preaching became the centerpiece of worship.* The Reformers altered the late medieval pattern of preaching by making it a part of the regular worship of the church rather than an *ad hoc* event reserved for special occasions or seasons of the liturgical cycle. Before the Reformation, sermons were often delivered outdoors in town squares and open fields. Both Bernardino da Siena and Savonarola were great outdoor preachers. The Protestant Reformers brought the sermon back inside the church and gave it an honored place in the weekly liturgical happening of the gathered community. In the Reformation, a new and prominent place was given to the pulpit, which was raised to a higher elevation.

In a famous painting of the interior of Le Temple de Paradis in Lyon, France, there is the pulpit—central and elevated. The pastor is shown delivering the sermon while the congregation is seated below around the elevated pulpit. Both men and women are present, although they are separated by gender. Children are also included in the congregation and sit in their designated pews with their Bibles or, more likely, their psalters or catechism books open. Even a stray dog has entered and appears to be listening intently to the sermon. Everything is focused around the pulpit in the center of the room. In the doorway coming into the painting, a couple is bringing a child, an infant who is to be baptized. Sitting right in front of the preacher is a couple about to be married. In the Protestant tradition, both of these important rites of passage were incorporated into the regular worship of the church and accompanied by the preaching of the Word.

Starting in 1528, Luther began to preach both marriage and funeral sermons. A number of these meaty, lengthy, complex, and exegetically rich sermons have survived.

While much has been made of the Reformation as representing a sudden move from the visual to the audible—and this certainly did happen—it was not as abrupt as we might think. There was a fluidity between eye and ear in the Reformation sermon. The Bible was meant not only to be read, studied, translated, memorized, and meditated upon, it was also to be embodied in preaching, baptism, the Lord's Supper, the singing (in the Reformed tradition especially of the Psalms), the prayers of the people, and the service of the congregation in the world. This was a part of a package deal. In time, these became dismembered and we sometimes think of them in discontinuous ways, but, at first, there was a holistic approach.

The Reformers introduced the faithful, regular, continuous preaching through a certain book of the Bible. When you visit Zurich today and go to the Grossmünster Church, on the door it says, "The Reformation of Huldrych Zwingli began here on January 1, 1519." That day could just as well mark the beginning of the Reformation as October 31, 1517, because on that day, Huldrych Zwingli, a *Leutpriester*, came to Zurich and began to preach chapter by chapter, verse by verse, starting with the Gospel of Matthew. When this was completed, he went on to the other books of the New and Old Testaments. Luther more or less followed the lectionary on Sundays but followed the *lectio continua* during the week, so that we have both kinds of sermons from Luther.

In 1541, Calvin returned to Geneva to resume his ministry after he had been expelled three years earlier by the city council. He entered the pulpit of the Cathedral of St. Pierre. Everybody was expecting an "I told you so" sermon, but he simply opened the Bible to the very text he had been preaching on three years earlier and continued an expositional sermon. What was he saying? He was saying that the Reformation is not about Calvin or any particular preacher, but rather about the hearing and proclamation of the Holy Scriptures.

Second, there was *a new theology of preaching* that came to the fore in the sixteenth century. In Reformation theology, preaching was understood as an indispensable means of grace and a sure sign of the true church. The Augsburg Confession, Article VII, states that where the gospel is preached in its purity and the holy sacraments are administered according to the gospel, there is the true church. These two things, the preaching of the gospel and the administration of the sacraments, are the indispensable marks of a true church, according to the Augsburg Confession. Calvin agreed with this.

Later, others in the Reformed tradition added a third mark: discipline. Calvin was big on discipline—read Book Four of the *Institutes*. But he wisely did not elevate discipline to an indispensable mark of the church, instead placing emphasis on the preaching of the Word and administration of the sacraments. Heinrich Bullinger, in the Second Helvetic Confession of 1566, put it as bluntly as it can be put: "The preaching of the Word of God *is* the Word of God."

A little over a year ago, we lost a great Reformation scholar, one of my former teachers, David C. Steinmetz. He explained this meaning of Bullinger's statement in terms of two different German words used first by Luther and then picked up by some others. The two words are *Heisselwort* and *Thettelwort*.[8] A *Heisselwort* is a word you use to identify something. In other words, it describes something that is already there: a book, a piano, a desk, a banner. It does not have the power to bring into existence things that are not already a part of creation. Rather, it is a "name" word.

But *Thettelwort* is different. It is a "deed" word—a word that once uttered, brings into existence a thing that did not exist before. In the creation, God spoke and worlds that were not yet present came into existence at the sound of His voice. That's a *Thettelwort*. In John 11, when Jesus stands at the grave of a dead man named Lazarus and says, "Lazarus, come forth!" resurrection happens. When Bullinger writes, "The preaching of the Word of God *is* the Word of God," he means that preaching is a *Thettelwort*. It is a performative word, as we would say today. It does not merely name something that already exists. Nor is it merely a witness to the Word of God, though it is surely that, but it is also the means by which God breaks into our mundane everyday world, and shakes it up, reorders it, and transforms it. It is the means by which those who are dead in their trespasses and sins, as Paul says in Eph 2, come alive in Jesus Christ.

---

8. Steinmetz, *Taking the Long View*, 83–84.

Steinmetz explains that, in its sixteenth-century context, just as Catholics believe that when Mass is spoken, Christ is really present in the creaturely elements of bread and wine (transubstantiation), so Protestants now claim that, in a sermon, the life-giving Word of God is really present in the creaturely elements of human speech. The Word of God is present because, through culturally determined human language, God again speaks in a culturally transcendent word. If you could think about this in terms of the sacrament of penance and confession, when the priest says *te absolvo*—that part of confession at which the priest absolves the penitent—something new happens. Sin is forgiven. A new situation emerges by the power of the word of the priest. That is what all preachers do (*te absolvo*) whenever they proclaim the words of promise and forgiveness in the name of Jesus Christ. Steinmetz puts it this way:

> The Protestant Reformers . . . redefined the role of the ministry in terms of the proclamation and teaching of the Word of God. The sermon is not merely doctrinal instruction or moral exhortation. It is a means of grace. From a Catholic perspective the sermon has now become a sacrament. God speaks through human language and uses human words to effect those changes in the human condition that Catholic theology restricts to the power of the sacraments.[9]

Now, to be a minister of the gospel in the service of such a calling and such a word is high and holy, but it is also scary, dangerous, and fraught with all kinds of problems that maybe we know more about on this side of Descartes and Kant than Luther, Zwingli, and Calvin did in their day. But however you understand it, this high and holy and scary and dangerous calling should not be undertaken lightly or unadvisedly, but as the *Book of Common Prayer* says about marriage, it should be entered into advisedly, carefully, prayerfully, and in the fear of God.

Bibliography

Butler-Bowden, W., trans. *The Book of Margery Kempe*. Oxford: Oxford University Press, 1936.

Duffy, Eamon. *The Stripping of the Altars*. New Haven: Yale University Press, 2005.

George, Timothy. *Theology of the Reformers*. Nashville: B&H, 2013.

---

9. Steinmetz, *Taking the Long View*, 95.

Luther, Martin. "The Second Sermon, March 10, 1522, Monday after Invocavit." In *Martin Luther's Basic Theological Writings*, edited by W. R. Russell and T. F. Lull, 294. Minneapolis: Fortress, 2012.

Niebuhr, Reinhold. *Leaves from the Notebook of a Tamed Cynic*. Cleveland: Meridian, 1957.

Schilling, Heinz. *Martin Luther: Rebel in an Age of Upheaval*. Oxford: Oxford University Press, 2017.

Steinmetz, David C. *Taking the Long View: Christian Theology in Historical Perspective*. Oxford: Oxford University Press, 2011.

Wabuda, Susan. *Preaching During the English Reformation*. Cambridge: Cambridge University Press, 2002.

Chapter Seven

Preaching in the Victorian Era in England and Scotland

Joel C. Gregory

Introduction

A dozen preachers in nineteenth-century England and Scotland made an impact unequalled in the history of English language preaching. The preaching of an era may be summarized by either generalizations or exemplary preachers. This little survey proposes representative preachers.[1] Although a score of names clamors for inclusion, this overview is limited to those in Victorian England and Scotland, which presents an embarrassment of riches. Preachers could be included on the basis of the impact they had on their own respective generations, while another canon would require their abiding influence on the present. An elitist view would include the Oxbridge worthies but exclude the autodidacts. The Anglican Church might be favored over the Nonconformists. The published pastors may be favored over those who live today only in memoirs or in fragments.

It is commonly noted that nineteenth-century England witnessed unprecedented transitions. The era began with the first photograph

---

1. For the general background of preaching in nineteenth-century England, see Ellison, *Victorian Pulpit*; Ellison, *New History of the Sermon*; Paz, *Nineteenth-Century English Religious Traditions*; and Reardon, *Religious Thought in the Victorian Age*.

taken, for example, and six years before it ended, the first wireless transmission sent by Marconi. Rapid innovations developed in industry, transportation, and communication, along with revolutionary philosophies espoused by the likes of Marx and Darwin. The stark divisions of Dickensian London whispered at some and shouted at others.

The nature of pulpit speech drastically changed from the ornate, embellished, and showy rhetoric of the scholastic preachers (who owed as much to Cicero as they did exegesis) to a clearer, simpler, and more transparent language sounded from Anglican and Free Church pulpits. A decisive homiletic movement pushed preachers away from reading pulpit essays to imparting a more passionate delivery.

Moreover, the romanticism of the era was not confined to Wordsworth, Browning, and Keats; the pulpit also saw in a flower "thoughts too deep for human tears." Whereas the showy, prolix, patristic-quoting preachers of the previous era wished to merely inform, the nineteenth-century pulpit urged active application of the text. Indeed, such pinning of the sermon to the practical and nailing it to the now may be the principal change that can be observed in the era.

Finally, the publication of sermons reached a zenith previously unparalleled by any previous historical period. What Spurgeon said Sunday morning was available on national newsstands by Friday, not to mention the review of sermons in various newspapers. Spurgeon's sermons were even telegraphed to America for a season until Southern papers deleted his abolitionist sentiments.

This survey gives precedence to abiding influence, representation of state church and free-church traditions, Oxford men and self-taught, and—in the case of one—sheer genius. You may not excuse the exclusion of Cardinal Newman, but his influence today rests in an essay, "The Idea of the University," more than in his sermons at St. Mary's. For obvious reasons he has suffered the reality of the trite Civil War metaphor: he wore a blue shirt and gray pants.

By the aforementioned categories, this survey focuses first on two Anglicans, Canon Henry Parry Liddon of St. Paul's and Frederick W. Robertson, the lamented genius of Brighton who died at the age of thirty-seven. In Liddon's instance, his impact on education and Anglicanism exceeds his current influence. Robertson was hardly known in his lifetime but has grown in reputation through his sermons published posthumously. The final four, Alexander Maclaren, Charles Spurgeon, Joseph Parker, and Alexander Whyte—Nonconformists all—have remarkable current influence due to the massive reprints of their sermons, which highlight their individual gifts.

Spurgeon towers over them all regarding sheer persistent interest. As is the case with C. S. Lewis, every generation seems to rediscover him. Unlike Spurgeon, Maclaren was a schoolman, acquiring a degree from the University of London. G. Campbell Morgan referred to Maclaren as "the greatest of us all." Parker was an eccentric Congregationalist in London's second largest church, and peculiarly obsessed with Spurgeon. From Scotland comes Alexander Whyte, the biographical preacher of Free St. George's in Edinburgh.

This overview of Liddon, Robertson, Maclaren, Spurgeon, Parker, and Whyte features brief thumbnail sketches of their lives that feature both their struggles and successes in their pastorates. Then, an analysis of their individual sermon styles reflects the impact they had on their congregations, both then and now.

Henry Parry Liddon (1829–90)

Life

As the Canon of St. Paul's Cathedral in London, Liddon combined an intense commitment to orthodoxy, in the aftermath of the Oxford Movement, with a sometimes rapier wit. Upon one occasion of deep fog in London, he observed that the fog "is commonly attributed to Dr. Westcott having opened his study window at Westminster."[2] Concerning a man whose defense of the faith did not rise to Liddon's exacting standards, the Canon noted, "The good man set his face against it—not like a flint—but like a pudding."[3]

Liddon's father was a captain in the British navy at the height of the Empire and displayed a stalwart, disciplined character. His mother was an evangelical who worried about her son's High Church inclinations.

This stalwart defender of Athanasian orthodoxy and instant inventor of the *bon mot* was educated at King's College School, London, and a lifetime student at Christ Church, Oxford. Eschewing the popular side of student life, Liddon focused on study, meditation, and spiritual direction.

---

2. Russell, *Dr. Liddon*, 174.
3. Russell, *Dr. Liddon*, 179.

The religious cross-currents of his Oxford years could have swept him to Rome, the Broad Church, or the High Church. After Newman's conversion to Catholicism, Liddon toyed with the notion of going over to Rome himself. He even visited with the Pope but could not consider him infallible. He then dedicated himself to High Church Anglicanism, even though he avoided the denomination's inclination towards rationalistic devotion to dogma without the common touch.[4] Liddon was so devoted to Dr. Edward B. Pusey, the celebrated Oxford Anglo-Catholic icon, that he retired early to write a four-volume biography of the great Tractarian.

Liddon was a curate at Wantage, where his health failed him; first vice-principal at Cuddesdon Theological College, where he was shown the door after five years because he was considered tolerant of Catholicism; and vice-principal of St. Edmund Hall, Oxford, where he established a national reputation for preaching through his lectures on the New Testament on Sunday evenings. In 1864, Liddon was appointed prebendary at Salisbury Cathedral.

He delivered the 1866 Bampton Lectures on "The Divinity of our Lord and Savior Jesus Christ" before his installation as Canon of St. Paul's in 1870, the same year he was appointed Dean Ireland professor of exegesis at Oxford. He used this double appointment to strengthen orthodoxy in the aftermath of the Oxford Movement, as well as to fight higher criticism.[5] Concerning the latter, his successor Henry Scott Holland opined that "his intellectual pivot was absolutely fixed" with a "clear hold by which the Church of the Councils" secured the faith. "For Teutonic speculation he had a most amusing repugnance."[6]

In the cavernous extensiveness of St. Paul's, the intellectual Liddon decided to preach on Sunday afternoons, drawing throngs of approximately four thousand—a mix of Nonconformists, intellectuals, and working people from London. Although these crowds were smaller than Spurgeon's multitudes, it was unprecedented for a high churchman, as well as for St. Paul's. As such, he was noted as a festal preacher on the high holy days, the feasts, and fasts of the Church.[7] He used the lectionary as

---

4. Fant and Pinson, *20 Centuries of Great Preaching*, 94.
5. Cross and Livingstone, *Oxford Dictionary of the Christian Church*.
6. Holland, *Personal Studies*, 143–44.
7. Olds, *Reading and Preaching*, 396–97.

the norming norm for his defense of orthodoxy, locating the lesson in the celebration of the Christian year.[8]

Although Liddon was never in robust health, his sermons at St. Paul's were often an hour long. Without any amplification, he strained to be heard within the church's reverberating stone walls, virtually screaming at the top of his voice. In fact, he was sick sometimes for three days after he preached.[9] They almost needed someone to catch him as he fell back and then fainted after trying to make himself heard. And it didn't help for him to see people quizzically looking up at him trying to hear what he said.

An orthodox preacher, Liddon sometimes seemed to be sparring against critics yet seldom to the point of being acerbic. His preaching was often characterized as "lofty." He was an avid reader of the newspapers, and some highbrow critics thought his journalistic references sullied his message.[10] One gets the impression that he was a devotee of the same basic Christianity popularized seventy years later by an Oxford Anglican layman across the city at Magdalene.

As a preacher Liddon was no spellbinder, but his charm, wit, remarkable face, and passion for orthodoxy engaged people.[11] It is interesting that in his magisterial 2004 *History of Preaching*, O. C. Edwards Jr., an Episcopalian, does not so much as mention Liddon.[12] Edwards' take on Victorian preaching emphasizes the romanticism of the rugged heroes, F. W. Robertson and John Henry Newman. Apparently Liddon does not fit into the romantic mold that Edwards uses as a lens for his Victorian preacher-picking.

---

8. Olds, *Reading and Preaching*, 398.
9. Fant and Pinson, *20 Centuries of Great Preaching*, 96.
10. Fant and Pinson, *20 Centuries of Great Preaching*, 98–99.
11. Olds, *Reading and Preaching*, 399.
12. Edwards, *History of Preaching*, 591–618. Edwards selects for his representative preachers of the era John Henry Newman and Frederick Robertson. Newman left the Anglican Church for Catholicism, and Robertson left the Evangelical Low Church for his own distinctive position. Liddon was a staunch defender of the Athanasian creed and an opponent of the critical approach of the German universities. Liddon preached to more people at St. Paul's than the other two together.

Sermon

Liddon preached at Saint Paul's on Sunday afternoon, February 17, 1867, a sermon on Creation. His text was Gen 1:1: "In the beginning God created heaven and earth," and he said, "That's enough." First of all, he—as was his wont—anchored that verse in the Creed by acknowledging God as the maker of heaven and earth.

But then, in contrast, Liddon invents a straw man unfamiliar with Christian culture or European thought, and places this Rousseau-like creature into the created world. He imposes on this straw man the questions of what causes this, what upholds it, and why is it here. But what does this noble savage think, who's not tutored in the Christian faith?

First of all, Liddon supposes that the man brings up the philosophy of materialism: "His eye rests on the forms and colours around him with the keen fresh delight of an unexercised sense. Earth, sky, sun, stars, clouds, mountains, valleys, seas, trees, animals, flowers, fruits, in groups and separately pass before him."[13]

This is a great quote indirectly reflecting the materialist, who avers there is only matter and form. That is all there is—nothing else. The storm and the sun come from the same impersonal matter and form. There is no resurrection, so there is no meaning. The materialist lies to both his heart and conscience.

Then, this straw man considers pantheism and dualism in the same breath: "Does God inhabit the natural elements, and is He equal with this?" He admits pantheism uses religious language that catches one off guard. And yet pantheism makes God immoral. A God trapped in nature causes man to look at both beauty and horror with indifference.

But then Liddon dismisses both of those and comes to this great piece of Victorian pulpit rhetoric:

> Out of millions and millions of chances that it might have been otherwise, one chance has carried the day in favor of order. . . . [Y]ou yourselves, brethren, with the marvelous organs that belong to each one of you, and with the even more remarkable moral and ethical faculties, are the product of mere chance. . . . The human mind with its faculties and its ability to turn around and look critically at nature is the product of chance.[14]

---

13. Liddon, "Creation," 4, a sermon by Henry Parry Liddon preached in St. Paul's Cathedral on Sunday evening, February 17, 1867.

14. Liddon, "Creation," 4.

Returning to Gen 1, Liddon insists that creation shows God's nature and character. Only God made the material with which He works. Humans can only combine and organize the material that's already been made.

> Humans can make a brick but they cannot make the clay from which the brick is made, humans can invent varied shades of color but humans cannot make the primary colors, humans can combine words to make sense but humans cannot make any sense out of a word invented themselves that has no reference to other words. Everything humans make is a recombination of givens that come from creation.[15]

Furthermore, science cannot explain life. Humans can build the Crystal Palace, Liddon observes, but they cannot create the life in the tiniest insect on one of its windows. That building of wrought iron and plate glass was built in Hyde Park, near today's Royal Albert Hall. It was part of the Great Exhibition of 1851, with fourteen thousand exhibitors in 990,000 square feet of space and an interior height that reached 128 feet. It was the greatest argument from lesser to greater that Liddon could produce. He suggests that God creates in majestic freedom to show His love. Then Liddon turns to his application. What good is all of this speculation? He pictures a typical self-sufficient Londoner at the height of the Empire, admiring the city, its buildings, and its government, who then considers that he himself is the cause of his own existence. But then, he notes, "The very 'I' at the center of your being is a gift. . . . The only thing we create is our own sin."[16]

He ends the sermon by fitting the pattern of Victorian rhetoric with his aim to persuade.

> Awake, thou that sleepest in some pantheistic or materialistic dream of error, or in some deadly sensual passion, or greed, or ambition. . . . [W]ake to acknowledge the awful blessedness of existence. . . . Awake, thou that sleepest and as thou contemplatest, that thou existest and must exist forever . . . remember that Christ only now and in eternity will give thee light if only thou wilt receive it.[17]

---

15. Liddon, "Creation," 6.
16. Liddon, "Creation," 8.
17. Liddon, "Creation," 8.

Frederick W. Robertson (1816-53)

Life

F. W. Robertson may be considered a study in contrasts. Although he received acclaim only in a narrow sphere during a six-year ministry at Brighton, on the seacoast of England, his posthumous reputation far exceeded his living notoriety. Even though he ardently desired to pursue a military career like his father, an officer in the Royal Artillery, shortly before receiving his commission, he decided to enroll at Brasenose College, Oxford, to study for the Anglican ministry after attending a French seminary. With no attraction to the Tractarian movement, however, he began his ministry as an evangelical. He left the narrow evangelical movement that criticized him, but he refused to align himself with Anglo-Catholics, criticizing their high view of the Eucharist and showing disdain for their lectionary and liturgical calendar. Although he was raised in a well-to-do family, he gave himself relentlessly to the poor to the point of damaging his health. While sympathetic to the cause of the working class, he never aligned himself with the international socialist movement of that day. F. W. Robertson was absolutely his own man.[18]

O. C. Edwards locates Robertson, along with John Henry Newman, in the depths of nineteenth-century Romanticism. A sensitive man who appreciated common people, Robertson loved poetry and nature. During the same century, another tragic Romantic, Van Gogh, was painting pictures of peasants and old shoes. In a way, Robertson was the Van Gogh of the pulpit. Just as Van Gogh never sold a painting in his life, Robertson only sold one sermon during his brief lifespan of thirty-seven years. In an utterly Romantic mystery, his sermons that have survived were recollections from relatives to whom he repeated his sermons or wrote in letters.[19]

Equally Romantic, Robertson had Byronic good looks and a chivalry associated with his military leanings, and yet he was the melancholy victim of tuberculosis, also called consumption. O. C. Edwards wryly notes that consumption and melancholy were "the ailments of artists; they made people interesting. Keats, Shelley, and, it seems, half of the poets of that time were consumptive."[20]

---

18. Olds, *Reading and Preaching*, 367.
19. Edwards, *History of Preaching*, 609.
20. Edwards, *History of Preaching*, 610.

Forty-five years after his father had gone, in 1898, Charles Boyd Robertson issued an affordable five-volume set of his father's sermons. Emblazoned at the top of the cover were the words, "People's Edition. Price One Shilling and Sixpence Net." That equals $30.23 in today's market value.

Charles also gave an explanation for his father's power in the pulpit. He said his father emphasized the constructive rather than the destructive: "a principle upon which he lays much stress: that of establishing the truth rather than directly combating the error."[21]

At his first post as a curate in Cheltenham, F. W. Robertson revolutionized that church during his four-year tenure, but he demonstrated the morose spirit and self-doubt that plagued his ministry. When he came to Cheltenham, he was an evangelical, but his morbid experience of church life there changed his position. False charges brought against his orthodoxy stung his thin skin, and when he responded to them, he lost his sense of proportion. In Maclaren's view, Robertson suffered from the lower quality of evangelicalism in England and mistook that for the genuine higher evangelicalism. The American evangelical Warren Wiersbe, says, "He was pained by the bitterness, narrowness and downright meanness that characterized some of his leaders. . . . He stood alone, like a theological Ishmael."[22]

Perhaps answering some of his father's critics, the younger Robertson stresses the centrality of the Incarnation in the elder's preaching, "The Incarnation was to him the blossoming of Humanity."[23] At that point, Robertson moved beyond his usual subjective Romantic preaching to actual argument. The son emphasizes his father's commitment to the real, the earnest, and the courageous.

After spending time on the Continent recovering from a lost friendship in the fray, for six years Robertson pastored Holy Trinity Church in Brighton, where he was a tourist attraction to holiday makers who would catch the train from London to that southern English seaside resort. Being considered by many as a tourist attraction burdened him greatly, and he was often depressed by that reality. In a famous confrontation, someone left the church at Brighton one day and said, "Oh, Dr. Robertson, that

---

21. Robertson, *Sermons*, xi.
22. Wiersbe, *Walking with the Giants*, 27.
23. Robertson, *Sermons*, xiii.

was a great sermon," and he said, "Thank you. The devil's already told me that."

On a train ride, Robertson was talking with a stranger who rhapsodized about the preacher he had heard the day before in Brighton. When Robertson commented, "I think I ought to stop you," the man was embarrassed that he did not recognize the preacher. The stranger asked where the voice was he had heard the day before. Robertson was depressed that he could so hide his inner self from his outer performance. He complained, "For myself, never have I felt a more fixed and settled depression."[24]

In a city with thirteen Anglican churches, Robertson was a superstar. Yet jealousy and slander hounded him in the Anglican evangelical magazine, *The Record*. When he came to his Brighton pastorate in 1847, he was swept by the great political changes of 1848 throughout Europe. Typical of his dialectical life, he was counted "too Conservative by the Radicals and too Radical by the Conservatives," while his balanced view kept both from excess.[25] Maclaren overstates the case but touches a nerve when he exclaims, "Under his teaching and spirit, the very face of preaching was changed in half the pulpits of our land."[26] Added to these recriminations was Robertson's personal preference for the working poor that offended his affluent congregation.[27]

More recently, Christina Beardsley, an Anglican chaplain who studied Robertson's life, noted that he fought ill health, felt himself to be a failure, afflicted himself with self-deprecation, and was slandered by other clergy. Early in his ministry, he was haunted by his desire to be a soldier: "Very unhappy, listless, motiveless and a broken spirit all before me seems a dull, dead, waste, so little. Am I subdued to God's will in denying my heart?"[28]

A contributing factor to his depression was an unfortunate marriage with Ellen Robertson, who lacked the ability to encourage him. He had "been attracted by a pretty face, only to discover that there was not much behind that face."[29]

---

24. Beardsley, *Unutterable Love*, 181.
25. Robertson, *Sermons*, xxxiii.
26. Robertson, *Sermons*, xxxv.
27. Wiersbe, *Walking with the Giants*, 28.
28. Beardsley, *Unutterable Love*, 41.
29. Beardsley, *Unutterable Love*, 86.

After a sermon on the death of the Queen Dowager, a national event, he was criticized by Lady Byron, and he realized the deficiency of the sermon—the only sermon published in his lifetime. Not long before he died, he lamented, "Life seems gathering all its fires for the last crisis and there's nothing more, and for that all is dark."[30]

The accumulation of physical weakness, perpetual misunderstanding, fraught nerves, and self-doubt led him to experience a painful death on Sunday, August 15, 1853. His last sermon was from 2 Corinthians, "Finally, brethren, farewell."[31] His last words, in agony, were, "My God, my Father . . . let God do His work."[32]

One observer notes his depression, isolation, and a sense that he should have been in the military. Yet these aspects of his life only made things worse. To some extent, Robertson is a ministerial Beethoven. The musician's most creative work came after crushing disappointments, such as his three bouts of depression, his loss of the immortal beloved, his inability to adopt his nephew, and his deafness. Nevertheless, it took the fire to produce the music. In Robertson's case, a light, momentary tribulation did work out an eternal weight of glory.

Olds contends that Robertson "blazed a trail in the nineteenth century that has become, at the beginning of the twenty-first century, a superhighway."[33] Ian Mclaren (aka John Watson, pastor of Scotts Free Church) affirmed that "in the Church of Christ no Englishman of this century more entirely fulfilled the idea of a prophet than Frederick Robertson of Brighton."[34] He showed his genius for portraying the humanity of Jesus, relating to the political and social issues of the day, and may well have been the first preacher who brought psychological insights to the text, long before Leslie Weatherhead would do so at City Temple a century later.[35]

---

30. Beardsley, *Unutterable Love*, 158.
31. Wiersbe, *Walking with the Giants*, 29.
32. Robertson, *Sermons*, xxxviii.
33. Olds, *Reading and Preaching*, 368.
34. Robertson, *Sermons*, xxv.
35. Olds, *Reading and Preaching*, 368.

Sermon

On August 12, 1849, Robertson preached a sermon entitled "Christian Progress by Oblivion of the Past," based on Phil 3:13–14. He begins anthropocentrically, noting Paul's willingness to identify himself with his readers. He, too, is a frail creature, as was Paul: "I count not myself to have apprehended." It is typical of Robertson to link himself and his listeners sympathetically with the text.

He turns adroitly to the usual perception of Paul as one so far above us that we have no more identity with him than with "a gliding swallow's flight," a Romantic touch from nature that recalls Robertson's ornithological hobby. Paul is so unlike us in respect to his lack of depression, even though he had no home; his superiority over jealousy, pride, and ambition; and his shedding of the slanders and calumnies of opponents. One must recognize Robertson's own depression in the face of jealousy and slander from other ministers gently whispering in these opening words.[36]

He then turns to the body of his sermon in his famed two-point style:

1. The apostle's object in this life.
2. The means which he used to obtain it.[37]

The object is nothing less than perfection. This is more than the negative absence of evil; it is "the attainment of conceivable excellence."[38] He employs a mathematical metaphor. In a difficult math problem, you can only approximate the answer, but every fraction you add makes it closer to the "millionth millionth."[39]

Robertson then leans into the phrase, "this one thing I do." He considers that easy enough for the minister but a challenge to the working person. All work would cease if the layperson literally did this one thing. Robertson distinguishes between doing and being. Every layperson can be a one-thing person in the midst of temptations to ill temper or, for that reason, the very changes of the weather in Victorian England.

He then addresses the difficult challenge of the Christian reward, the "prize." This is not the prize of the student who studies to get a good

---

36. Robertson, *Sermons*, 55–56.
37. Robertson, *Sermons*, 57.
38. Robertson, *Sermons*, 58.
39. Robertson, *Sermons*, 58.

job. Rather, it is the prize of the learner who learns for the sheer joy of learning.

> To those who seek knowledge for its own sake, the labour is itself reward.... The man who is honest because honesty is the best policy, has not integrity in his heart.... God for His own sake—goodness because it is good—truth because it is lovely—this is the Christian's aim.[40]

One familiar with C. S. Lewis's discussion on Christian rewards finds here the fountainhead of Lewis' thought, whether from this well or someone else who drank from this well.

Robertson considers the ultimate motive for this is the promise of heavenly rest, but "the rest which is not of indolence, but of powers in perfect equilibrium. The rest which is deep as summer midnight, yet full of life and force as summer sunshine, the Sabbath of Eternity."[41] One must be moved by these words from an other-worldly soul whose life was lived in pain and restlessness.

Robertson then turns to the means of attaining this perfection, "forgetting those things behind." He labors more than we would today, telling his congregants to forget their loss of innocence that lays behind them. They cannot regain innocence, and that loss is no more to be regretted than the blossom is to be regretted when fruit is hardening in its place.[42]

One almost hears here the Wordsworth's poem, "Intimations of Immortality from Recollections of Early Childhood." Pining over lost innocence belongs to the Victorian psychology more than our own. (My generation is closer to regretting the loss of the bright colors seen under the influence of psychogenic drugs.)

He then persuades us to forget the loss of youth. By mid-life, we are heading downhill. His prose is prettiest when he looks at the older person: "There is a second youth for man, better and holier than his first, if he will look on and not back. There is a peculiar simplicity of heart and a touching singleness of purpose in Christian old age, which has ripened gradually and not fitfully."[43] These words were from one who would be gone in four years at thirty-seven. He felt the shadow.

---

40. Robertson, *Sermons*, 60.
41. Robertson, *Sermons*, 61.
42. Robertson, *Sermons*, 63.
43. Robertson, *Sermons*, 64.

His sermon reaches an empathetic zenith when he urges us to forget our mistakes. These include mistakes based on our circumstances, such as choosing the wrong career. One wonders if this is the rueful memory of Robertson wishing to be a soldier. His best words come when he turns to our past guilt: "Bad as the results have been in the world of making light of sin, those of brooding over it too much have been worse. Remorse has done more harm than even hardihood."[44] He points to Judas.

In a stirring peroration, he turns the tables on the congregation by describing that person who looks forward without Christ: "It will be winter soon—desolate, uncheered, hopeless winter—old age with its dreariness and disappointments, and its querulous broken-heartedness; there is no second spring for you."[45]

In another day and time, Robertson is closer to a Norman Vincent Peale or Robert Schuller in their anthropocentric positivism than he is to a John Piper or John MacArthur in their rational biblicism, but he is not close to any of those. He has too much theology to be a Peale and too much humanity to be a MacArthur.

Charles Haddon Spurgeon (1834–92)

Life

In the remote Essex village of Kelvedon and under the shadow of Cambridge University, Charles Haddon Spurgeon was born in 1835.[46] His father was a Congregationalist preacher who was so poor that baby Charles had to live with his Congregationalist pastor grandfather in the

---

44. Robertson, *Sermons*, 66.

45. Robertson, *Sermons*, 66.

46. Spurgeon's biographies are as numerous as diverse. He began his autobiography, and it was completed by his wife and private secretary. It was originally issued in four coffee table–sized volumes (1897–1900) and later reprinted, *C. H. Spurgeon, Autobiography*. There were volumes written shortly after his death—Northrop, *Life and Works of Rev. Charles H. Spurgeon*; and Hope, *Spurgeon*. More recent biographical treatments include Drummond, *Spurgeon, Prince of Preachers*; Nettles, *Living by Revealed Truth*; and Morden, *C. H. Spurgeon, The People's Preacher*. Thielicke's *Encounter with Spurgeon* surprised the homiletical world as the renowned German academic preacher heralded Spurgeon as the example to follow. Even "how to do it" books point to Spurgeon: Michael, *Spurgeon on Leadership*; as well as a guided tour of Spurgeon locations, Anderson, *C. H. Spurgeon*. Midwestern Baptist Theological Seminary now houses Spurgeon's library and artifacts, and its curator, Christian George, is publishing lost and previously unpublished sermons from his earliest ministry.

even more remote Stambourne. From these rural roots this self-taught youth would explode—and that is the word—on the scene as the premier preacher in London at nineteen, and by the time of his death in 1892, his image was as well-known as Victoria herself. A case is easily made that Charles Spurgeon holds a firm place in Christian history as the ablest pastoral preacher in the history of Protestantism. He built the first megachurch, published more sermons than anyone in history, founded a college, established an orphanage, and presided over the first church in history that was open from dawn until midnight and operated more than sixty ancillary ministries. No building in England was able to hold the crowds when he was preaching. He preached to the largest indoor crowd in history at the Crystal Palace.

How did this historical phenomenon develop? At sixteen the teenager got lost in the midst of a snowstorm at the village of Colchester and accidentally wandered into a primitive Methodist church. Huddled with a few people braving the storm, Spurgeon listened to a substitute preacher. No church service in a snowstorm was more consequential than that because he was converted there. He walked eight miles to be baptized in the River Lark at Isleham Ferry, a site marked by a monument today.

Spurgeon's first sermon was unexpected. As he and a friend were walking to the Essex village of Teversham, his friend assured Spurgeon that he would pray for him as he preached. But Spurgeon thought his friend was the preacher. Out of this providential misunderstanding, the teenage preacher first preached in a humble cottage within a remote village. At the same time, his Sunday school class at St. Andrews Baptist in Cambridge drew more persons than the pastor's sermon, creating a bit of a sensation. Ironically, as a dissenter he could not have attended the University of Cambridge since he could not sign the 39 Articles of the Anglican Church.

A strange providence marked Spurgeon's potential educational experience that never developed. Dr. Angus, the principal of Regent's Park College, was scheduled to meet Spurgeon in a private home. A servant seated Angus in one room and Spurgeon in another. They sat in the same house but missed one another, each thinking that the other had failed to show. Shortly after that, Spurgeon was called to London. Even stranger is the fact that Spurgeon's brother and later associate pastor, James Archer Spurgeon, did attend the college while Spurgeon did not. Spurgeon chalked all this up to providence and his call to London.

Spurgeon became pastor of the small Baptist church in Waterbeach, a village in Essex, during 1851, the same year he preached his first sermon. The village was considered a vile backwater. The youthful preacher jammed the church with crowds, the town was transformed, and his fame spread. He received a letter from the New Park Street Baptist Church in London in 1854 asking him to come and preach. Thinking the letter was sent to the wrong Spurgeon, he returned it, but they promptly responded that they meant him. He journeyed to London, where he preached to the slender crowd in the two hundred-member church in the morning. By nightfall the church was filled for the evening service.

Spurgeon had found his life's work. His life and religion in London would no longer be the same in that Victorian era. This village lad would preach to more people than any Oxbridge-educated pastor in the capital of the Empire and command the attention of the nation for the rest of his life. And he was only nineteen.

In 1855 he began the publication of his sermons, preached to enormous crowds in Exeter Hall, and worked with his first ministerial student. In 1856 he married Susannah Thompson and soon became the father of twin sons. That year also witnessed the great disaster of his ministry. To accommodate the crowds that wished to hear him, the church met at Surrey Gardens. Apparently, one Sunday during his sermon, some conspirators yelled out "Fire," and seven persons were trampled to death in the aftermath of the stampede. The newspapers, already vilifying the young preacher, crucified him over the melée—and it almost ended his ministry.

Rather than leaving the ministry, Spurgeon nevertheless progressed. In 1857 he founded the Pastor's College, which continues to this day. Its graduates would plant churches in London and all over the world. The strictly abolitionist college welcomed black students from its beginning. In 1861, seven years after coming to London, the barely twenty-seven-year-old Spurgeon preached to the largest indoor crowd in history—23,654 in the Crystal Palace, which was built for the world exhibition. He was so exhausted after preaching, he slept for three days. That same year his new church building, the Metropolitan Tabernacle, which seated fifty-six hundred people, opened free of debt. It would be the world center of preaching for the next three decades.

The 1860s would be a decade of achievement for Spurgeon. In 1865 he began his influential magazine, *The Sword and the Trowel*. The next year he founded the Colportage Association to distribute Christian literature. During the following year, he broke ground for the Stockwell Orphanage, which exists to this day. It cared for children off the streets of Dickensian London. When Spurgeon preached, he took up offerings for his orphanage. He would go to the orphanage and greet the children with great joy, as well as teach at his college on Friday afternoons.

Spurgeon was no ascetic, living in a grand home in South London with a household staff like any British gentleman. He was not a teetotaler until later in life when the abstinence movement enlisted him, but one gets the sense he did not do this with great glee. He loved cigars so much that a tobacco company quoted his approval in an advertisement. All of these indulgences, plus the typical diet of an English gentleman, left him with a great girth. His health broke in his early forties. He suffered from painful gout that drove him to leave in the winter months for Mentone on the Riviera, his perpetual retreat. While visiting there, he would sometimes preach in the commons room of the small hotel where he stayed.

His publications went far beyond his weekly sermons. His *Treasury of David* became a classic collection of homiletical notes on Psalms. His daily devotional book, *Morning and Evening*, is digitized today and available on the Internet. His *Lectures to My Students* remains a classic. He also wrote pithy epigrammatic books of homespun humor. The greatest phenomena, however, were Spurgeon's sermons that he preached on Sunday and made available by Friday all over the United Kingdom. People would wait on the docks in Wales for his sermons to be unloaded from the ships. David Livingstone was found with a Spurgeon sermon on his person when he died in Africa. Spurgeon wrote these sermons while often preaching ten times a week for various occasions.

In 1887 he became embroiled in a controversy that overshadowed the latter years of his life, the Downgrade Controversy. First in his magazine, and then more publicly, he accused unnamed members of the British Baptist Union of heresy, especially regarding the atonement and eternal reprobation. The controversy caused him to quit the Union in late 1887 and be censured by the same body in 1888 for not naming the heretics. The controversy became a public phenomenon when the most famous Baptist in British history quit his own denomination and became essentially an independent Baptist. Spurgeon's health in his later years raised a chicken-and-egg question: Did his health cause the controversy, or did the controversy further damage his health? He vehemently denied that his declining health led to the controversy, but he also refused to name the heretics because of a pledge he made to the executive of the Union.

His last illness took him to Mentone on the Riviera, where he died on January 31, 1892. His London funeral on February 12th was such an astonishing public event that most of London south of the Thames shut down. Tens of thousands in an enormous procession filed by his casket. He was buried at West Norwood Cemetery, a then new Victorian cemetery in south London. His gravesite is a place of pilgrimage even today. His sermons continued to be published until World War I yielded a paper shortage. In 1916 his thirty-five hundredth sermon was published, capping off a remarkable sixty-one years of published sermons. After his death, sermons were published from transcriptions of evening and midweek sermons.

Sermon

In 1879, Spurgeon was in his forty-sixth year. Managing the leadership of the largest Protestant church in history and its related enterprises had taken its toll. His health had broken several years previously. He had been staying at his Mediterranean retreat, Mentone on the Riviera, during the harsh London winter. Besides suffering other maladies, he was aching severely with gout, so much so that his portly knees gave him torment and sometimes his hands could not hold a pen. Still, the sermons preached on Sunday morning at the Tabernacle were revised and issued the same week. When he was away ill, he would revise older sermons—often from Sunday nights earlier preached—and those would be published without dates.

Another dozen years awaited him before he died at Mentone in 1892. He had been preaching to the masses in London for twenty-six years. This sermon shows the remarkable fertility of his mind that was yet tempered by the gathering years and suffered pain. This is the 1,469th published sermon in the twenty-fifth volume of the series.[47] The sermon chosen here was selected at random on purpose to demonstrate his typical pulpit work.

Spurgeon was the most famous preacher in the world. His aptness of metaphor, pastoral theology, and experiential Christianity gleam through this particular sermon. Unlike some preachers, somehow the vitality of his delivery and the charm of his presence still permeates the pages of his written sermons more than a century later. With an urgency

47. Spurgeon, "Prayer Perfumed with Praise," 217–28.

and empathy, his sermons have retained a sense of now rather than then, here rather than there. He speaks here with a captivating urgency that makes thankful prayer the most significant thing.

As always, Christian experience at its highest forms the basis of his preaching. God is real, Christ is risen, life is preparation for eternity, and every day is aglow with spiritual life. He tells you how to experience all that as the most significant thing in the world.

Spurgeon had just returned that Sunday after his long recovery in Mentone. One can imagine the crushing resumption of responsibilities he experienced the week before this sermon, yet he retains his freshness.

The text for the sermon is typical of his usual short texts: "In everything, by prayer and supplication with thanksgiving, let your requests be made known unto God" (Phil 4:6). He will hold these few words up in the light of revelation, rotate them around, and let the light refract from them into life.

He begins with a brief exegetical observation that "prayer" refers to general, usual praying, but "supplication" indicates immediate and pressing needs.[48] From there he conducts a biblical survey of those who joined together prayer with praise, whether it was Abraham or Elijah. His burden is to emphasize the necessity of thanksgiving with prayer.

As always, he was quick with the metaphor: "No matter though the prayer should struggle upward out of the depths, yet must its wings be silvered o'er with thanksgiving."[49] Such a pithy metaphor characterizes the preaching of Spurgeon. Here, prayer is conceived as a bird in the depths. As the bird rises, one notices that the edges of its wings appear to be overlaid with silver. So also is prayer. Spurgeon seemed to have an endless supply of such metaphors. Of course, in the world of Wordsworth, Shelley, and Keats, not to mention Trollope and Dickens, such decorative language was not uncommon. Spurgeon claimed to have read *Pilgrim's Progress* three hundred times. Allegory came as easily to him as the cigars that he regularly placed in his mouth.

He then turns to the use of a common biblical word, "Hosanna." With his peculiar ability to find new meaning in old words, he reminds the reader that "Hosanna" involves both prayer and praise. As a prayer it means "Save, Lord," and as praise "it is tantamount to 'God save the king,'

---

48. Spurgeon, "Prayer Perfumed with Praise," 217.
49. Spurgeon, "Prayer Perfumed with Praise," 218.

and it is used to extol the Son of David."[50] Thus, Spurgeon finds in one word the burden of his entire sermon. He continues to demonstrate the combination of prayer and thanksgiving in the psalms as well as in the Pauline epistles. He has thus laid the groundwork in a longer than typical introduction for his sermons, showing the canonical pervasiveness of prayer mixed with thanksgiving. He is now ready to begin the body of the message.

Spurgeon always announced all of the "heads" of his sermons at the end of his introduction. This harked back to earlier preachers, but he persisted in the practice. Thus, the preacher pauses to say, "With this as a preface, I invite you to consider, carefully and prayerfully, first, *the grounds of thanksgiving in prayer*; secondly, *the evil of its absence*; and thirdly, *the result of its presence*."[51] What has fascinated the ages is the brevity of his pulpit notes. He would take to the pulpit these headings, along with a few subheadings, on a half sheet of paper. When printed, the sermons were typically a dozen pages of smaller typeface. His delivery was extemporaneous. Added to the well-established habit that he did not select his text until Saturday evening, the whole of it cannot fail to astonish the current reader.

Spurgeon turns to his first "head," which covers the reasons for joining thanksgiving with prayer. He has no less than nine subdivisions of this first main point, each a paragraph. The very possibility of prayer ought to be cause for gratitude, but that is not enough. The fact that we have the power to pray is another cause for praise. We look at back at past mercies, and they add to prayers of thanksgiving.[52]

When we pray about present trouble, we should be thankful that it is sent in love. We are thankful in praying because God has sent so many answers before. We ought to thank God as if the gift had already been received. Here he points to a contemporary, George Müller, who was famed for prayers in running his orphanage.[53] Moreover, we should thank God in prayer whether He says yes or no.

He uses another metaphor to plead, "Let your prayers be like those ancient missals which one sometimes sees, in which the initial letters of the prayers are gilded and adorned with a profusion of colors, the work of

---

50. Spurgeon, "Prayer Perfumed with Praise," 218.
51. Spurgeon, "Prayer Perfumed with Praise," 220.
52. Spurgeon, "Prayer Perfumed with Praise," 220–21.
53. Spurgeon, "Prayer Perfumed with Praise," 220.

cunning writers."[54] Those letters Spurgeon compares to illuminating our prayers with thanksgiving.

In his second "head," Spurgeon turns to the evil of praying without thanksgiving. He quotes Aristotle's observation against ingratitude. This division of the sermon, divided into five subdivisions, is marked by typical Spurgeonic humor. He told the story of a very bad little boy who resisted his parents' correction. His parents told him it was hypocritical to pray. The little boy responded to the accusation of hypocrisy, "No, mother, indeed it is not, for I pray God to lead you and Father to like my ways better than you do."[55]

He follows up this humor with a sad story about a personal friend who lost a daughter but refused to accept the providence of God in the loss. His Reformed theology comes across in his exclamation that prayer does not alter the mind of God: "Prayer is the shadow of the decrees of the Eternal. God has willed such a thing, and he makes his saints to will it, and express their will in prayer. Prayer is the rustling of the wings of the angels who are bringing the blessing to us."[56]

Time evidently pressed the preacher because his third "head" was shorter. This should be an encouragement to the rest of us mere mortals. Here he gives the results of the presence of thanksgiving with prayer—it brings peace and warms the soul. If you feel thankless in prayer, he encourages you to take down the hymnbook and sing.

Then he uses a creative illustration from contemporary mining in Victorian England. The miners would use the full wagons atop the mine to pull the empty wagons up as the full wagons descended. Even so, prayers filled with the praise of God pull our emptiness up to heaven.[57]

Spurgeon then turns to an apt Old Testament intertextual exposition. Jehoshaphat's army went into battle led by the praise singers of Israel (2 Chr 20:21). Victory came to Israel when the army was led forth with praise.[58] This appeal to sentiment sets Spurgeon apart from some of the rather dour preaching of earlier Reformed preachers in the Puritan tradition. There is an inescapable presence of joy in his sermons that reflects the attitude of his heart.

---

54. Spurgeon, "Prayer Perfumed with Praise," 224.
55. Spurgeon, "Prayer Perfumed with Praise," 225.
56. Spurgeon, "Prayer Perfumed with Praise," 225.
57. Spurgeon, "Prayer Perfumed with Praise," 227.
58. Spurgeon, "Prayer Perfumed with Praise," 227.

He ends with an emotional story that appeals to common empathy. If you promised food to a poor woman with a little girl, you would likely keep the promise. But if the little girl showed up with an empty basket that already had a thank-you note in it for the food you would put in it, you would doubtless do anything to give her the food. So also, our thanks moves the heart of God when we express it to Him with our requests.[59] At the end of the sermon, Spurgeon turns to the unconverted. Their prayer must be the sinner's prayer, which God is as happy to answer as the father of the prodigal was to receive the returning son.

Chosen at random, this is not the most spectacular of Spurgeon's sermons, by any means. Yet even on an average day, one can imagine the kind of congregation that gathered to listen to this stolid, practical, encouraging, and pastoral preaching. The greatness of Spurgeon rested in what counted for the consistency of his average sermons over so long a period of time. Now, in a world so far removed from the Victorians, they are still read the world over. He is the most quoted preacher today and will likely remain so.

Alexander Maclaren (1826–1910)

Life

In a volume on the leaders of the century, Alexander Maclaren achieved a standing among the most eminent.[60] Hugh Price Hughes, ministerial orator and editor of the *Methodist Times,* called him "supreme as the highest modern exponent from the pulpit of the spoken word."[61]

A private person, Maclaren avoided publicity, so newspapers had little to quote regarding his opinion on social and political public questions. He proclaimed basic orthodox Christianity while standing apart from theological controversy, evidenced by his refusal to join fellow Baptist Spurgeon's departure from the Baptist Union in the Downgrade Controversy. He had a quiet confidence that "not one grain of the true wheat should fall to the ground, though a million Satans had the Church to sift. There is an exaggerated conservatism that does not love the old so much

---

59. Spurgeon, "Prayer Perfumed with Praise," 228.

60. Carlile, *Alexander Maclaren, D.D.,* 8. For a popular devotional treatment, see Wiersbe, *Walking with the Giants,* 35–40. For other biographies by his contemporaries, see Mclaren, *Mclaren of Manchester*; and Williamson, *Life of Alexander Maclaren.*

61. Carlile, *Alexander Maclaren, D.D.,* 8.

as it hates the new, and which understands neither. The men who stoned Stephen for the sake of Moses would have stoned Moses for the sake of Abraham."[62] This came from the man who opened the first meeting of the Baptist World Alliance by reciting the Apostles' Creed.

Alexander Maclaren was born on February 11, 1826. His typically Scottish bi-vocational preaching merchant father David, pastor of John Street Baptist Church, Glasgow, was a participant in the plural eldership of Scottish Baptists. David was an able expositor and stamped on his son the equal obligation of the laity with ministers. In the evangelical fervor of the time, David transferred from the Church of Scotland to Congregationalists to Baptists. Extended members of the family included the Giffords of the eponymous lecture fame. Politically, the family was liberal and progressive in social causes of the times.[63]

David went away to Australia on business, and Alexander was baptized at Hope Street Baptist Chapel on May 17, 1838. While in a Glasgow high school, Alexander acquired the habit that shaped his preaching more than anything else—reading a chapter of Hebrew and Greek every day. At sixteen, Alexander matriculated at the Baptist College, Stepney, in East London, which was affiliated with the University of London and later became the present-day Regent's Park College of Oxford. His student years spanned a four-year period, 1842 to 1846. Samuel Green told his son "the Committee had passed a Scotch lad named Maclaren, who would cut all the others out."[64] Reclusive and painstaking in his studies, he earned the BA from the University of London.

The new principal of Stepney was Benjamin Davies, PhD (Leipzig), a stickler for the painstaking reading of biblical languages and a major influence on Maclaren. While at Stepney, Alexander developed a lifelong love for Hebrew that informed his striking Old Testament preaching.

Maclaren's earliest ministry was marked by his youth, devotion to study, and certain mentors. He delivered his first sermon to six old men of the college committee sitting at the other end of a conference table. They only said, "He would do."[65] His first public service was held at a nearby chapel with seven people present, yet he was considered too youthful to release to the public.

---

62. Carlile, *Alexander Maclaren, D.D.*, 8.
63. Olds, *Reading and Preaching*, 393.
64. Carlile, *Alexander Maclaren, D.D.*, 18.
65. Carlile, *Alexander Maclaren, D.D.*, 25.

Two persons influenced the young Maclaren: the eccentric Thomas Binney, who pastored a church near the Monument on Fish Street Hill, and Edward Miall, MP, editor of the *Non-Conformist*. Miall stoked Maclaren's passionate devotion to religious freedom and his early ardent support of the disestablishment of the Anglican state church. Maclaren trumpeted the virtues of a free church in a free state. He gathered from St. Augustine the reality of sin and the sovereignty of God and devoured the works of Thomas Carlyle, Emerson, and John Ruskin. In fact, Maclaren was so touched by Emerson that he often used the transcendentalist's beautiful nature metaphors.

The London where Maclaren studied was very Dickensian. A thin upper crust of wealthy people reveled in ease while the sullen masses lived in cringing poverty. Regarding religion, his student days were marked by the Oxford Movement, the sacerdotalism of Pusey, and the departure of John Henry Newman that shook the state church and the nation. The Stepney common room buzzed with all of this revolutionary thought.

Twenty years after college, Maclaren spoke to students at another Baptist school, Rawdon College. He described two types of ministerial students: those who were lazy through their college years, impatient to get to the work, and those who so loved the academy that they forgot why they were there in the first place and became "reviewers, schoolmasters, or the like."[66]

On November 16, 1845, during his last year as a student, the congregation at Portland Chapel, Southampton, heard him preach as a supply. The church had a fractious past but called him while waiting a year for him to finish his degree. His call involved a three-month probationary period.

From the beginning, he was noted for his individuality in content, dress, and verbiage. He spoke to the masses by clothing the old orthodoxy with new language. Once, after twenty minutes of preaching, he bluntly remarked, "I have no more to say," and sat down.[67] Determined to preach without a manuscript, he sometimes paused to think of the right word for so long, visitors thought he had broken down or ended his sermon. One old Scotswoman said "she often wished to be in the pulpit to whisper in the lad's lug the word he waited for."[68] He did suffer from

---

66. Carlile, *Alexander Maclaren, D.D.*, 25.
67. Carlile, *Alexander Maclaren, D.D.*, 49.
68. Carlile, *Alexander Maclaren, D.D.*, 50.

what today is called stage fright. But later he got better at preaching. By the time he accepted the pastorate at Union Chapel in Manchester, he became, according to a literary critic in that city, the greatest determiner of style in that city.

Maclaren sternly avoided having newspapers and periodicals in the study. Instead, he considered the study a place for meditation and the root of a successful ministry, and disdained desultory reading.

Even early on, Maclaren avoided the typical round of tea-drinking ministerial social calls. Yet he was a student of people. A biographer once observed, "He knows men as a botanist knows flowers."[69] During his Southampton days, he vehemently voiced his opposition to the social ills of poverty, overcrowding, intemperance, and slums. Yet, he maintained that the gospel changes the individual first, then society. He opined, "The willful blindness of many good people to the sufferings of the masses is little less than criminal."[70]

Maclaren's preaching method astonished people from this distant time because he did not practice *lectio continua*. Worried that Englishmen might not appreciate that old Scottish style, he often agonized over his texts. He left us one volume of *lectio continua*, "Colossians" in the Expositor's Bible.[71] Unlike other Victorian pulpit giants, his preaching style was more classical than Romantic. Although he devoured Italian art and English literature, these aesthetics made no appearance in his straightforward and simple sermons.[72] By today's standards, however, his sermons appear to be literary masterpieces. In his own time his language was *koine* for his congregation. Yet, a college principal considered Maclaren a chief literary influence, if not *the* chief literary influence in Manchester.[73] A memoirist believed his pulpit power rested on two foci, a sympathetic instinct for souls and remarkable power for meditation on the text.[74]

Usually, he made a few notes on some ideas for his sermon but did not take them to the pulpit. Considering the beauty of his pulpit speech from today's standpoint, his extemporaneous preaching seems as likely as Wordsworth citing his poetry as an extemporaneous improvisation for

---

69. Carlile, *Alexander Maclaren, D.D.*, 53.
70. Carlile, *Alexander Maclaren, D.D.*, 67.
71. Olds, *Reading and Preaching*, 394.
72. Olds, *Reading and Preaching*, 395.
73. Carlile, *Alexander Maclaren, D.D.*, 73.
74. Carlile, *Alexander Maclaren, D.D.*, 82–83.

the public. We owe his sermons not to manuscripts but to stenographers who captured seven thousand sermons and lessons spanning his long ministry. He spent his last years editing these sermons, from 1904 to 1910.[75]

His performance exhibited few gestures, relying on his striking thought rather than any artifice. He had "a rich, musical voice, clear and penetrating; the undoubted Scotch accent adds to his force by giving a suggestion of greater volume than it really possesses, though the Doctor is clearly heard in our largest London buildings."[76]

Sermon

Consider a typical Maclaren exposition from a seldom preached, relatively obscure passage, 1 Sam 8. Here, the elders of Israel confront Samuel about his age, his derelict sons, and their desire for a king like their neighbors. God tells Samuel they have not rejected the old man but God Himself. He tells Samuel to let them have their visible king but warn them about what kings do. Samuel warns the people, but they do not relent.

Maclaren's divisions of the text are never forced, and often enchanting. In this exposition he calls on us to "1) note the ill-omened request; 2) note God's concession of the foolish wish; 3) note the obstinancy, with eyes open to the consequences, persists in its demands; and 4) note the divine purposes which use man's sin as its instrument in advancing its designs.[77] As always, his clear, simple language catches the essence of each movement in the briefest terms. It is never forced or complicated.

Maclaren moves with gracious ease from the "then" of the text to the "now" of the listener. Concerning Israel's desire for a visible rather than invisible king: "We too are ever being tempted to prefer the solid security, as our foolish senses call it, of visible supports and delights, to the shadowy help of an unseen Arm. . . . Note, too, that we cannot combine reliance on the seen and the unseen. Life must be molded by one or the other."[78]

In dealing with the hidden grace behind God's grudging concession of giving a king to Israel: "The surest way to disgust men with their own

---

75. Olds, *Reading and Preaching*, 395.
76. Carlile, *Alexander Maclaren, D.D.*, 71–72.
77. Maclaren, *Expositions*, 295–97.
78. Maclaren, *Expositions*, 294–95.

folly is to let it work out its own results, just as boys in sweetmeat shops are allowed to eat as much as they like at first, and so get a distaste for the dainties. 'Try it, and see how you like it' is not an unkind thing to say, and God often says it to us."[79]

Concerning Israel's obstinacy and ours, "Like bulls that shut their eyes when they charge, we rush at our mark, and often dash ourselves to pieces on it."[80] Concerning God's ultimate will being done, even by using our sin, "No barriers can stop the march of His great purpose through the ages, any more than a bit of glass can stay a sunbeam. However the currents run and the streams howl, they carry the ship to the haven; for He holds the helm and all winds help."[81]

Anywhere you touch Maclaren, you find these quick, vivid metaphors from life and nature. He observes boys at a candy shop in Manchester, he watches a bull in the pasture, he looks up in his own study and sees the light coming through the wavy Victorian glass, and he remembers a nautical principle. Maclaren may virtually be called an expositor by metaphor. His figures of speech seem to spring up instantly, like homiletic mushrooms. All the more to admire because he spoke extemporaneously. He claimed only to know the opening sentence when he began. He was a metaphor machine.

Always evangelical, Maclaren sees in their sinful desire for a king the manner God uses our sin to further His purposes. Providentially, the elders' miscalculated desire for a king led to David and the greater Son of David, the Messiah. Indeed, their misguided desire initiated the very idea of the Messiah. The Cross itself is just like their mistake; when humans did their worst, God did His best.

One is compelled to agree with Robertson Nicoll: "Maclaren touched every text with a silver hammer, and it broke up into three natural and memorable divisions."[82] Whatever gave three-point preaching a bad name, it was not the work of Maclaren.

Deep calls unto deep. The late and lamented Dr. Gardner C. Taylor devoured Maclaren. Bishop J. D. Wiley of New Orleans has Taylor's volumes of Maclaren. Taylor never, ever parroted Maclaren, but it is moving to see how the great wordsmith of the twentieth century loved

---

79. Maclaren, *Expositions*, 296.
80. Maclaren, *Expositions*, 297.
81. Maclaren, *Expositions*, 298.
82. Larsen, *Company of the Preachers*, 581.

his counterpart of the nineteenth. I can never read Maclaren without his pitch-perfect outline grasping my brain and overcoming all other ideas about dividing the text.

Joseph Parker (1830–1902)

Life

As pastor of the second largest church in London, the City Temple, Joseph Parker stood with Spurgeon as one of the two dominant contemporary autodidacts in the capital of the Empire.[83] He was born four years before Spurgeon and lived a decade longer. His birthplace was Hexham-on-Tyne, a small town on England's northernmost county, barely thirty miles from the border of Scotland and a short trip away from Edinburgh. His father was a stonemason and a devout Congregationalist. Parker matured by listening to earnest theological debates in a humble home. His formal education amounted to that of an American high school. Yet, at an early age he showed interest in ministry and arose at six o'clock in the morning to be tutored in Greek. His first sermon was on the village green, and he later professed surprise that he had preached. Parker honed his craft as a temperance preacher from 1845 to 1850.

In 1851 Parker married the daughter of a farmer, Ann Nesbitt, also from a devout family. She died after twelve years of marriage. He remarried in 1864, but then lost his second wife in 1899, a bereavement from which he did not recover.

In 1852 he joined John Campbell at Whitfield's Tabernacle as his assistant at twenty-two years of age. From there he accepted a pastorate at a church in Banbury, Oxfordshire, in the shadows of the oldest university in England, but he could not attend the school because he was not an Anglican. The church mushroomed, and he turned down seven calls to other churches. He finally relented and went to Cavendish Street Congregational Church in Manchester; the same year Maclaren went to Union Chapel in the same city. The two became lifelong friends. At Cavendish, he preached both to management and labor in that center of the Industrial Revolution. Then the call came from the oldest congregational

---

83. For treatments of Parker, see Fant and Pinson, *20 Centuries of Great Preaching*, 238–73; Gammie, *Preachers I Have Heard*, 39–41; Olds, *Reading and Preaching*, 411–21; Wiersbe, *Walking with the Giants*, 51–59. For Parker's autobiography, see Parker, *Joseph Parker, A Preacher's Life*.

church in London, the Poultry Chapel. The church had diminished, so he declined the call. But in 1868 the church called again, and he began his thirty-three-year ministry that was overshadowed only by that of Spurgeon.

It may be an unfair judgment, but Parker was widely regarded as an egotist. With his leonine hair and massive frame, he could indeed sound a narcissistic tone. When he was asked what style, he wished his new suburban City Temple to take, he replied that it should be designed so that when Queen Victoria asked who preached there, people could answer, "Joseph Parker." When a smaller church asked him to leave City Temple, he retorted, "An eagle does not roost in a sparrow's next."

Yet, more perceptive observers consider this Parker's defense mechanism against an inferiority complex that haunted him throughout his ministry. He was obsessed with Spurgeon, worried that the London weather would take his congregation, and thin-skinned about his critics. But none of his anxieties kept him from building the then striking City Temple five years into his London ministry. Along with Liddon's St. Paul's and Spurgeon's Tabernacle, this became the destination church for a London visitor.

In 1884 he made the announcement that thrilled the Romantic churchgoers of the era. In a planned program that would last seven years, he intended to preach a thousand sermons through the Bible and publish them in twenty-five volumes—which he did. He delivered his sermons with his famous extemporaneous style; often he stated that he did not know what he would say first in a sermon. His secretary transcribed and edited them because he could not stand to read his own sermons, unlike Spurgeon, who tediously edited his own sermons. Parker began at his desk at 7:30 a.m. with newspapers and correspondence and then worked out his sermons while walking in the London public parks.

Sermon

A typical Parker sermon, chosen at random, is "Memorial Stones," an inventive pulpit discourse about the stone monument in the Jordan. Parker jumps into the image immediately: life should be full of cairns. Yet, was it not too early for Israel to have built a monument? They have conquered nothing yet, and Jericho looms before them. No! Crossing the Jordan means that we have already defeated every Jericho before us. All of life is a single sentence, and the first step contains the last. When Jesus turned water into wine at Cana, He already had turned His dead body into a risen Savior.[84]

Parker's sermons are similar to entering a grand home and being arrested by the beauty of the foyer. Yet, you are led down a hallway to a grander room. Suddenly, you are shuttled off into a side room that is amazing in and of itself.

He next observes that in education, the reading of the first book has the reading of all others in it. The person who never read the third book never read the first. So also, it is with Euclid—the person who masters the first equation has already mastered all the rest. This is the tragedy of the church: It never dares to get past its first principles, so it cannot go forward. The Devil mocks the church because it never goes beyond the basics.[85]

Then, we are led back into the main room of the sermon. He warns us that in our own lives, we should never stray far from the last memorial stone. When we are tempted, we must run back under its shadow. When the enemy comes, run back to the last stone. That is why it's wrong not to keep a diary or journal about our spiritual lives. If you do not use pen and ink, at least keep a diary written in your own heart. Let everything in life become a memorial so that you have so many memorials they crowd out everything else. Then, all of the past becomes a memorial, a whole subdivision of memorials.[86]

Parker then takes a visit to another side room. He says that when your children ask you why you have wrinkles on your face, why you have white hair, why you're talking to an invisible Presence, or why you're singing anthems all of the time, be ready to tell them your own history with God. Do not give them a philosophy of speculation, but rather give them concrete memories.[87] The stones in the Jordan remind us of our own cairns to which we return that bear witness to others.

Then, you peep into another chamber off the hallway. There, Parker takes you down an English countryside road, where there are stones aplenty, scattered and without meaning. Then, you discover a construction of stones intentionally put together. You are compelled to ask, "What

---

84. Parker, *Preaching Through the Bible*, 107.
85. Parker, *Preaching Through the Bible*, 108.
86. Parker, *Preaching Through the Bible*, 109.
87. Parker, *Preaching Through the Bible*, 110.

do these mean?" When you see a meaningful construction, you intuit purpose, design, and intention. No one asks what shapelessness means. Yet when you see a great manor house, you ask who built it and who lives there. That is how we should live our lives, so that those who come after us ask who lived that life.[88]

At the end of the sermon, Parker drops the figure of speech and speaks plainly about how we ought to see a Providence in our own lives and others should see it as well.[89] Then he goes back to the well-known metaphor of having to cross the final Jordan someday to get to the other side. Yet, we can already erect an Ebenezer because the other side has been conquered.[90]

Parker was not an expositor or an exegete. His sermons were often creative implications of an image in the text. In that style, he was unexcelled. When Parker died, he was the last of a type, the gifted nineteenth-century autodidact who enthralled the citizens of the Imperial capital. He would be very pleased that we mentioned him today but still pouting that he is in Spurgeon's shadow.

Alexander Whyte (1836–1921)

Life

Born in poverty to a single mother in Kirriemuir, County Angus, an ecclesiastical center on the west coast of Scotland, Alexander Whyte became one of Scotland's most famous leaders as well as a world-famous preacher.[91] In his long career as the pastor at Free St. George's, Edinburgh, his work as the moderator of the General Assembly of the Free Church of Scotland and his professorate and subsequent appointment as the principal of New College at seventy-three framed a career that was as passionate as it was disciplined. Counting his time as the associate pastor, he spent forty-seven years at the same church.

---

88. Parker, *Preaching Through the Bible*, 111.
89. Parker, *Preaching Through the Bible*, 112.
90. Parker, *Preaching Through the Bible*, 113.
91. The standard biography is Barbour, *Life of Alexander Whyte*. See also Fant and Pinson, *20 Centuries of Great Preaching*, 235–78; Gammie, *Preachers I Have Heard*, 11–13; Olds, *Reading and Preaching*, 688–95; and Wiersbe, *Walking with the Giants*, 89–102.

Whyte's mother nurtured his faith in a humble home. Meanwhile, he worked with cattle and learned the local trades of weaving and shoemaking. From his early childhood, he announced his intention to be a preacher. Perhaps the day Robert Murray M'Cheyne handed him a tract reinforced that aspiration. Through it all, his consuming passion was books. Whyte would even pay someone to read to him while he worked.

His early development was marked by a revival in north Scotland, education from 1858 to 1866 at Aberdeen and New College, Edinburgh, and a four-year apprenticeship at Free St. John's in Glasgow. In 1870 he was given his life's work when Robert Candlish, pastor of Free St. George's Church, called the young Whyte as his assistant. Candlish died three years later and Whyte began his storied pastorate. His early ministry was greatly influenced by the Dwight Moody revival in Edinburgh.

The heart of Whyte's ministry beat in the midst of the Belle Epoque, the fin de siècle optimism that characterized the intersection of the nineteenth and twentieth century. Optimism in inevitable progress, the belief that everything was headed toward a golden age, and the brimming confidence that a new century would be better than anything that had gone before defined the times.

Yet the preaching of Whyte was known for its almost monomaniacal emphasis on the depravity of humans, most especially his own. At one time he said from his pulpit, "I have discovered the most wicked man in Edinburgh." After a dramatic pause to await the congregation's rapt attention, he intoned, "His name is . . . Alexander Whyte."

Of course, this optimistic era ended with the horrors of trench warfare, which took the life of one of his promising sons. Adversity struck again when he took on the new post at New College at the age of seventy-three in addition to his pastorate. He suffered his first heart attack, followed by a second, but he resolutely soldiered on.

Unlike his fellow Scot, Alexander Maclaren, Whyte insisted on the necessity of pastoral visitation. Conscientious in calling on his congregants, he considered it a great sin to fail to do so. He excelled in appreciation for anyone who did anything for him. Even though he was a very conservative theologian, Whyte was broad-minded in his sympathies, sometimes too much. He demonstrated naïvete in welcoming the leader of Bahá'i to his home and surprised many by his warm interest in John Henry Newman. As an evangelical, he gave a passionate defense for a faculty member dismissed from New College for progressive theological views. He continually demonstrated his absence of fear regarding the perseverance of the truth.

His noted biographer and kinsman, G. F. Barbour, gave an intimate portrait of his methods and work. Whyte freely opened his heart to his people about the temptations and victories of a preacher. He was equally forthright in addressing the Assembly. A man of Herculean labors, he roared: "I would have all lazy students drummed out of the college, and all lazy ministers out of the Assembly.... I would have laziness held to be the one unpardonable sin in all our students and in all our ministers."[92] Yet Whyte must not be perceived as a demanding master of ministry. One of his earliest assistants, after noting Whyte's indefatigable discipline, remarked, "There is a certain tenderness about him, a large sympathy, a sweet and gracious courtesy, that are infinitely attractive and endearing."[93]

As incredible as it may sound to American ministerial ears, Whyte took two or three months away from his pulpit in the summer, as well as significant breaks at Christmas and Easter. Yet, these were not vacations in the normal sense of the word. Instead, they were intense times of prayer, meditation, and preparation for lectures.

Apart from the holidays, he kept an ironclad weekly schedule. Beginning at 9:00 a.m., he kept the next four hours as a sacred time for study. He spoke five times a week to large congregations in the church, not counting other places. Unless he was doing pastoral work, he spent his evenings at his desk with his books. He did take a break on Saturday after finishing both sermons for Sunday by 1:00 p.m. During this time, he would gather with friends, read periodicals, order new books, and forward magazines to friends. One Sunday he was awake at 6:00 a.m., brought porridge before seven o'clock, and then spent two or three hours before breakfast for prayer and revision of the message. At 10:30 he was in the vestry thirty minutes before the service.[94]

From childhood, Whyte was plagued by his faulty memory. So, to help with his studies, he used an interleaved Bible. His favorite gifts that he received were notebooks of any number and size. He told a ministerial friend that for forty years he never read anything without writing it in his interleaved Bible adjacent to that which it illustrates. He was passionate

---

92. Barbour, *Life of Alexander Whyte*, 282.
93. Barbour, *Life of Alexander Whyte*, 285.
94. Barbour, *Life of Alexander Whyte*, 289.

about sending such interleaved Bibles to others, and would then hound the recipients to fill up the pages of his gift![95]

Style did not come easily to Whyte, and he often expressed his struggle with finding the right style in light of his many ideas. He once told a friend, "I have more ideas than I know what to do with," but he suffered great travail in finding the most arresting form in which to express his ideas.[96] His biographer estimated that Whyte was in his sixth decade before his mature style marked his work. He once told his children, "Style!—it's the march of language: it's the way one word is married to another, the way the words lean upon one another, the way they walk together."[97]

Sermon

Alexander Whyte's biographical sermons combine peculiar insight into the text with a soaring imagination. Congregations would always breathlessly await the first striking sentence. Consider these opening words of his biographical sermons:

Terah—"The first Jew was a Gentile."[98]

Abraham—"I did not know before that God had ever needed a friend."[99]

Miriam—"Watch well, Miriam, and never let thine eyes off that ark of bulrushes. Watch that little ark with all thy wit, for no other maiden shall ever have such another watch till the fulness of time, when another Miriam shall watch over another child still more fair to God."[100]

Jeroboam—"God may have that in his heart for you, which you must not once let enter your heart for yourself."[101]

Jonah—"The Prophet Jonah was both elder son and the unmerciful servant of the Old Testament."[102] In one sentence, he shoves Jonah up against two parables of Jesus, the elder brother in the story of the prodigal

---

95. Barbour, *Life of Alexander Whyte*, 290.
96. Barbour, *Life of Alexander Whyte*, 292.
97. Barbour, *Life of Alexander Whyte*, 292.
98. Whyte, *Bible Characters*, 65.
99. Whyte, *Bible Characters*, 74.
100. Whyte, *Bible Characters*, 130.
101. Whyte, *Bible Characters*, 341.
102. Whyte, *Bible Characters*, 381.

son and the unmerciful servant in the story about forgiveness. He puts into Jonah's mouth the complaint about music and dancing in the father's house, and then puts into Jehovah's mouth the fateful words of the forgiving potentate, "Ought not you to have had mercy."

One of the complaints about Whyte's sermons is a certain lack of structure. He does take some unusual detours, but the scenery is so gorgeous, his hearers would forget all about the highway and enjoy the view. The spare pulpit prose still vibrates, and even more so when you imagine the great Scot rolling his r's and growling his gutturals.

Consider, chosen at random, his sermon on Terah. Not many would preach on the father of Abraham, fearing that the shadow cast from the great mountain would obscure anyone on the windward side. Yet, Whyte opens the front door of the sermon to a completely unexpected hallway. Why did God wait so long to select the man with whom He made His covenant and started His great plan? Why not start with Adam? Did Adam consider his fall too much to be used, or did he take it too lightly? God could have started with Abel, but we know what happened to him. Why not Enoch? Heaven needed him more than earth. Or why not Noah? The abstemious, teetotaling Scot excuses Noah as the head of all those who drown their faith in the "wine-vat."

That brings us to Terah. Then, "the star came and stood over the house of Terah." In a remarkable thought, Whyte assumes that Terah was a pagan idolater who raised his devout son to be the same. "But those two Gentile men, father and son, served their Gentile gods with such truly Jewish service that God was constrained to wink at their unwilling ignorance."[103] That is one of those sermons gems that may be wrong, but it is good enough until something better comes along or until we get a direct report from Iraq four thousand years ago.

Whyte then speculates that it would have been the expected thing for God to have called Terah, and Abraham, as his submissive son, would have marched into the desert with his father. But here, the elder father patriarch submitted to the vision of his son. We would expect a thousand resistant excuses from an old geezer "but not one word of such stagnation, stubborn, unbelieving speeches came out of the mouth of Abraham's noble father."[104]

---

103. Whyte, *Bible Characters*, 66.
104. Whyte, *Bible Characters*, 67.

Whyte continues, "Far from that. Nay, I know not that we would have ever have had an Abraham, or would ever have heard his name, unless his humble-hearted, youthful-hearted, brave-hearted and believing-hearted father had taken his chosen son by the hand, and chosen son's wife, and said, Yes."[105] Whyte uses the image of an adventuresome old father to commend to all aged men. Terah becomes the great type of "all those men old in years, whose eye is not dim, nor their intellectual nor their spiritual strength one iota abated."[106] It is good to see a son who is loyally subservient to a father "but a still teachable, tractable, pliable-minded, genial-minded, hopefull-minded father is a still finer sight to see."[107] Terah is that Pauline person whose outer man is perishing but whose inner man is being renewed.

You will observe again Whyte's inclination to empty the thesaurus, which he loved to read. He may have had an advanced copy of David Buttrick's *Homiletic*, which suggests synonymous repetition in delivered speech to build faith-consciousness. Whyte says the same thing with different words to marinate the mind in the concept.

Whyte then turns to Abraham's trial when Terah died at Haran. With typical Scottish pathos, he pictures Abraham walking arm in arm with Terah, praying with him and praising with him. Then Terah is gone. All that Abraham loved as an immigrant had come from Iraq with him: his father, his beautiful wife, and his managerial brother Lot. Now the little company is diminished. The long walk to Shechem is longer because of the loss. Abraham was left with Lot, who whined that they should have stayed at Haran and listened to their neighbors. After Bethel's altar came grief upon grief. A famine is added to the loss of Terah.

Whyte points out that all of us will have to move on with some Terah in a grave in our own Haran. He then develops the implications of going forward without Terah and then ends with a stirring reminder of the journey of life as we leave behind others and our very previous selves. A person moves from "youth, man, married man, father, master, citizen and so on. Maid, wife, mother, mistress, widow indeed, and so on."[108]

---

105. Whyte, *Bible Characters*, 67.
106. Whyte, *Bible Characters*, 68.
107. Whyte, *Bible Characters*, 68.
108. Whyte, *Bible Characters*, 73.

Conclusion

And thus, the inventiveness of these famed Victorian preachers comes through so clearly. It is interesting at this symposium to look at these different characters in hopes that in some corner of that world, where eye has not seen and ear has not heard they sit together in eternal joy. Perhaps there is a Victorian preacher's corner in heaven such as the Poet's Corner in Westminster Abbey. Perhaps Spurgeon places his hand on Joe Parker, enabling the pastor of the Tabernacle to admit, "You did well." And Parker could put his hand on Alexander Whyte and say, "Alex, you weren't as bad you thought you were." And they all gather around Frederick Robertson, the depressed pastor, and say, "Fred, had you lived, you might have been the greatest to all of us."

Bibliography

Anderson, Clive. *C. H. Spurgeon: In the Footsteps of the "Prince of Preachers."* Epson, Surrey: Day One, 2002.

Barbour, G. F. *The Life of Alexander Whyte*. 8th ed. London: Hodder and Stoughton, 1925.

Beardsley, Christina. *Unutterable Love: The Passionate Life and Preaching of F. W. Robertson*. Cambridge: Lutterworth, 2009.

Carlile, John C. *Alexander Maclaren, D.D.: The Man and His Message*. New York: Funk and Wagnalls, 1902.

Cross, F. L., and E. A. Livingstone, eds. *Oxford Dictionary of the Christian Church*. 3rd rev. ed. Oxford: Oxford University Press, 2009.

Drummond, Lewis. *Spurgeon, Prince of Preachers*. Grand Rapids, MI: Kregel, 1992.

Edwards, O. C., Jr. *A History of Preaching*. Nashville: Abingdon, 2004.

Ellison, Robert H., ed. *A New History of the Sermon: The Nineteenth Century*. Boston: Brill, 2010.

———. *The Victorian Pulpit: Spoken and Written Sermons in Nineteenth-Century Britain*. Selinsgrove, PA: Susquehanna University Press, 1998.

Fant, Clyde E., Jr., and William M. Pinson Jr. *20 Centuries of Great Preaching: An Encyclopedia of Preaching*. Vol. 5. Waco: Word Books, 1971.

Gammie, Alexander. *Preachers I Have Heard*. London: Pickering & Inglis, n.d.

Holland, Henry Scott. *Personal Studies*. London: Gardner and Daron, 1905.

Hope, Eva. *Spurgeon: The People's Preacher*. London: Walter Scott, n.d.

Larsen, David L. *The Company of the Preachers: A History of Biblical Preaching from the Old Testament to the Modern Era*. Vol. 2. Grand Rapids, MI: Kregel, 1998.

Liddon, Henry Parry. "The Creation." In *Nineteenth Century Collections Online, British Politics and Society*. Reprinted from "The Preacher," CCXVII. "Preaching for the Millions," 136; "Special evening services," no. 7, "New series," no. 205, 4.

Maclaren, Alexander. *Maclaren's Expositions of Holy Scripture*. Vol. 1. Grand Rapids, MI: Eerdmans, 1959.

Mclaren, E. T. *Mclaren of Manchester: A Sketch*. London: Hodder and Stoughton, 1912.
Michael, Larry J. *Spurgeon on Leadership*. Grand Rapids, MI: Kregel, 2003.
Morden, Peter. *C. H. Spurgeon, The People's Preacher*. Franham, Surrey, UK: CWR, 2009.
Nettles, Tom. *Living by Revealed Truth: The Life and Pastoral Theology of Charles Haddon Spurgeon*. Fern, Scotland: Mentor, 2013.
Northrop, Henry Davenport. *Life and Works of Rev. Charles H. Spurgeon: Being a Graphic Account of the Greatest Preacher of Modern Times*. [Washington] Memorial Publishing, 1892.
Olds, Hughes Oliphant. *The Reading and Preaching of the Scriptures in the Worship of the Christian Church: The Modern Age*. Vol. 6. Grand Rapids, MI: Eerdmans, 2007.
Parker, Joseph. *Joseph Parker, A Preacher's Life: An Autobiography and an Album*. London: Hodder and Stoughton, 1899.
———. *Preaching Through the Bible*. Vol. 5. Grand Rapids, MI: Baker, 1978.
Paz, D. G. *Nineteenth-Century English Religious Traditions: Retrospect and Prospect*. Westport, CT: Greenwood, 1995.
Reardon, Bernard M. G. *Religious Thought in the Victorian Age: A Survey from Coleridge to Gore*. 2nd ed. New York: Longman, 2001.
Robertson, Frederick W. *Sermons: First Series*. London: Kegan, Paul, Trench, and Trubner, 1898.
Russell, George William Erskine. *Dr. Liddon*. London: Mowbray, 1905.
Spurgeon, Charles Haddon. *C. H. Spurgeon, Autobiography*. 2 vols. London: The Banner of Truth Trust, 1967.
———. "Prayer Perfumed with Praise, A Sermon Delivered on Lord's-Day Morning, April 20th, 1879." In *The Metropolitan Tabernacle Pulpit: Sermons Preached and Revised by C. H. Spurgeon During the Year 1879*. Vol. 25. Pasadena, TX: Pilgrim Publications, 1972. 217-228.
Thielicke, Helmut. *Encounter with Spurgeon*. Philadelphia: Fortress, 1963.
Whyte, Alexander. *Bible Characters: The Old Testament*. London: Oliphants, 1952.
Wiersbe, Warren. *Walking with the Giants: A Minister's Guide to Good Reading and Great Preaching*. Grand Rapids, MI: Baker, 1976.
Williamson, David. *The Life of Alexander Maclaren*. London: Clarke, 1910.

Chapter Eight

Preaching in Early America

The Preaching of George Whitefield

Thomas S. Kidd

On October 12, 1740, in the fading light of a cool autumn evening, twenty-five-year-old evangelist George Whitefield ascended a platform on Boston Common. Before him stood twenty thousand people. If the crowd estimates were reasonably accurate, this was the largest assembly ever gathered in the history of England's American colonies. (Boston's entire population was only seventeen thousand in 1740.) Whitefield had already seen crowds this massive—even larger—in the great city of London, but the teeming New England throngs, gathered in the region's small fishing villages and provincial towns, amazed him.[1]

Sometimes the press of the people frightened him, too, because of their volcanic outbursts of emotion. He regularly had to cut his preaching short, unable to be heard over the cacophonies of weeping and screeching. At the Common, Whitefield implored people to put their faith in Jesus Christ, the kind of sincere faith their Puritan forefathers embraced. It did not matter if their parents were Christians. It did not matter if they

---

[1]. This chapter appeared in earlier form in sections of my book, *George Whitefield: America's Spiritual Founding Father.*

prayed, attended church, or read their Bibles. Whitefield wanted to know if they had experienced the "new birth" of conversion.

Concluding the sermon, his countenance falling, he told them that it was time for him to go because other audiences needed his gospel preaching too. "Numbers, great numbers, melted into tears, when I talked of leaving them," Whitefield wrote. He had begun to forge a special bond with the American colonists. "Boston people are dear to my soul," he confessed.[2]

Reports about this boy wonder began to appear in the colonies' newspapers in 1739. By 1740 he had become the most famous man in America. (Remember, in 1740 George Washington was eight years old, John Adams was four, and Thomas Jefferson was not even born. Ben Franklin's fame as a printer, which did not extend much beyond Philadelphia, was enhanced considerably by becoming Whitefield's publisher.) Whitefield was probably the most famous man in Britain, too, or at least the most famous aside from King George II.

Three hundred years after his birth, George Whitefield is not entirely forgotten, but his fame now is far dimmer than it was on that fall evening in Boston. Today Whitefield's renown is surpassed by other evangelical contemporaries, especially Jonathan Edwards, the great pastor-theologian of Northampton, Massachusetts. The sensational success of Whitefield's ministry was both a reflection of and against the traditional preaching culture of the colonies, especially in New England. In early New England, families routinely attended church multiple times a week to hear lengthy doctrinal sermons read from a manuscript. A New England colonist who lived to an average age probably heard about seven thousand sermons in his or her lifetime.[3]

In spite of Whitefield's relative lack of fame today, there have been a number of biographies written about him. Christian treatments of Whitefield have been highlighted by Arnold Dallimore's monumental two-volume biography written in the 1970s. Most American history survey courses and textbooks also mention Whitefield, thanks to two major academic biographies, Harry Stout's *The Divine Dramatist* (1991) and Frank Lambert's *"Pedlar in Divinity"* (1994). These biographies, as well as a surge of recent studies of the Great Awakening, have established Whitefield as a fixture in the standard narrative of American history.

2. Whitefield, *Continuation of the Reverend Mr. Whitefield's Journal*, 41, 43.
3. Kidd, *American Colonial History*, 92.

Stout, Lambert, and other scholars have helped us interpret Whitefield within the framework of eighteenth-century Anglo-American culture. Lambert examined Whitefield in light of the "consumer revolution" of the eighteenth century. As the "Pedlar in Divinity," Whitefield mastered the use of publicity, newspapers, and inexpensive print to promote his preaching tours and the gospel he expounded. Stout, on a related theme, presented Whitefield as "Anglo-America's first religious celebrity, the symbol for a dawning modern age." Even though Whitefield denounced the theater following his conversion, his background as an actor, along with his familiarity with England's theater culture, prepared him for a fabulously successful preaching career.[4]

In his two recent books on Whitefield, communications scholar Jerome Mahaffey has expanded earlier proposals by Stout and historian Alan Heimert by considering how Whitefield became the "Accidental Revolutionary," or the man most responsible for shaping an American culture primed for the Revolution. Whitefield was the "central figure" in the process by which disparate colonists became Americans, prone to think in zealous, adversarial terms about religion, rights, and liberties. Whitefield's Awakening may not have caused the Revolution, Mahaffey argued, but it had a profound conditioning influence on Americans as the Revolution approached. Heimert memorably argued that whether Jefferson, "the enlightened sage of Monticello knew it or not, he had inherited the mantle of George Whitefield."[5]

Whitefield and commerce, Whitefield and religious celebrity, Whitefield and the Revolution. All of these arguments have considerable merit, even if I have doubts about certain aspects of them. The main problem with these approaches, however, is that they do not really focus on Whitefield's primary significance, or the way he viewed himself. My argument regarding Whitefield is straightforward: George Whitefield was the key figure in the first generation of Anglo-American evangelical Christianity. Whitefield and legions of other evangelical pastors and laypeople helped establish a new interdenominational religious movement in the eighteenth century, one committed to the gospel of conversion, the new birth, the work of the Holy Spirit, and the preaching of revival across Europe and America. My work on Whitefield places him fully in the dynamic, fractious milieu of the early evangelical movement. And

4. Lambert, *"Pedlar in Divinity,"* 6; Stout, *Divine Dramatist*, xvi.
5. Mahaffey, *Accidental Revolutionary,* 188; Heimert, *Religion and the American Mind*, 148.

of course, Whitefield's fame derived substantially from the power and notoriety of his preaching.

Indeed, if people know anything about Whitefield, they know that he was a remarkably gifted preacher and evangelist. Scenes from his ministry are among the most powerful from the whole Great Awakening of the mid-eighteenth century, from the titanic throngs he drew to Moorfields and Kensington Common in London as he began his "field preaching" ministry, to the pressing crowds who came to see him in America: sometimes more people came to his meetings in the colonies than the entire population of the town hosting him. To pick one particularly evocative scene, let's consider Whitefield's role in the Cambuslang revival in Scotland in 1742. In that year, intriguing news of awakening came to the itinerant from the small parish of Cambuslang, southeast of Glasgow, where he had not yet preached on an earlier visit he took to Scotland.

Cambuslang's fifty-one-year-old pastor, William McCulloch, reported to Whitefield that under McCulloch's ministry, three hundred people (in a town of less than a thousand) had come under conviction of sin, and of those, perhaps two hundred had experienced authentic conversion. Many more descended on the town on Sunday mornings, and the estimated crowds numbering as many as ten thousand on recent Sabbaths. (Note that Whitefield often built upon the momentum generated by the ministry of local pastors.) McCulloch pled with Whitefield to come to Cambuslang as soon as possible. Arriving in Edinburgh in early June of 1742, Whitefield told McCulloch, using language from 1 Kgs 18, that "the cloud is now only rising as big as a man's hand; yet a little while, and we shall hear a sound of an abundance of gospel rain."[6]

Whitefield finally came to Cambuslang in July. Over a long weekend, throngs gathered in a natural amphitheater setting on a hillside the Scots called a "brae," near McCulloch's church. Congregants built two wooden-framed preaching tents and set up Communion tables in the fields. On consecutive days, Whitefield preached to crowds he estimated at twenty thousand. The twenty-one-year-old John Erskine, who would go on to become one of Scotland's leading evangelical ministers, described the

---

6. Extract of a letter from Mr. T. L. and J. K. of Edinburgh, to the Reverend Mr. George Whitefield, Dec. 26, 1741, in *Weekly History*, Feb. 13, 1742; William McCulloch to Whitefield, Feb. 14, 1742, in Whitefield Papers, Library of Congress; [William McCulloch] to Whitefield, Apr. 28, 1742, in *Weekly History*, May 29, 1742; Whitefield to [William] M[cCulloch], June 8, 1742, in *Letters of George Whitefield for the Period 1734–1742*, 401.

brae as "the most commodious [place] for hearing ever I saw." Although the number of attendees was disputed, Erskine was "certain a voice near as good as Mr. Whitefield's could have reached a greater number had they been there."[7]

On the Sabbath, it came time, for those who qualified, to take Communion. Church members, meaning those who had made a convincing profession of faith in Christ, received small lead tokens with which they gained admission to the tables. Different churches, from Scotland to Ulster to the Scots-Irish settlements in America, had designed different shapes for these tokens. Some were plain circular pieces with the minister's initials; those used at a great Dunfermline revival featured two hearts becoming one, just as the believer was united with Christ.[8]

McCulloch estimated that perhaps seventeen hundred of the tens of thousands of attendees received tokens at the July assembly. Whitefield attempted to help serve the communicants, but as he moved down the line, people got out of their seats and pressed around him, thanking him for coming and sharing prayer requests. Lest he become a distraction, he left the tables and allowed the other ministers to finish.[9]

Once everyone had been served, the whole assembly gathered before a tent, where Whitefield preached on Isa 54:5 (KJV), "Thy Maker is thy husband; the Lord of hosts is his name." Although Whitefield preached numerous sermons at Cambuslang, this is the one that converts remembered best, and it was a standard sermon in his preaching repertoire. There was considerable variation between the preached versions and the published one, as Whitefield appears to have used a memorized skeleton outline, but in the estimation of an early Scottish church historian, he delivered it each time "as his own feelings and a sense of duty prompted."[10]

---

7. Whitefield to J[ohn] C[ennick], July 15, 1742, in *Letters of Whitefield*, 409; Fawcett, *Cambuslang Revival*, 115; William McCulloch, July 14, 1742, in *Glasgow Weekly History* 30, 2; John Erskine to [Thomas Prince], July 17, 1742, in ed. Jonathan Yeager's, "John Erskine's Letterbook, 1742–45," *Miscellany of the Scottish History Society* XIV (2013) 234.

8. Schmidt, *Holy Fairs*, 108.

9. Whitefield to J[ohn] C[ennick], July 15, 1742, in *Letters of Whitefield*, 409; Fawcett, *Cambuslang Revival*, 115; William McCulloch, July 14, 1742, in *Glasgow Weekly History* 30, 2.

10. Fawcett, *Cambuslang Revival*, 116; Smout, "Born Again at Cambuslang," 115; Beebe, "McCulloch Manuscripts," appendix ia: 229; MacFarlan, *Revivals of the Eighteenth Century*, 66; Hindmarsh, *Evangelical Conversion Narrative*, 183 n.63, 194.

In the published version of the sermon, Whitefield emphasizes his simple preaching method: "I came not here to shoot over people's heads, but to reach their hearts. Accordingly, I shall endeavor to clothe my ideas in such plain language, that the meanest [lowliest] Servant, if God is pleased to give a hearing ear, may understand me." He speaks directly to the correct practice of the Communion many had just taken that day, urging ministers only to serve the Lord's Supper to those who have united with Christ in spiritual marriage. Those who receive Communion in a worthy manner, he exclaims, are "one with Christ, and Christ with them," and "they dwell in Christ, and Christ in them."[11]

Referring to the matrimonial metaphor of his text, Whitefield insists that the "poorest and most illiterate person here present [may] easily know, whether or not he is really *married to Jesus Christ*." Furthermore, he or she can often (though not always) know the time and circumstances under which that union occurred. "The day of our espousals is, generally, a very remarkable day; a day to be had in everlasting remembrance," he notes. Most true believers, he contends, can remember the moment of their conversion, just as they would remember their own wedding.[12]

To Whitefield, Christ is the spiritual husband of all believers. They are Christ's possession—body and soul. Whitefield's comparison of the believer's union with Christ to earthly marriage was common among early evangelicals. As seen in Isa 54:5, the Song of Solomon, and a number of other scriptural passages, the theme of marital union between God and his people frequently appeared in the Scriptures as well.[13]

Laypeople resonated powerfully with the itinerant's message. Margaret Lap, an unmarried twenty-nine-year-old, heard Whitefield preach first on his initial visit to Scotland in 1741, and found that his evocation of the dangers of hell summoned "great confusion" in her. She also listened to his sermon, "Thy Maker is Thy Husband." The message lodged in her mind, staying with her for months and even years afterward. She frequently had Scripture passages vividly impressed on her as she gained assurance, but early one Friday morning, while she still lay in bed, "these words, 'Thy Maker is thy Husband,'" came rushing into her thoughts, along "with several notes of a sermon of a certain minister." She became

---

11. Whitefield, *Five Sermons*, 5–6, 11.
12. Whitefield, *Five Sermons*, 11 [emphasis in original], 16.
13. Whitefield, *Five Sermons*, 22; Anderson, *Imagining Methodism*, 85–87.

physically overwhelmed—"sick," she said—with love for Jesus, and the Spirit made her believe that Christ was indeed her spiritual husband.[14]

Margaret Clark, a married forty-two-year-old, saw one of the most remarkable visions described by any Cambuslang convert (and a number of converts did report visions as part of their conversion experience). For some time she had experienced deep consternation over her sins, thinking she could never be forgiven. But as she listened to one of Whitefield's sermons, she thought she saw "with [her] bodily eyes, Christ as hanging on the cross, and a great light about him in the air, and it was strongly impressed on [her] mind; that he was suffering there for [her] sins." Evangelical pastors like William McCulloch, who recorded these testimonies, were cautious about visions seen with "bodily eyes" (as opposed to visions occurring in the mind or spirit). Clark noted, probably with McCulloch's prompting, that she had never seen the cross again, nor did she desire to see it again, and she never "laid any stress of [her] salvation upon [her] seeing this sight."[15]

Whitefield's spectacular ministry continued to generate hostility in personal encounters (he survived several assassination attempts and attacks from lynch mobs during his career), as well as printed assaults. The work at Cambuslang only deepened his rift with the Associate Presbytery of Scotland, comprising ministers called the Seceders, who had recently broken away from the established Church of Scotland. Because Whitefield—befitting his interdenominational evangelical tendencies—would preach at both Associate Presbytery and Church of Scotland parishes, some of the Associate Presbytery ministers denounced him in tracts, such as the floridly titled "Declaration, Protestation and Testimony of the Suffering Remnant of the Anti-Popish, Anti-Lutheran, Anti-Prelatick, Anti-Whitefieldian, Anti-Erastian, Anti-Sectarian, true Presbyterian Church of Christ in Scotland." Whitefield was "an abjured prelatick [Anglican] hireling, of as lax toleration-principles as any that ever set up for the advancing of the Kingdom of Satan." He was a "limb of Antichrist," and a "boar and wild beast from the Antichristian field of England." Cambuslang was a "mere delusion of Satan." Instead of leading participants to reject the apostate churches of England and Scotland, this faux

---

14. Beebe, "McCulloch Manuscripts," appendix ia: 9, 13, see also appendix ia: 59; Landsman, "Evangelists and Their Hearers," 133.

15. Beebe, "McCulloch Manuscripts," appendix iib: 450; Kidd, *Great Awakening*, 285.

revival birthed corrupt interdenominational cooperation and false shows of enthusiastic ecstasy, the Seceders insisted.[16]

As seen in his tangles with the Associate Presbytery, Whitefield was a man familiar with denominational and theological conflict. If all we knew about Whitefield was his rhetorical skill, we might get the impression that he was all show and no substance. But nothing could be further from the truth. Whitefield was no brilliant theologian like his contemporary Jonathan Edwards—and really, isn't it unfair to compare almost anyone to Edwards?—but he was a solid, principled, Bible-centered Calvinist evangelical thinker. If he was not solidly grounded in his theology, then he could have saved himself a lot of time and energy because his career was marked by repeated difficulties with fellow evangelicals, from the Wesleys to the German-based Moravians, over key points of theology.

Whitefield was the first celebrity pastor of the evangelical movement, but in his case, popularity did not equal vacuity, nor need it be so among celebrity pastors today. While his besetting feuds within the evangelical camp are troubling in one sense—should Christ's followers not manifest more unity?—there's another sense in which those theological battles are actually comforting because they tell us that doctrine mattered to Whitefield. But what was the key to Whitefield's celebrity? I suspect that many of us would love just to have a taste of the kind of preaching and evangelistic success that Whitefield did. Many Christians would argue that God used Whitefield powerfully through the preaching and evangelistic gifts that Whitefield zealously employed. Whitefield was also rooted in biblical doctrine, sound education (he was an Oxford man, after all), and church history, all of which thoroughly informed his preaching.

Because of Whitefield's rhetorical talents and mastery of media, sensationalism and the crass aspects of celebrity were always risks, but they did not seem to capture Whitefield. This is not to say that he was a perfect man—not at all, as anyone reading my biography will find out. His relationship with his wife was often hampered because of his ministry, and she paid a hefty price for his relentless travels. The most disturbing aspect of Whitefield's career was his involvement with chattel slavery, which he worked hard to introduce to colonial Georgia, where he had founded the Bethesda orphanage. (Georgia officials had initially banned slavery from the colony.) Whitefield envisioned the orphanage thriving on the

---

16. *Declaration of the True Presbyterians*, 6, 16–17, 23.

proceeds derived from Georgia plantations worked by slaves. Through the gifts of South Carolina plantation masters who were converted under his ministry, Whitefield became a slave master himself in the 1740s. Although he had a few anti-slavery friends around him, his conscience never seemed to have been especially pricked about that issue, and he did not free Bethesda's slaves at his death. Some critics of Whitefield today have understandably questioned whether we should admire this man at all, given his support for slavery.

These sobering truths about Whitefield remind us that even great heroes of the faith still struggle with sin and limited vision. For the Christian biographer, trying to hide or excuse such failings not only risks dishonesty, but it also turns away from the biblical mode, where the greatest saints are often also great sinners—from David to Peter to Paul. God graciously redeems and uses sinners in His kingdom work, and for that I am thankful.

To return to the reasons for Whitefield's success: all of Whitefield's talent and preparation would have meant nothing had Whitefield been averse to hard work, creative risk, and entrepreneurial ministry. Time will not allow me to unpack every detail here, but let's begin with the obvious: Whitefield made an incredible thirteen transatlantic voyages to bring the gospel to the American colonies. Each one of these could easily have ended in Whitefield's death, and some nearly did. He knew the risks full well, but through prayer and conversation with Christian associates, he determined to follow God's leading wherever it took him. He was never a model of physical health, both from bodily disposition, as well as the toll of his rigorous—some said reckless—preaching tours.

But working hard was not the whole story either, because many pastors have worked extremely hard yet followed the same old paths in ministry tactics. Whitefield was an entrepreneur, and especially as a young man pioneered innovative methods of preaching and communication that fueled the attention his ministry garnered. The key developments here were his extemporaneous preaching methods, his field meetings, and especially his use of the latest forms of media and communications to spread the word. Note again: these tactics did not alter his basic message or undermine his orthodoxy.

But in an era when many pastors gave long sermons that might have been doctrinally sound but were as dull as dirt, Whitefield revolutionized the sermonic form with a rhetorical style that captured the imaginations of the Anglo-American people. (Those of you who pastor local churches will note that Whitefield, as an itinerant, also had the advantage of really polishing a short list of memorized sermons, instead of having to come up with new material every week.) And when crowds could not fit into the era's small churches, or when local ministers banned Whitefield from their pulpits, Whitefield shifted gears and went into the commons and fields in order to reach the people where they were. "We've never done it that way before" was not a deal-breaker for George Whitefield.

Whitefield similarly employed the latest communications technology—especially cheap print and newspapers—to publicize his ministry and the gospel he preached. People began hearing about his travels months or even years in advance, and they were drawn by the media to witness his work. Whitefield also surrounded himself with the best experts in the new media of his time, most notably the Philadelphia printer and newspaperman Benjamin Franklin, with whom Whitefield became a lifelong friend.

Theirs was a peculiar relationship, because Franklin was no evangelical. Franklin could readily appreciate the power of Whitefield's preaching, however. "His eloquence had a wonderful power over the hearts and purses of his hearers, of which I myself was an instance," the printer wrote. Once, in Philadelphia, Franklin attended one of the itinerant's sermons. Suspecting that he would ask for money, Franklin wrote that he "silently resolved he should get nothing from me. I had in my pocket a handful of copper money, three or four silver dollars, and five pistoles in gold. As he proceeded, I began to soften and concluded to give the coppers. Another stroke of his oratory made me ashamed of that, and determined me to give the silver; and he finished so admirably, that I emptied my pocket wholly into the collector's dish, gold and all."

This passage from Franklin's autobiography poked fun at Whitefield's incessant requests for money to help fund his Bethesda orphanage in Georgia. But Franklin was adamant that the revivalist had an impeccable character. Many spread rumors that Whitefield spent the charity's money on himself, but to Franklin, those charges were absurd. Whitefield was "in all his conduct a perfectly honest man. And methinks my testimony in his favor ought to have the more weight, as we had no religious connection," Franklin said.[17]

17. Labaree et al., *Autobiography of Benjamin Franklin*, 177–78; Whitefield to Mr. F[ranklin], Nov. 26, 1740, in *Letters of Whitefield*, 226; B[enjamin] Franklin to John Franklin, Aug. 6, 1747, in Labaree, *Papers of Benjamin Franklin*, 3:169.

Because they both knew that Franklin was not a believer, Whitefield would routinely implore Franklin to accept Christ for salvation. For example, in 1752, he commended Franklin for his growing fame related to his scientific experiments. "As you have made a pretty considerable progress in the mysteries of electricity," Whitefield said, "I would now humbly recommend to your diligent unprejudiced pursuit and study the mystery of the new-birth . . . one at whose bar we are shortly to appear, hath solemnly declared, that without it, 'we cannot enter the kingdom of heaven.'" In spite of Whitefield's prodding, Franklin recalled in his autobiography that the itinerant would "sometimes pray for my conversion, but never had the satisfaction of believing that his prayers were heard." Nevertheless, Franklin insisted that he admired Whitefield's character and benevolent ministry. At Whitefield's death, Franklin wrote, "I knew him intimately upwards of 30 years: his integrity and zeal in prosecuting every good work, I have never seen equaled, I shall never see exceeded."[18]

In any case, Whitefield's relentless effort and entrepreneurial methods emerged from his conviction that the gospel demanded tireless work and creative tactics. Far from being a sign of theological shallowness, doctrinal conviction actually drove his innovations in method. Again, Whitefield had glaring personal inconsistencies, but there can be little doubt about his commitment to proclaiming the new birth of salvation through Christ. It took him to an early grave on his last visit to America in 1770. The gospel was that important, God's grace was that wonderful, and God had promised to draw the lost to Himself through the proclamation of the gospel. To Whitefield, there was no greater imperative.

Bibliography

Anderson, Misty G. *Imagining Methodism in Eighteenth-Century Britain: Enthusiasm, Belief, and the Borders of the Self.* Baltimore: Johns Hopkins University Press, 2012.
Beebe, Keith Edward, ed. "The McCulloch Manuscripts of the Cambuslang Revival, 1742: A Critical Edition." PhD diss., University of Aberdeen, 2003.
Fawcett, Arthur. *The Cambuslang Revival.* Carlisle, PA: Banner of Truth, 1971.
Gillies, John. *Works of Whitefield.* Shropshire, UK: Quinta, 2001.
Glasgow Weekly History. Printed by William Duncan, 1743. Gale ECCO (print editions and online), 2010.

---

18. Whitefield to Mr. F[ranklin], Aug. 17, 1752, Gillies, *Works of Whitefield*, 2:440; Labaree, *Autobiography of Benjamin Franklin*, 178; B[enjamin] Franklin to Noble Wimberly Jones, Mar. 5, 1771, in Wilcox, *Papers of Benjamin Franklin*, 18:53.

Heimert, Alan. *Religion and the American Mind: From the Great Awakening to the Revolution.* Cambridge: Harvard University Press, 1966.

Hindmarsh, Bruce. *The Evangelical Conversion Narrative: Spiritual Autobiography in Early Modern England.* Oxford: Oxford University Press, 2005.

Kidd, Thomas S. *American Colonial History: Clashing Cultures and Faiths.* New Haven: Yale University Press, 2016.

———. *George Whitefield: America's Spiritual Founding Father.* New Haven: Yale University Press, 2014.

———. *The Great Awakening: The Roots of Evangelical Christianity in Colonial America.* New Haven: Yale University Press, 2007.

Labaree, Leonard W., et al. *Autobiography of Benjamin Franklin.* 2nd ed. New Haven: Yale University Press, 2003.

———. *The Papers of Benjamin Franklin: January 1, 1745, through June 30, 1750.* New Haven: Yale University Press, 1961.

Lambert, Frank. *"Pedlar in Divinity": George Whitefield and the Transatlantic Revivals, 1737–1770.* Princeton: Princeton University Press, 1994.

Landsman, Ned. "Evangelists and Their Hearers: Popular Interpretation of Revivalist Preaching in Eighteenth-Century Scotland." *Journal of British Studies* 28 (April 1989) 133.

Mahaffey, Jerome Dean. *The Accidental Revolutionary: George Whitefield and the Creation of America.* Waco: Baylor University Press, 2011.

MacFarlan, D. *The Revivals of the Eighteenth Century, Particularly at Cambuslang.* London: Forgotten, 2017 (reprint).

Schmidt, Leigh Eric. *Holy Fairs: Scotland and the Making of American Revivalism.* 2nd ed. Grand Rapids, MI: Eerdmans, 2001.

Smout, T. C. "Born Again at Cambuslang: New Evidence on Popular Religion and Literacy in Eighteenth-Century Scotland." *Past and Present* 97 (Nov. 1982) 115.

Stout, Harry S. *The Divine Dramatist: George Whitefield and the Rise of Modern Evangelicalism.* Grand Rapids, MI: Eerdmans, 1991.

Whitefield, George. *A Continuation of the Reverend Mr. Whitefield's Journal, From a Few Days after His Return to Georgia to His Arrival at Falmouth, on the 11th of March 1741.* London: W. Strahan for James Hutton, at the Bible and Sun, without Temple-Bar, 1741.

———. *Five Sermons on the Following Subjects.* London, 1747.

———. *Letters of George Whitefield for the Period 1734–1742.* Carlisle, PA: Banner of Truth, 1976.

Whitefield Papers, Library of Congress.

Wilcox, William B., ed. *The Papers of Benjamin Franklin: January 1 through December 31, 1771.* New Haven: Yale University Press, 1974.

Yeager, Jonathan, ed. "John Erskine's Letterbook, 1742–45." *Miscellany of the Scottish History Society* XIV (2013) 234.

W. E. B. Dubois, one of the first African American PhDs in the country, highlights African American preachers' importance to the African American community: "The Preacher is the most unique personality developed by the Negro on American soil. A leader, a politician, an orator, a 'boss,' an intriguer, an idealist. . . . The combination of certain adroitness with deep-seated earnestness, of tact with consummate ability, gave him his preeminence, and helps him maintain it."[2] Thus, the preacher's communally affirmed sense of calling, along with his ability to offer a relevant interpretation and application of God's Word, ultimately heighten the significance of the preacher in the African American community.

A critical criterion for the masses' acceptance of the preacher and message includes some evidence of "the call." For African Americans, there must be some visible, tangible manifestation of the Holy Spirit that provides confirmation in the human spirit that the preacher is one who was sent, not one who simply went. The apostle Paul raises the rhetorical interrogative in Rom 10:14-15 (ESV): "How then will they call on him in whom they have not believed? And how are they to believe in him of whom they have never heard? And how are they to hear without someone preaching? And how are they to preach unless they are sent? As it is written, 'How beautiful are the feet of those who preach the good news!'"

The sense of "the call" for the preacher and the hearers, therefore, has historically facilitated and still creates an openness to hear and believe what "thus saith the Lord." Moreover, communal affirmation and acceptance of a preacher's call creates an equality of the voice of the preacher with the voice of God. Note that the communal affirmation of "the call" has historically been significant in the African American community. The preacher became the *Vox Dei*, the *Kohl YHWH*—that is, the voice of God to the people of God. Therefore, the preacher became a person of great significance in the African American faith experience.

When I was a student and Martin Luther King Jr. chapel assistant at Morehouse College, I was asked to participate in a play entitled *God's Trombones*. The play is based on James Weldon Johnson's 1927 publication of the same title, which presents poetic renderings of African American folk sermons. He casts the preacher in the role of God's trombone, intoning the sermon commencing with creation and concluding with judgment. Johnson determines the preacher to be the greatest influence on African Americans in the country because the preacher speaks for God. Thus, Gardner C. Taylor warned, "Preaching is a presumptuous

---

2. DuBois, *Souls of Black Folks*, 149.

Chapter Nine

The African American Preaching Tradi[tion]

Claybon Lea Jr.

African American preaching is much like jazz music which [is in]triguingly diverse in its numerous expressions but obviously di[ffers] from all other major music genres. African American preaching, i[n the] expanse of Judeo-Christian preaching, is unquestionably unique. It[s sig]nificance in the history of preaching in America is undeniable. Whil[e this] lecture cannot exhaustively treat the subject matter under considera[tion,] I will highlight several features of African American preaching tha[t are] significant and add significance to its place in the history of preachi[ng in] America.

Olin P. Moyd published a work entitled *The Sacred Art: Preac[hing] and Theology in the African American Tradition*. In this monograph, [the] author espouses two fundamental suppositions. First, African Ameri[can] preaching has historically been and remains the primary medium [for] communicating the *euangelion*, the gospel, and its values to the masse[s of] African Americans in the diaspora—and beyond. Week after week si[nce] the long and dark night of slavery in America, African Americans ha[ve] received a word from the Lord through the preacher. Moyd aptly asse[rts] that the preacher has been and continues to be the mass communicat[or] of spiritual and moral truths and values by which the community is [to] live.[1]

The preacher, then, must be included in any evaluative attributio[n] of African American preaching's significance. In *The Souls of Black Folk*

---

1. Moyd, *Sacred Art*, 6.

business. If the undertaking does not have some sanctions beyond human reckoning, then it is, indeed, rash and audacious for one person to dare to stand up before or among other people and declare that he or she brings from the Eternal God a message for those who listen which involves issues nothing less than those of life and death."[3]

Second, Moyd notes that the core content of African American preaching is practical theology. Like King Zedekiah in Jer 37:17 raising the query: "Is there a word from the Lord?" African Americans look to the preacher to indeed affirm, even as Jeremiah did, "Yes, there is a word from the Lord." The people anticipate proclamation that speaks to their particular circumstances, context, concerns, and consternations. In other words, the African American community would often listen to preaching with an ear bent towards a clear connection between what the Word of God says and how the Word of God helps them find meaning in their life experiences.

Like all theology, African American preaching as practical theology emerges out of and addresses a particular contextual reality. Its origins involve the combination of West African oral traditions and the torment of American slavery. Frank Thomas surmises that West African oral traditions, the slave experience, and post-slavery realities shaped the preacher's verbal and nonverbal expressions (sounds and gestures) that were inherently and necessarily rhetorical and theological.[4] The oppression of slavery, racism, Jim Crow, segregation, and injustices experienced by African Americans forged a unique form of preaching, faith, and hope in a context of degradation, dehumanization, and despair.

The experiential realities of inequitable existence in an unjust society birthed a form of preaching that is simultaneously redemptive and hope-filled, biblical and instructive, creative and engaging, artistic and argumentative, rhetorical and theological, spiritual and practical, moral and ethical, worshipful and joyful, comforting and accountable. As Kenyatta Gilbert writes, "It is the very disinheritance and dehumanization that inspired the African to hold in tension, perhaps a dialectical tension, both 'theology from above' and 'theology from below.'"[5] Hence, African American preaching is sensitive to the universal and particularized plight of humanity. As Frank Thomas notes, "The African American preaching

---

3. Taylor, *How Shall They Preach?*, 24.
4. Thomas, *Introduction to the Practice*, 55.
5. Gilbert, *Journey and Promise*, 36.

tradition has been shaped by faithful responses to centuries of racial, sexual, social, cultural, political, economic, and gender oppression, and as a result, is uniquely able to minister to all people, and especially hurting and oppressed people, in America and all over the globe."[6]

Whenever you begin to study preaching, particularly African American sermons, you will come across the name Henry Mitchell. Henry H. Mitchell's 1970 monograph, *Black Preaching*, initiated academic reflection on African American preaching's nomenclature. In both *Black Preaching* and *Celebration and Preaching* (1990), Mitchell emphasizes the importance of context in preaching. For him, the congregational context, along with the reception of and response to the spoken Word, are part and parcel of the authentication of African American preaching.

In their respective surveys of African American preaching, both Thomas and Gilbert view African American preaching as inherently theological and rhetorical. While Thomas effectively uses rhetorical analysis to examine African American preaching, he does not settle on a definition. Gilbert also argues for the theo-rhetorical nature of African American preaching but offers with it the following definition: "African American preaching is a ministry of Christian proclamation—a theo-rhetorical discourse about God's good will toward community with regard to divine intentionality, communal care, and the active practice of hope—that finds resources internal to black life in the North American context."[7]

Cleophus J. LaRue advances the discussion by acknowledging Mitchell's performative-rhetorical understanding of preaching, and does not seem to be at odds with Thomas' and Gilbert's theo-rhetorical view of African American preaching. Yet LaRue seems to push the envelope further. LaRue sees the need, as do I, to highlight the biblical hermeneutic that emerges in sermons preached by African American clergy, as well as the role and function of Scripture therein. In *The Heart of Black Preaching*, LaRue posits that,

> Where black preaching differs from traditional understandings of the faith is in its interpretation of the witness of scripture in light of blacks' historical and contemporary experiences.... A God who is unquestionably for them is what blacks see when they go to the scriptures. Thus the distinctive power of black preaching is to be found, first and foremost, in that which blacks

---

6. Thomas, *Introduction to the Practice*, 85.
7. Gilbert, *Journey and Promise*, 11.

believe scripture reveals about the sovereign God's involvement in the everyday affairs and circumstances of their marginalized existence.[8]

Having mentioned the significance of the African American preacher and acknowledged the fundamental prism through which certain scholars on the subject view African American preaching, I would like to share some of the significant characteristics of African American preaching.

Thomas identifies seven characteristics of African American preaching, to which eighth and ninth characteristics may be added.

1. *The centrality of the Bible.* This suggests that the rhetoric and theological understanding of the faith is rooted centrally in the Word of God. Now, this may not seem to be significant to any preaching, and you might presume that all preaching should have this same center; but you must not allow yourself to remove African American preaching from its context. Its context is that it has been forged and birthed in a context of oppression—slavery. The very same Bible that African Americans preach is the Bible taught and preached to them in order to facilitate their docility—to make them quiet, to make them subservient—and to say to them that slavery was indeed God's will, so they were supposed to submit to their masters as unto God.

    For the centrality of Scripture to be at the heart of African American preaching is a miracle. It's a miracle that a people who were oppressed by the same book can take that book and see in it liberation, freedom, and the ability to have a relationship with God irrespective of their present plight and predicament. The centrality of Scripture is vital to our understanding of the heart of African American preaching. LaRue contends that "more than a mere source for texts, in black preaching the Bible is the single most important source of language, imagery, and story for the sermon."[9] When you understand this, you appreciate all the more the centrality of the Bible in African American preaching. We do not preach it simply because it is the Word of God, we preach it because we also *believe* that it is the Word of God.

---

8. LaRue, *Heart of Black Preaching*, 2–3.
9. LaRue, *Heart of Black Preaching*, 10.

2. *The importance of experiential preaching.* African American preaching is an experience! It is so much more than a rhetorical act. Instead, it enlists and stirs the five senses to create a moving and often life-changing experience. For example, I heard both E. K. Bailey and Jasper Williams Jr. preach from the Book of Hosea in first person. In *"I Fell in Love with a Prostitute,"* E. K. Bailey, dressed in overalls, assumed a first-person narrative position for his message. He brought to life the narrative from the prophet Hosea. As he preached, one could see himself in the ancient narrative as an eyewitness. You could see Hosea relentlessly seeking to love and reclaim his wayward wife, Gomer. You could also feel the pain and disappointment in Hosea's heart. Moreover, you began to see yourself as Gomer and feel the heart of God for you—His love for the wayward. By the time E. K. Bailey finished preaching that story of Hosea, it was an unforgettable experience.

   Thomas also offers an example as told by James Forbes about hearing Gardner C. Taylor preach the biblical story of the prodigal son. At a certain juncture in the sermon, Taylor said, "Look, the boy is coming up the road now!" Forbes says he turned around, looked to the back of the church, and saw the boy coming up the road.[10]

3. *Existential exegesis.* African American preaching exegetes the biblical text and context of human need. It is always connected to both the historical-critical truths excavated through an exegesis of Scripture and the existential realities of the socio-cultural experiences of its hearers. African American preaching finds points of responsible connection between the exegetical and the existential. For example, James H. Cone expresses a historical and theological identification of the lynching of blacks with the cross of Jesus in his book *The Cross and the Lynching Tree*. "While the lynching tree symbolized white power and "black death," the cross symbolized divine power and "black life"—God overcoming the power of sin and death."[11] African American preaching makes connections that transform tragic experiences into triumphant expectations and realities.

4. *The inspiration of the Holy Spirit.* The preacher does not and cannot preach in his or her own power. The inspiration of the Holy Spirit is essential. The uniqueness of the African American tradition is

---

10. Thomas, *Introduction to the Practice*, 87.
11. Cone, *Cross and the Lynching Tree*, 18.

that African Americans can sense and observe when the Holy Spirit shows up. If you've ever been in African American church services, you might hear the preachers say these words: "I feel my help," which means that they have felt such an overwhelming sense of the Spirit's presence and power that they are no longer the one who is preaching to you—the real preacher has shown up. The Spirit is the real preacher! The Spirit informs, illumines, inspires, and empowers. The Spirit makes the Word come alive through the preacher in the ears and hearts of the hearers.

5. *The call and response nature of the sermon.* This phenomenon involves the dynamic interaction between the pulpit and the pew which allows the congregation/audience to partner in the preaching experience. Preaching becomes a dialogical communal event. That is, it is marked by creative Spirit-empowered speech and congregational response. It is, in effect, antiphonal preaching. The preacher talks to the people and the people talk back to the preacher. The call and response nature of African American preaching facilitates realtime improvisation on the sermon score the Spirit has crafted in the preacher's preparation.

6. *Rhetorical-linguistic eloquence of the sermon.* African American preachers have historically used linguistic bridges via poetry, imagination, illustration, quotes, and the like. Mitchell notes that African American congregations enthusiastically respond to beautiful language and well-turned phrases.[12] (Black preachers balance their rhetorical-linguistic artistry with globally and culturally recognizable references: Homer and Hughes, Dickinson and Angelou, Greek and Egyptian philosophy, John Newton and Isaac Watts, James Cleveland and Jay-Z, etc.)

Moyd lifts a sermon entitled *"The Inviter,"* taken from Matt 11:28 and preached by Manuel L. Scott Sr. as an example of the rhetorical-linguistic prowess of the African American preacher. Scott said, "Something can be gained ... by pointing out ... the audience to whom this invitation was first addressed." Then in powerful, poetic language, Scott conjectured,

> This audience was parked in poverty pockets and gathered in ghettos. They were Jews, second class citizens of the Roman Empire. . . . They were the culturally deprived and the

12. Mitchell, *Black Preaching*, 173.

socially disadvantaged. They were underfed, under housed, and under clothed. They were overworked and underpaid. These citizens were like cogs in other men's machines, compelled to be bearers of other men's burdens. They were moved about like checkers on a board, according to the whims and wishes of the dominant group.... They were the people against whom institutions were rigged—the courts, the government, the schools, and even the churches. It was people in such a plight, and listeners with such a lot on whose ears the Great Invitation was the first to fall.

Scott then raised the query, "Who is the Inviter?" His response came from Daniel: "He is the stone cut out of the mountain without hands breaking down idol gods and vanishing immoral kingdoms."[13] Scott's rhetorical-linguistic brilliance caused African American hearers to identify with the original audience and see themselves as recipients of the great invitation. Moreover, the hearers saw Jesus as the one who would redeem them, not only from sin but also from unjust kingdoms, and vindicate the hopes of the oppressed.

7. *The prophetic posture.* Gilbert states that the prophetic voice "speaks to the predicament of human suffering from the perspective of God's justice."[14] The African American preacher and congregation view the preacher in terms of the prophetic continuum. That is, prophets communicate God's compassion to the oppressed without diluting God's anger at injustices perpetrated by oppressors. Prophets indeed afflict the comfortable and comfort the afflicted. The African American preacher as the prophet is always, as Martin Luther King Jr. said of Amos, "maladjusted."

Walter Brueggemann asserts that the prophet's work "is nothing less than an assault in the consciousness of the empire, aimed at nothing less than the dismantling of the empire both in its social practices and its mythic pretensions." The prophet, therefore, must blow the trumpet and make what Samuel DeWitt Proctor could call "a certain sound" that rebukes evil oppressors and evil systems, as well as offers hope and restoration to the downtrodden, hopeless, and backslidden. William August Jones Jr. would often say, "Where the trumpet is needed, the flute will not suffice."

---

13. Moyd, *Sacred Art*, 53–54.
14. Gilbert, *Journey and Promise*, 12.

Gardner C. Taylor was an exemplar of the prophetic preaching tradition. In his Lyman Beecher Lectureship on preaching at Yale Divinity School in 1975 to 1976, published in 1977 in his book entitled *How Shall They Preach?* Taylor proclaimed,

> The preacher has no warrant to speak to our social ills save in the light of God's judgment and God's grace. For instance, racism is not merely an oppression by one people of another with all of its resultant group guilt, group degradation and social disorder. Racism is set against the "one blood" tie which God ordained in our creation. Racism, whether it be the rapacity of a majority position or the reactionary toughness and terrorism of an outraged minority, assaults the mandate of our creation that we human beings are to have dominion over the "fish in the sea, the birds of the air, and every living creature that crawls on the earth," not over each other.[15]

8. *The performative nature of the sermon.* The preacher embodies the sermon within his or her total person. Rationality, emotionality, and physicality are all engaged in African American preaching. In a sense, the preacher becomes an incarnation of the sermon as his/her total person embodies it. Hence, it becomes performative in nature without being relegated to mere dramatic performance.

9. *Suspense that leads to celebration.* In the African American preaching tradition, every sermon builds suspense and/or anticipation of a powerful and uplifting conclusion. People are made to listen, think, respond, and anticipate at the same time. One of the most effective uses of suspense found in contemporary African American preaching is presented by Frederick Douglas Haynes III. Haynes often shares a story in his sermon introduction that he does not conclude. Rather than share the outcome of the story, he proceeds to develop the sermon based upon the selected text. This creates intentional suspense that causes the hearer to listen, though distracted. Then, at the end of the sermon, Haynes will return to the formally open-ended story to offer a resolution that ties the introduction and conclusion together around the sermonic thesis in a homiletical bow, which then segues to a natural intoned celebration. Celebration in African American preaching makes the sermon melodic, musically intoning the message with varying styles of vocality. The ultimate

---

15. Taylor, *How Shall They Preach?*, 84.

celebration in African American preaching includes both the cross and empty tomb, irrespective of the biblical text chosen for the message. Celebration is just not celebration unless the preacher reminds the people of what Jesus did for us: "He died" and "He arose"!

Thomas includes an excerpt from C. C. Lovelace's 1929 sermon on "The Wounds of Jesus" and captures Lovelace's intoning of Jesus dying on the cross as he brings the sermon to a climax:

> He died until the great belt in the wheel of time
> And de geological strata fell aloose
> And a thousand angels rushed to de canopy of heben
> With flaming swords in their hands
> And place their feet upon blue ether's bosom and looked back at de dazzling throne
> And de arc angels had veiled their faces
> And de throne was draped in mournin
> And de orchestra had struck silent for the space of half an hour
> Angels had lifted their harps to de weepin willows
> And God had looked off to-wards immensity
> And blazin worlds fell of His teeth
> And about that time Jesus groaned on de cross and said, "It is finished."
> And then de chambers of hell explode.[16]

Having noted characteristics that highlight the significance of the African American preaching tradition, I will conclude with comments regarding the future significance of African American preaching. Gilbert is probably correct when he describes the future of African American preaching as "indistinct."[17] The world has changed and is still changing rapidly. There are challenges to our preaching that accompany societal change.

First, we preach to very distracted hearers. Multi-tasking has become more the norm than ever before. Technology can be both a bane and blessing for the preacher who seeks to be an effective communicator. People are completely engrossed in their smart devices, and they are only disengaged from their lives' simultaneous foci when they are asleep. Attention spans are shorter and retention is uncertain.

---

16. Thomas, *Introduction to the Practice*, 72–73.
17. Gilbert, *Journey and Promise*, 23.

Second, people communicate and listen differently. Millennials are used to communicating in 120 characters or less via video with FaceTime, Facebook Live, Snapchat, Instagram, and the like. People listen in a hurry. Many seem to appreciate as well as prefer the brevity and succinct nature of Ted Talks.

Third, meta-narrative is challenged by vignettes, plots with multiple subplots, and stories within the story to keep people engaged. The *Harry Potter* and *Game of Thrones* series are masters of this.

Fourth, the attire and positioning of the preacher on a Sunday or during a mid-week service or Bible study may look quite different in the immediate future. Standing behind "the sacred desk" may become less common because it has become a barrier in an age when people long for connection. Whatever the future trajectory holds for the methods of the African American preaching tradition, however, the core of its message should remain the same. Paul's words continue to ring from 1 Cor 1:21 (NIV): "For since in the wisdom of God the World through its wisdom did not know him, God was pleased through the foolishness of what was preached to save those who believe."

Bibliography

Cone, James H. *The Cross and the Lynching Tree*. Maryknoll, NY: Orbis Books, 2011.
DuBois, W. E. B. *The Souls of Black Folks*. Edited by David W. Blight and Robert Gooding-Williams. New York: Bedford Books, 1997.
Gilbert, Kenyatta R. *The Journey and Promise of African American Preaching*. Minneapolis: Fortress, 2011.
LaRue, Cleophus J. *The Heart of Black Preaching*. Louisville: Westminster John Knox, 2000.
Mitchell, Henry. *Black Preaching*. New York: Harper and Row, 1970.
Moyd, Olin P. *The Sacred Art: Preaching and Theology in the African American Tradition*. Valley Forge, PA: Judson, 1995.
Taylor, Gardner C. *How Shall They Preach?* Elgin, IL: Progressive Baptist, 1977.
Thomas, Frank A. *Introduction to the Practice of African American Preaching*. Nashville: Abingdon, 2016.

Chapter Ten

The Preaching of the Great Evangelists
Finney, Moody, Sunday, and Graham

Winfred Neely

Isaiah 52:7 (NASB) reads, "How lovely on the mountains are the feet of him who brings good news, who announces peace and brings good news of happiness, who announces salvation, and says to Zion, 'Your God reigns!'" Echoes of these words are found in Eph 6:15 which reads, "And having shod your feet with the preparation of the gospel of peace." Preparation and readiness to preach the gospel is a part of the Christian's spiritual armor. Of course, not all of us have the gift of evangelism but the church ministry should be characterized by an evangelistic kind of work. My presentation will center on several men who were gifted evangelists and how their gift expressed itself in their evangelistic preaching and ministries. I center my thoughts mainly around Charles Finney, with some thoughts about D.L. Moody and Billy Graham, along with some brief observations about Billy Sunday.

Charles Grandison Finney

(1792–1875)

Charles Finney was an evangelist, revivalist, Christian social reformer, theology professor, college president, and a man who knew God through personal experience. His contribution to Christ's kingdom and the redemptive betterment of the human condition was immense.

A faculty member of Oberlin College, Finney eventually became the second president of this institution. In the Finney years, Oberlin was an avant-garde haven of Christian social reform. For example, in 1835 and 1837, respectively, Oberlin was the first white collegiate institution in the United States to admit African American males[1] and females. Oberlin's glory days revolved around Finney's example, teachings, and educational leadership.

Finney's preaching left a massive imprint on his generation. Five hundred thousand people received Christ directly or indirectly through him. Local churches grew in number due to conversion growth through Finney's preaching.

Arguably, Finney was the most important figure in the Second Great Awakening and the greatest revivalist in American history in his ministry impact and enduring influence on evangelistic practice. One historian observed, "If American theological thought is a series of footnotes to Jonathan Edwards, American evangelistic practice would be a series of footnotes to Finney."[2]

Finney, of course, was more than an evangelist. He was a revivalist as well. In his book, *Lectures on Revival*,[3] Finney defines revival in the following way: "Revival is the renewal of the first love of Christians, resulting in the awakening and conversion of sinners to God. A revival of true Christianity arouses, quickens, and reclaims the backslidden church and awakens all classes, insuring attention to the claims of God."[4] Some years later, in his book entitled *Finney's Systematic Theology*, he defines

---

1. Until the early 1900s, one-third of African American professionals received their training at Oberlin. In 1940, the late Gardner Taylor, former pastor of Concord Baptist Church in New York, graduated from the Oberlin School of Theology, an institution whose legacy is deeply rooted in Finney.

2. Fackler, "Maker of Modern Revivalism," 2.

3. Not long after the Rochester ministry was over, Finney accepted the call to pastor Chatham Street Chapel in New York City. During this time Finney gave lectures to his congregation about revival, and those lectures were published as *Lectures on Revival*. See Johnson, "Charles G. Finney," 8.

4. Finney, *Lectures on Revival*, 15.

revival as "a supernatural visitation from God which awakens hearts and produces joyful[5] obedience."[6]

Revival, as Finney understood it, includes supernatural visitation from God, the renewal of the church, and the awakening of lost people. What is distinctive about Finney's understanding of revival is his notion that such divine visitations may be promoted through the church's repentance, prayer, innovative evangelistic strategy, and faithful and wise preaching, etc.[7]

Finney championed innovative approaches to promoting revival because he believed that the church was free to be effective. He notes, "In preaching the gospel, there must be measures or methods used. The gospel must be put in front of people's minds, and strategies must enable them to hear it and induce them to pay attention—by building churches, holding meetings, and so on. Without some plan of operation, preaching can never be effective."[8]

Some of Finney's contemporaries blistered him with words because of his new methods. Three of those methods involved special objects of attack: anxious meetings, extended meetings, and the anxious seat. Anxious meetings were special meetings held for the sole purpose of talking with troubled, lost people seeking Christ and then helping them come to faith in Christ. Many people rejected this strategy simply because it was new.

Extended meetings were meetings held outside of the regularly scheduled church meetings. Today we call these extended services evangelistic meetings. Some considered such meetings to be irregular.

Finney describes the anxious seat in these words: "The anxious seat is a seat set aside at a meeting where the spiritually anxious can come and be addressed specifically and be prayed for and talked with individually. Lately this practice has met with more opposition than any other."[9] The anxious seat was public. In Finney's mind, the public nature of the seat allows people to humble themselves and express publicly that they want to commit themselves to Jesus. The principle of the public nature of the

---

5. Echoes of Finney's definition may be discerned in John Piper and his emphasis on glad submission of people to Christ. Piper's emphasis is clearly an intentional or maybe non-intentional echo of Finney.

6. Finney, *Finney's Systematic Theology*, 433.

7. Finney, *Lectures on Revival*, 29.

8. Finney, *Lectures on Revival*, 162.

9. Finney, *Lectures on Revival*, 170.

anxious seat would morph into Billy Graham's public invitation to come forward in his crusades during the twentieth century.

Finney's homiletical aim was revival—divine visitation evinced by the church's renewal and consequent awakening, conviction, and conversion of lost people. His itinerant revivalist efforts reached their pinnacle in Rochester, New York, in 1830 through 1831. During that year, his meetings resulted in thousands coming to Christ with observable dramatic life transformation. Some historians consider the Rochester revival to be the zenith of the Second Great Awakening and the year of the greatest divine visitation, renewal, and awakening in American history.[10]

Rochester's Spirit-empowered revival winds blew across the United States with awakening and saving force, impacting people from the least to the greatest. Crime rates went down dramatically and stayed down for years in spite of population growth. Establishments of ill repute even closed down for lack of patrons.[11]

In addition to aiming for revival, Finney employed some of the homiletical insights that mark much of effective biblical preaching today. Even though he was a fiery preacher, Finney was also conversational and often used stories to illustrate abstract ideas in his messages. He felt deeply about his subject while anticipating the unbeliever's objections and addressing them in his preaching.[12]

Soteriological and eschatological concerns also informed Finney's preaching and his Christian social reform efforts. He emphasized that the Lord's death on the cross—the infinite price paid to save people—along with the unfathomable suffering Jesus endured for lost people meant that the human soul had incredible worth before God. "All people matter to God!" was one of the overarching themes of his sermons.

Finney was a postmillennialist. In this eschatological scheme, Christ will return after the millennium of vibrant and Spirit-empowered Christian living, which will impact the whole of the human experience. He, along with others, maintained that America was on the verge of the millennium—the golden age of human history that would usher in the second coming of Christ. Due in part to his eschatology, Finney was a Christian social reformer.

10. Curtis, "Did You Know?," 4.
11. Cowles and Finney, *Sermons on Gospel Themes*, 4.
12. Finney, *Lectures on Revival*, 136–39.

Despite being on the verge of the millennium, according to Finney, the obstacle impeding progress was the institution of slavery. In early 1831 Finney told his own congregation that the sin of slavery was a hindrance to revival. Finney declared, "I believe revival in America will continue no further and faster than the church acts righteously regarding the slaves. Slavery is primarily the church's sin, because the very fact that pastors and professing Christians from different denominations hold slaves is what sanctifies the whole abomination in the eyes of the ungodly."[13] Finney took the matter so seriously that he did not allow slave owners in his church to participate in Communion. Before the American Civil War, during his Oberlin years, Finney denounced slavery in a sermon entitled "God's Love for A Sinning World":

> How much does it costs to rid society of certain forms of sin, as for example slavery. How much has been expended already, and how much more yet remains to be expended ere this sore evil and curse and sin shall be rooted from our land! This is part of God's great enterprise, and He will press it on to its completion. Yet at what an amazing cost! How many lives and how much agony to get rid of this one sin![14]

At the time most people had no idea about how much agony and blood would be spilled to uproot this sin. After 620,000 soldiers died in the Civil War, the 13th amendment was passed, ending slavery in the United States. The hope that revival would bring slavery to an end were not realized, however. The wrongs that revival would not solve in a fallen world, war and human legislation did.

In my judgment, the most significant factor in Finney's preaching was his break with Old School Calvinism and the consequent emphasis on human responsibility to believe the gospel. Finney was trained as a lawyer, so he thought like one. Finney's emphasis on human responsibility was the logical outcome of his theological conviction that Christ died on the cross for all: people could decide for or against Jesus. In communicating these ideas, Finney's language sometimes lacks nuance, but his emphasis on human responsibility to believe the gospel was a needed corrective at the time that has shaped the practice of evangelistic preaching to this day.

---

13. Finney, *Lectures on Revival*, 189.
14. Finney, *Sermons on Gospel Themes*, 15.

Finney faced his times, challenging the social status quo for biblical and theological reason as he understood them by moving beyond the confines of Old School Calvinism to extend the gospel invitation to all. From the vantage point of the twenty-first century, it is also obvious that Finney laid the foundation for the subsequent evangelistic ministries of D. L. Moody, Billy Sunday, and Billy Graham.

Dwight Lyman Moody

(1837–99)

D. L. Moody was converted to Christ through the evangelistic efforts of his Sunday school teacher. After he moved to Chicago to pursue his business dreams, Moody worked in the YMCA and developed a Sunday school designed to reach marginalized and at-risk children in one of Chicago's worst neighborhoods. Lyle Dorsett writes,

> Moody found himself increasingly attracted to children forced to live in the most degrading conditions imaginable. Most city missionaries avoided going to the neighborhoods and dwelling places of those on the lowest rung of society's ladder. Moody was one of the few who had the audacity and courage to go into the worst district of Chicago, "the Sands." Sometimes labeled "Little Hell," this is where Moody went to rescue souls. The Sands, located just north of the Chicago River on Lake Michigan's shore, was a place where children usually had only one parent—and that one was typically an alcoholic or drug addict. Children in Little Hell were usually illiterate. . . . These children were emotionally and physically wounded. Often beaten, sexually abused, malnourished, and exposed to drinking, gambling, fighting, and prostitution, these youngsters were discarded and treated like rats and other vermin that roamed their wooden shanties and tenement hovels.[15]

Like his Savior, Moody launched his Sunday school in one of the darkest places in Chicago. "The people who were sitting in darkness saw a great light, and those who were sitting in the land and shadow of death, upon them a light dawned" (Matt 4:16).

Like Finney, Moody emphasized the necessity of offering the gospel invitation to all people. Since Christ died for all people, then the logic of

---

15. Dorsett, *Life of D. L. Moody*, 64–65.

the scope of Christ's death demands that the invitation be offered to all people—to every tribe, tongue, and nation. Moody also underscored human responsibility to believe the gospel. Wherever Mr. Moody preached, he proclaimed, "Whosoever will, let him come."

As Moody grew in his experiential understanding of God, he sought to woo people to Christ by highlighting God's love for them. Moody believed that since humanity's fall in the garden, the Lord was on a mission to woo people to Himself by His love. In one of his sermons entitled "The Love of God," Moody says,

> I have often thought I would need only one text. If I thought I could make the world believe that God is love, I would take that text alone and go up and down the earth trying to counteract what satan has been telling people—that God is not love. He has made the world believe that lie. . . . It would take 24 hours to make the world come to God if you could just make people believe that God is love. . . . If I could only make people really believe that God loves them, what a rush we would see for the kingdom of God! Oh, how they would rush in! But man has a false idea about God, and he will not believe that He is a God of love. It is because he doesn't know Him.[16]

For Moody, stressing God's love in his messages served as an evangelistic apologetic to win people to Christ. While Moody was not the theological and philosophical revivalist Finney was, he believed that revivals could occur in answer to prayer.

Not long after he experienced personal revival and a fresh encounter with God in 1872, Moody was prompted to return to England, mainly for the purpose of studying under some British Bible teachers. In London, Rev. John Lessey saw Moody in a prayer meeting and invited him to preach at the New Court Congregational Church. The reluctant Moody preached the following Sunday morning to an apathetic congregation. He also preached that night, and when he extended the invitation to receive Christ, people all over the church stood up, expressing their desire to trust Jesus as their Lord and Savior. The next day, Moody left for Ireland but had to rush back to England after learning that more inquirers came out on the following Monday than were present at the Sunday evening service. D. L. Moody then preached at the church for ten days, leading four hundred people to Christ, increasing Lessey's congregation through

---

16. Moody, "Love of God," 11.

conversion growth.[17] This movement from God was unexpected. Moody himself was surprised, but this ten day experience led Moody to continue to preach in the United Kingdom with powerful effects.

Moody knew that God was at work, but he also sensed that someone must be in prayer. I suspect this notion that prayer and revival are linked is associated with Finney's idea that revival may be promoted. After careful inquiry, Moody believed that the revival was due to the prayer of a bedridden young girl named Marianne Adlard.[18]

Marianne had prayed for years that God would send revival to her church. After reading about D. L. Moody and his work among poor children, she asked the Lord to send him to New Court Congregational Church. And indeed, God answered her prayer. Upon learning about her, Moody visited her, and she asked him to write his name in her birthday book. Moody did so and Marianne prayed and interceded for the evangelist until the day he went home to be with the Lord.[19] The revival, this divine visitation from God, was granted in response to prayer.

Space will not allow a discussion about Billy Sunday, but it must be noted that the revivalist tendency as Finney understood it was a part of Sunday's thinking and shaped the way that he approached ministry. Sunday wanted his evangelistic work to be done in conjunction with local churches. The principal way to involve local churches was by obtaining pastoral support from these congregations. Sunday learned that if the pastors experienced personal revival, they, in turn, could encourage the renewal of their own churches, and "from there they could reach out and confront nonchurched people with Christ's claims and promises and then follow that up with prayer for growing churches, more dedicated members, and a morally transformed community."[20]

William Franklin "Billy" Graham

(1918–2018)

Much more could be said, but as we move on to Billy Graham, it is interesting to note how prayer was such a central element in his ministry.

---

17. Moody, "Love of God," 160–66.
18. Moody, "Love of God," 161.
19. Moody, "Love of God," 161–62.
20. Dorsett, *Billy Sunday*, 53.

In a 1934 prayer meeting held on the pasture of Billy Graham's father, Vernon Patterson prayed that out of Charlotte, North Carolina the Lord would raise up someone to preach the gospel to the ends of the earth.[21] The evangelistic ministry of Billy Graham was the answer to that prayer.

Billy Graham entitled his autobiography *Just As I Am*. The title itself is drawn from the invitation hymn sung on the night the Billy Graham trusted Christ and subsequently sung as people were coming forward to trust Christ in Graham's own evangelistic crusades.

> Just as I am
> Without one plea,
> But that Thy blood was shed for me
> And that Thou biddest me come to Thee
> O Lamb of God, I come.

The choice of this title for Graham's autobiography also provides us some insight into Graham himself. He is also one who has responded to the Master's bidding—just as he was, without one plea. Graham has devoted most of his life to bidding the fallen world to come to Jesus. The hymn captures much of the theological essence of Graham's understanding of the evangelistic invitation. We come to Jesus in faith just as we are, without any plea or claim to merit. The only plea involves the shed blood of Jesus as the redemptive basis for our coming.

Graham has preached to gospel across the United States, the United Kingdom, Africa, Australia, the Middle East, Moscow, Poland, Yugoslavia, and Asia. Over a million people showed up to hear Billy Graham preach in Yeouido Park (South Korea) in 1973.[22] Billy Graham has traversed the planet, extending the invitation to salvation in Christ and challenging men and women to respond to the gospel in faith.

The echo of Finney is heard in the invitations of Billy Graham. Graham preached with power and persuasion, "You have a decision to make. God himself cannot make that decision for you. So I am going to ask you to get up out of your seats!" This is vintage Finney dressed in twentieth-century evangelistic clothes. Indeed, every one of Billy Graham's evangelistic messages "ends with a specific invitation to receive the gospel. This invitation is presented in the tradition of American revivalism."[23]

---

21. Graham, *Just As I Am*, 24.
22. Graham, *Just As I Am*, xviii.
23. Old, *Reading and Preaching of Scriptures*, 64.

Like Finney, Graham also has a revivalist strain in his preaching. As a result of his preaching, many believers have rededicated their lives to Jesus. This rededication is a form of revival.

Finney, Moody, and Graham all had life-transforming encounters with God Himself. This seems to be the supreme factor in the preaching of these evangelists. At the crossroads of his own life, hurricanes of doubt were unleashed in Graham's soul, and he had no answers. He wrote,

> I had to have an answer. If I could not trust the Bible, I could not go on. I would have to quit the school presidency. I would have to leave pulpit evangelism.... [Dropping to my knees in the woods] I prayed, "O God! There are many things in the book I do not understand. There are many problems with it for which I have no solution. There are many seeming contradictions. There are some areas in it that do not seem to correlate with modern science. I can't answer some of the philosophical and psychological questions ... others are raising."[24]

Graham continues to write,

> I was trying to be on the level with God, but something remained unspoken. At last the Holy Spirit freed me to say it, "Father, I am going to accept this as your word—by faith. I'm going to allow faith to go beyond my intellectual questions and doubts, and I will believe this to be your inspired word." When I got up from my knees at Forest Home that August night, my eyes stung with tears. I sensed the presence and power of God as I had not sensed it in months. Not all my questions were answered, but a major bridge has been crossed.[25]

After this encounter with God in the woods, Graham preached with new power. In the Los Angeles campaign of 1948, the Lord used Graham in such a way that hundreds of thousands heard the gospel and thousands responded in faith. Thousands of Christians came forward to rededicate their lives to Christ. This combination of rededication and conversion was reminiscent of Finney's understanding of revival. After that campaign, some considered Billy Graham and his small evangelistic team to be the hope for national and international revival.[26] Of course, Graham knew that they were not the hope, but Jesus was and still is. Interestingly

---

24. Graham, *Just As I Am*, 139.
25. Graham, *Just As I Am* 139.
26. Graham, *Just As I Am*, 158.

enough, Graham traced the wonderful work of God in the Los Angeles to prayer. He traces the stream of prayer back to some little girls.[27]

In short, while our evangelistic efforts in many respects today may be a footnote to Finney, the bigger and more significant element in the lives of these evangelists is the work of the Lord Himself in these men. The Lord met each one in significant, life-transforming ways. The big picture for them all involved their encounter with the risen Lord through the ministry and power of the Spirit, based on God's Word, the basis of impactful preaching in any age of human history. In this regard, Finney, Moody, and Graham stand in the stream of the hosts of men and women who encountered God Himself, and out of fresh God-encounters had the principal and abiding requisite for effectiveness and power in preaching.

Bibliography

Cowles, Henry, and Charles Finney. *Sermons on Gospel Themes: The Preface.* Classic Domain, 2014.
Curtis, A. K. "Did You Know?" *Christian History* 20 (1988) 4.
Dorsett, Lyle W. *Billy Sunday and the Redemption of Urban America.* Grand Rapids, MI: Eerdmans, 1991.
———. *The Life of D. L. Moody.* Chicago: Moody, 1997.
Fackler, Mark. "Maker of Modern Revivalism." *Christian History* 20 (1988) 2.
Finney, Charles G. *Finney's Systematic Theology.* Minneapolis: Bethany, 1976.
———. *Lectures on Revival.* Minneapolis: Bethany, 1988.
———. *Sermons on Gospel Themes.* Classic Domain, 2014.
Graham, Billy. *Just As I Am: The Autobiography of Billy Graham.* San Francisco: HarperCollins Worldwide, 1997.
Johnson, James E. "Charles G. Finney: Father of American Revivalism." *Christian History* 20 (1988) 8.
Moody, D. L. "The Love of God." In *Classic Sermons on the Attributes of God,* compiled by Warren B. Wiersbe, 11–22. Grand Rapids, MI: Kregel, 1989.
Old, Hughes Oliphant. *The Reading and Preaching of Scriptures in the Worship of the Christian Church.* Vol. 7, *Our Own Time.* Grand Rapids, MI: Eerdmans, 2010.

---

27. Graham, *Just As I Am*, 158.

Chapter Eleven

Preaching in Mainline Protestantism

ELESHA J. COFFMAN

MY DISCUSSION OF PREACHING in the mainline tradition starts in Red Oak, Iowa, in 1891. There, Charles Clayton Morrison, son of a Disciples of Christ preacher, became a preacher himself at age sixteen, when his father's illness necessitated an emergency backup speaker. Soon, Morrison became a celebrated "boy preacher," speaking throughout western Iowa and eastern Nebraska. Two years later, the summer before he enrolled at Drake University, he was already serving as summer pulpit supply at a Disciples church a hundred miles from his family's home.

The lack of religious training prior to this temporary pastorate did not bother young Morrison, for, as he recalled years later in his unfinished autobiography, "I knew my Bible, many of its great paragraphs I knew by heart. And my mind was well furnished with Father's interpretations." Only much later did this homiletical preparation strike him as woefully inadequate. To the mature Morrison, his long-ago sermons seemed *biblical* in a negative sense, "enclosed" in the text, using the Bible to interpret itself rather than applying insights from biblical studies, theology, and other disciplines. In short, he confessed, "I had not yet learned to read books."[1]

---

1. Charles Clayton Morrison, *Autobiography*, b2-4. The autobiography was never finished or published. The manuscript resides in the Christian Century Foundation Archives, Special Collections Research Center, Morris Library, Southern Illinois University, Carbondale, Illinois. This anecdote is recounted in Coffman, *Christian*

Preaching in the mainline tradition does have much to do with reading books. In this article, I will describe four ways in which books and reading are relevant to my topic. First, though, I want to back up a bit and clarify how I define mainline Protestantism.

One method of delineating this tradition centers on the "Seven Sisters of American Protestantism": the Episcopal Church, the Evangelical Lutheran Church in America (ELCA), the Presbyterian Church (PCUSA), the United Methodist Church, the American Baptist Church, the United Church of Christ, and the Disciples of Christ. Other denominations might be included, depending on who's making the list and what characteristics they're interested in. You might see Quakers, or the Reformed Church in America, or any group affiliated with the National Council of Churches. You might see African-American churches, such as the African Methodist Episcopal Church.

As with the study of American evangelicals, Pentecostals, or Roman Catholics, it can be difficult for scholars to decide what to do with racial differences—you don't want to focus only on white people, as if only white people were important, but you also don't want to write as if these traditions were racially diverse but otherwise unified because sadly, they're not. White, black, Asian, and Hispanic believers with similar theological convictions seldom worship together during what remains, as Dr. Martin Luther King Jr. called it, "the most segregated hour in this nation." I want to be clear that I am going to focus on the white mainline tradition here because Dr. Claybon Lea Jr. has written about the African-American preaching tradition, and unfortunately, my historical sources feature little racial diversity.

So I am going to describe the white mainline tradition, and include a discussion about preachers in those "Seven Sisters" denominations—but not all of them, because the mainline tradition is more sharply defined than that. Jonathan Edwards was a Congregationalist, and the Congregational Church is now part of the UCC, but that doesn't make him a mainline figure. Charles Finney was a Presbyterian, but no one thinks of him as a mainline figure either. If the mainline tradition is to be defined sharply enough to be of analytical use, it needs to start more recently in history and include some, but not all, of the preachers in the supposedly "mainline" denominations. This is not a value judgment but merely an analytical choice. I think it's great that some people in these churches

---

Century, 15–16.

would identify themselves as evangelical, charismatic, or something other than "mainline"—although it does make for some uncomfortable denominational meetings!

The mainline tradition emerged in the late nineteenth century and was associated with what we typically think of as "modernism." (Incidentally, a friend of mine argued in the book *Dispensational Modernism* that fundamentalists were every bit as modern as their modernist foes if you look at their epistemology rather than their theology, but that's a conversation for another day.)[2] In this late nineteenth-century period, Christians were reacting to a spate of academic developments, prominent among them evolutionary science, including the geological evidence for a very old earth; the emerging fields of psychology and sociology; biblical higher criticism; and the development of historical consciousness. Let me say a bit more about those last two.

Higher criticism, or the historical-critical method, applied the same tools that scholars used to study *other* ancient texts to the texts of the Bible. Scholars working in this vein have asked many questions: Were there sources behind the texts we have in front of us, lost documents we might label J, E, D, P, and Q? How do literary genres and oral traditions affect our reading of the texts? What was the historical context of the original writing, and how might the documents have been edited over the years?

Overall, the proponents of this approach did not view the biblical texts as having been dictated, timelessly and perfectly, by God, but considered the texts as human products—in some sense inspired and definitely "true" at a deep level, but not word-for-word infallible, and certainly not transparently self-disclosing to all readers. The Bible, for modernists, was a set of documents best handled by trained experts—those who had "learned to read books."

Related to this, modernism embraced historical consciousness. Not only was the *Bible* the product of human forces in human time, modernists asserted, but so was *every* facet of culture. Nothing falls like a sacred meteor from the sky, as my graduate adviser, Grant Wacker, often said. The way you structure your church, with bishops or presbyters or congregational polity, or the way you understand race or gender or government—none of this, modernists insisted, was dictated, timelessly and

2. Pietsch, *Dispensational Modernism*.

perfectly, by God. It was all in flux, all bound to historical context, and guaranteed to vary across time and space.[3]

Once again, to get a handle on all of this, you must learn to read books: History books. Philosophy books. Anthropology. Comparative religions. Theology. These books won't all be on the shelves of the average church attender, but preachers had better have them in their study. And they had better keep up with the latest scholarly developments, because knowledge is forever growing and changing. Human history, modernists believed, was a fairly steady march of progress. Answers from the past could not necessarily be trusted. It was important, therefore, to keep asking questions and seeking out new answers.

This is the first sense in which you might call the mainline preaching tradition "bookish": it values erudition and academic credentials. It's no coincidence that mainline clerical vestments resemble academic regalia. Although this varies somewhat by denomination, and lay preachers are becoming more common amid shrinking church budgets, mainline clergy will generally have at least an MDiv, maybe a Doctor of Divinity or even a PhD. Often they have to pass ordination exams. (This reminds me of the one Presbyterian joke that David Steinmetz, the late Reformation historian at Duke, used to tell: At the end of a grueling oral examination, a candidate for Presbyterian ministry was asked by his committee, a stern bunch of Calvinists, if he was willing to be damned for the glory of God. The candidate stared back and said, "I'm willing that everyone in this room be damned for the glory of God!") The point here involves credentials. You have to read a lot of books to be a mainline pastor.

Sometimes this erudition has manifested itself in sermons full of literary allusions, dense with names of theologians and scholars, or loaded with technical terms like "koine Greek" and "pericope." Here's an example from *The American Pulpit: A Volume of Sermons by 25 of the Foremost Living Preachers, Chosen by a Poll of All the Protestant Ministers in the United States, Nearly 25,000 of Whom Cast Their Votes*. The book came out in 1925, a seminal decade for modernism and the mainline tradition. The clergy survey was conducted by the magazine *The Christian Century*, the mainline journal of record, and the book was edited by the gentleman referred to in the opening anecdote, Charles Clayton Morrison, who also edited *The Christian Century* from 1908 to 1947.

---

3. On this topic, see Wacker, *Augustus Strong*.

This particular Easter sermon was preached by Dr. Charles Gilkey, who had studied at Harvard, Union Seminary, Berlin, Marburg, Scottish universities, and Oxford before becoming the minister at Hyde Park Baptist Church, adjacent to the University of Chicago. In the course of his sermon, Dr. Gilkey managed to name-check Ralph Waldo Emerson; Rudyard Kipling; poet Josephine Preston Peabody; Kenneth Grahame, author of *The Wind in the Willows*; Alfred, Lord Tennyson; and a book about Alice Freeman Palmer, the former president of Wellesley. He didn't do this just to dazzle his audience or pad the sermon. His point was that the loftiest of human words and sentiments were compatible with the Christian message, so his audience didn't have to choose between being learned and being faithful. Here, he reads his text from Ps 139 (in the poetic King James, not the Revised Version generally embraced by modernists) and gives his interpretation:

> Whither shall I go from thy Spirit?
> Or whither shall I flee from thy presence?
> If I ascend up into heaven, thou art there:
> If I make my bed in Sheol, behold, thou art there.
> If I take the wings of the morning,
> And dwell in the uttermost parts of the sea;
> Even there shall thy hand lead me,
> And thy right hand shall hold me.

> Surely this must mean that the living God stands ready to be our guide on all high intellectual adventure, when our exploring minds, urged by our deep instincts and our pressing needs, go forth to new discoveries of the world about us, better understanding of the life that is given us, broader conceptions of the God we "ignorantly worship," worthier hopes of the immortality our hearts desire. Some of us have faith to believe that when our theology is considerably less provincial than much of it is now, and our science perhaps just a little less provincial than some of it is now; when our thinking minds and our aspiring souls understand each other better and help each other more; we shall then at least recover the fullness of what is after all an ancient Christian faith, that God is the God of all truth. His guiding presence within the mind man lights us along the narrow and difficult way that leads into larger truth. If some of us have been busy throwing overboard our childish conceptions of religion because they have seemed too small for so great a voyage as we

are now finding human life to be, we shall do well not to miss the point of Emerson's assurance:

When the half-gods go,
The gods arrive.[4]

The same theme animated probably the most famous sermon in the mainline tradition, Harry Emerson Fosdick's "Shall the Fundamentalists Win?" which he preached at the First Presbyterian Church, New York City, in May of 1922. Note a few of the oft-quoted paragraphs:

> As I plead thus for an intellectually hospitable, tolerant, liberty-loving church, I am, of course, thinking primarily about this new generation. We have boys and girls growing up in our homes and schools, and because we love them we may well wonder about the church which will be waiting to receive them. Now, the worst kind of church that can possibly be offered to the allegiance of the new generation is an intolerant church. Ministers often bewail the fact that young people turn from religion to science for the regulative ideas of their lives. But this is easily explicable.
>
> Science treats a young man's mind as though it were really important. A scientist says to a young man, "Here is the universe challenging our investigation. Here are the truths which we have seen, so far. Come, study with us! See what we already have seen and then look further to see more, for science is an intellectual adventure for the truth." Can you imagine any man who is worthwhile turning from that call to the church if the church seems to him to say, "Come, and we will feed you opinions from a spoon. No thinking is allowed here except such as brings you to certain specified, predetermined conclusions. These prescribed opinions we will give you in advance of your thinking; now think, but only so as to reach these results."
>
> My friends, nothing in all the world is so much worth thinking of as God, Christ, the Bible, sin and salvation, the divine purposes for humankind, life everlasting. But you cannot challenge the dedicated thinking of this generation to these sublime themes upon any such terms as are laid down by an intolerant church.[5]

---

4. Gilkey, "Journeys Out and Home," 96–97.

5. This sermon is widely anthologized and available online. One print source is Warner, *American Sermons*, 775–86.

I found an alliance between mainline Christianity and advanced learning all over my research for this article. Our guest William Willimon edited a volume of sermons from Duke Chapel, and in his own sermon for the collection, he admonished the assembled students:

> You know what really gets me about some of you? It's not your behavior at parties on Saturday night, it's that some of you are making judgments about Jesus on Sunday morning on the basis of a puerile, nay, infantile, understanding of Jesus that you had when you were eight. I can't stand for an adult, with an arrested religious development, to dismiss Jesus on the basis of what that adult thought he knew about Jesus at age six.
>
> Taking physics this semester? "No, I took physics at my exclusive, expensive elementary school where I learned that whatever goes up comes down, and it all seemed so obvious and trite to me, so, no, I've had it with physics." That attitude, applied to Jesus, gets me.[6]

There are many reasons for this alliance between the mainline tradition and higher education. As mentioned previously, ministers in these churches generally must complete extensive training and credentialing. Pulpits at or near universities—such as Hyde Park Baptist Church and Duke Chapel—exert an outsize influence on the tradition, because people who preach in these places get their sermons published, write for periodicals such as *The Christian Century*, teach homiletics and publish books about homiletics, and are generally mainline rock stars. We could call those all supply-side factors.

There's also the demand side. Mainline preachers are routinely facing congregations full of doctors, lawyers, MBAs, professors, teachers, and even biblical scholars. (My own pastors, Rev. Dr. Leslie King and Rev. Dee Dee Carson, admit that it makes them a bit nervous to preach on the New Testament with Baylor's own Dr. Beverly Gaventa in the audience.) Speaking more broadly, according to a 2016 Pew Research survey, the American Christian denominations with the highest percentage of members holding at least a college degree were Anglican, Episcopal, Presbyterian USA, and United Church of Christ, followed by Orthodox, then United Methodist and ELCA.[7] A bookish sort, all around.

It's worth noting that the alliance with higher education and, along with it, modernism hasn't entirely been a winning strategy for the

---

6. Willimon, "Confused, Yet Curious About Jesus," 364.
7. Murphy, "Most and Least Educated."

mainline. I documented in my book, *The Christian Century and the Rise of the Protestant Mainline*, how pastors who got their fancy seminary training and then took a parish in Dazey, North Dakota, or Dayton, Tennessee, felt estranged from their congregations, as if no one in the pews spoke their language. As the percentage of Americans attending college rose in the second half of the twentieth century, the percentage of Americans attending mainline churches fell. The problem identified by Gilkey, Fosdick, and Willimon remains, however. A 2011 Barna study asked why young people leave church, and among the top responses were the following:

- Christians are too confident; they know all the answers.
- Churches are out of step with the scientific world we live in.
- Christianity is anti-science.
- I'm unable to ask my most pressing life questions in church.[8]

Mainline preaching cannot catch all of these folks before they leave the church, but it is conscious of the need to try.

A second way in which books and reading have been significant for mainline preaching pertains to psychology and self-help books. Historian Matthew Hedstrom, in his book *The Rise of Liberal Religion*, documented countless connections between mainline preachers, mainline institutions, and publishing houses in the middle of the twentieth century, all working together to promote liberal ideas including ecumenical and interfaith cooperation, positive psychology, and social progress.[9]

Here again, Harry Emerson Fosdick was a central figure. From 1930 to 1946, Fosdick led Riverside Church in New York City, a stronghold of the social gospel built by John D. Rockefeller Jr. For nineteen years, Fosdick's sermons were broadcast on the radio, on the *NBC National Vespers Hour*. At its height, the program reached between two-and-a-half to three million listeners weekly, and between 1936 and 1946, more than a million copies of his sermons were mailed to listeners on request.[10] Fosdick also served as an adviser to the Religious Book Club, a marketing program that aimed to spread liberal religious ideas to the middlebrow public through affordable bestsellers. Selected titles of Fosdick's books

---

8. Barna Group, "Six Reasons Young Christians Leave Church."
9. Hedstrom, *Rise of Liberal Religion*.
10. Godfrey and Leigh, *Historical Dictionary of American Radio*, 169.

(he wrote dozens) show his early contributions to the promotion of modernist theology, followed by a therapeutic turn. Many of his books were collected sermons:

- *Christianity and Progress* (1922)
- *Science and Religion: Evolution and the Bible* (1924)
- *The Modern Use of the Bible* (1924)
- *The Secret of Victorious Living* (1934)
- *Successful Christian Living* (1937)
- *On Being a Real Person* (1943)
- *On Being Fit to Live With: Sermons on Postwar Christianity* (1946)
- *A Faith for Tough Times* (1952)
- *What Is Vital in Religion: Sermons on Contemporary Christian Problems* (1955)
- *Dear Mr. Brown: Letters to a Person Perplexed about Religion* (1961)

To be clear, mainline Protestantism was not alone in taking a self-help turn in the twentieth century. In a 2005 study, sociologists Chris Smith and Melinda Lundquist Denton found "moral therapeutic deism" to be the default spirituality of American teenagers.[11] A sort of anodyne pleasantness has, however, been persistently and negatively attributed to mainline preaching specifically.

When historian Randall Balmer visited twelve churches in the 1990s for his book *Grant Us Courage: Travels Along the Mainline of American Protestantism*, he didn't say much about the preaching he heard, but his comments sketched a pattern as he used terms such as: "aphorisms," "very little of theological substance," and "tame and uplifting homilies"; and genial, undogmatic, and optimistic. He wryly comments, "If any boundary remains between theology and pop psychology, the preacher clearly trespassed into the territory of the latter."[12] These observations comport with much of what I heard when I asked friends, many of them mainline preacher themselves, what I should say in this article. The first comment about mainline preaching was usually along the lines of, "Well, most of it is really bad." (This refrain raises the question of whether mainline preaching is reputed to be unusually bad, or whether American

---

11. Smith with Denton, *Soul Searching*.
12. Balmer, *Grant Us Courage*.

Christians lament the quality of preaching across the denominational spectrum.)

Alongside the "tame and uplifting homilies," there has been a contrasting current within mainline preaching, summed up in the quote commonly attributed to Karl Barth, that one should preach with the Bible in one hand and the newspaper in the other. Especially in times of national crisis (i.e., World War I and II, civil rights, and Vietnam) but in other periods as well, mainline preachers have delivered messages that supporters described as "relevant" and "prophetic" while critics derided them as "too political."

One of the leading theories of mainline decline in the latter part of the twentieth century suggests that progressive, "political" preaching, echoed and amplified in statements from denominational leaders and the National Council of Churches, drove people away. In fact, the first use of the term "mainline" I could find in national journalism came from a 1960 *New York Times* article that began, "Protestant leaders in the Midwest and in Texas believe a concerted effort is being made by extreme economic and religious conservatives to keep ministers and church councils from speaking out on social issues and force them to 'stick to the Gospel.'"[13] I imagine that most mainline preachers have at least one story of a parishioner storming out of a "political" sermon, never to return. If they didn't have such a story before this year, they probably do now.

As part of my research for this talk, I checked in (online) with those same twelve churches Randall Balmer visited in the 1990s, which had originally been featured in a 1950 *Christian Century* series entitled "Twelve Great Churches." The twelve churches, like the twenty-five sermons in the *American Pulpit* book, were selected by a survey of *Century* readers. (Remember when I mentioned a dearth of racial diversity in my sources? When that article series ran in 1950, Gardner Taylor, then the thirty-two-year-old pastor of Concord Baptist Church in Brooklyn, wrote a scathing letter to the editor, pointing out that there were no black churches on the list, nor any that had taken a public stand against racism. "You have not named a single great Christian church in the series," he wrote, "for you have not named a single Christian one."[14] Kudos to the *Century* for printing the letter, but they were pretty sluggish to respond to Taylor's critique in the body of the magazine. They were doing better

---

13. Coffman, *Christian Century*, 213.
14. Coffman, *Christian Century*, 175.

by 1963, when the *Century* became one of the first places of publication for Martin Luther King's "Letter from a Birmingham Jail."

When I digitally visited these churches in August of 2017, I was trying to get a sense of their most recent sermons, based on texts or audio posted on the church website. I happened to be doing this research the week after the white supremacist rally in Charlottesville, Virginia, that left one anti-racism activist dead. Not all of the churches addressed the topic, and, it should be noted, not all of them still fit my definition of mainline. (One of the original twelve, Bellevue Baptist Church in Cordova, Tennessee, was always fundamentalist; another, First Presbyterian Church of Hollywood, California, has always been on the evangelical edge of the PCUSA; and a third, tiny Olive Chapel Baptist Church in Apex, North Carolina, was progressive enough to have called its first female pastor around the time of Balmer's visit but appears to have swung to the right since then.)

In the remaining group, about half featured August 13th sermons on what might be termed a psychological, therapeutic topic: "The Problem of Pain," "Limping Towards Heaven," "God Is With Us," and "In God We Nearly Trust." The other half hit white supremacy head on, an especially impressive feat considering that the relevant events had happened less than twenty-four hours before Sunday morning. At First United Methodist Church in Orlando, Rev. Tom McCloskey turned the Gen 19 story of Joseph being sold into slavery by his brothers into a forceful sermon on the risks faced by dreamers. "Our challenge as individuals and the church is not to see the world as we see it, but as God sees it," he said, noting that the attempt could get you killed.

I couldn't access that Sunday's sermon at Collegiate United Methodist in Ames, Iowa, but Reverend Jill Sanders preached the previous week about showing hospitality to all, including immigrants and participants in an upcoming LGBT pride event. Her sermon the following week was titled "Nevertheless . . . She Persisted," so I'm reasonably sure that the August 13th sermon was "political" as well.

Meanwhile, Rev. Elliott Munn told First Church of Christ Congregational in West Hartford, Connecticut:

> Those of you appalled by what you saw and nervous that there is no one else willing to speak out against the idol of White Supremacy, you have found the right place. You have allies here at First Church. I confess that we as a church have at times perpetuated its ill effects. That does not mean that this congregation

lacks desire to change. In this 500th anniversary of the Reformation year, the First Church staff is striving to reform the way we relate to White Supremacy as a church. We will host lectures on the prison industrial complex and hold antiracism trainings. We will read together Debby Irving's *Waking Up White*, and invite her to lead us in a workshop. Through these efforts and many more, we hope to move beyond simply condemning White Supremacy's most egregious manifestations to also confronting its more subtle and insidious forms.[15]

So, is mainline worship basically like a meeting of the College Democrats with two hymns and an offertory? I'm going to say no, in part because of my fourth and final point about learning to read books: the lectionary. Following the liturgical reform program of the Second Vatican Council, in the 1960s Roman Catholics developed a three-year lectionary (a planned cycle of biblical texts) for use in Mass. Mainline Protestants thought this was a great idea to build ecumenical consciousness and encourage people to engage the Old Testament, the New Testament, and the Psalms regularly. The lectionary isn't binding, but every week it gives preachers a selection of texts from which they might preach—the same selections being considered by preachers from multiple denominations around the world. The variety of August 13th sermons I've described, varied as they were, mostly sprang from the lectionary texts. The more "political" of the preachers used the scheduled Genesis or 1 Kings selections, while the more "therapeutic" preachers used the Matt 14 story of Jesus calming the sea.

I will confess to being a big fan of the lectionary. With my previous job at a seminary in Dubuque, Iowa, I had to preach in chapel once a semester—even though I don't have an MDiv, even though I'm not ordained, even though I was just there to teach church history. It was terrifying. I hadn't read the books! I don't know any of the languages! Instead of a blank canvas, I needed a coloring book with some lines to color inside, and the lectionary provided me that structure. I pulled up the lectionary website at Vanderbilt and looked at the texts for my assigned week. When one of them sparked something in my mind, I went to commentaries, looked up other sermons on the same texts, and sought help from my colleagues in biblical studies and homiletics. I checked out liturgical resources written to accompany the lectionary. I'm not going to claim that these shortcuts were equivalent to a theological education,

---

15. Munn, "Sound of Sheer Silence."

but they made the daunting task possible. At a Presbyterian seminary, surrounded by books and the authors of books, even I could join in on the adventure of preaching in the mainline tradition.

Bibliography

Balmer, Randall. *Grant Us Courage: Travels Along the Mainline of American Protestantism*. New York: Oxford University Press, 1996.

Barna Group. "Six Reasons Young Christians Leave Church." Barna Research Releases, September 27, 2011. https://www.barna.com/research/six-reasons-young-christians-leave-church/.

Coffman, Elesha J. *The Christian Century and the Rise of the Protestant Mainline*. New York: Oxford University Press, 2013.

Gilkey, Charles W. "Journeys Out and Home: An Easter Sermon." In *The American Pulpit*, edited by Charles Clayton Morrison, 96–97. New York: Macmillan, 1925.

Godfrey, Donald G., and Frederic A. Leigh, eds. *Historical Dictionary of American Radio*. Westport, CT: Greenwood, 1998.

Hedstrom, Matthew S. *The Rise of Liberal Religion: Book Culture and American Spirituality in the Twentieth Century*. New York: Oxford University Press, 2013.

Munn, Elliott. "The Sound of Sheer Silence: Hearing Aids." First Church West Hartford, August 13, 2017. http://www.whfirstchurch.org/wp-content/uploads/2017/08/SER-2017-08-13-The-Sound-of-Sheer-Silence.pdf.

Murphy, Caryle. "The Most and Least Educated U.S. Religious Groups." Pew Research Center, November 4, 2016. http://www.pewresearch.org/fact-tank/2016/11/04/the-most-and-least-educated-u-s-religious-groups/.

Pietsch, B. M. *Dispensational Modernism*. New York: Oxford University Press, 2015.

Smith, Christian, with Melinda Lundquist Denton. *Soul Searching: The Religious and Spiritual Lives of American Teenagers*. New York: Oxford University Press, 2009.

Wacker, Grant. *Augustus Strong and the Dilemma of Historical Consciousness*. Macon, GA: Mercer University Press, 1985.

Warner, Michael, ed. *American Sermons: The Pilgrims to Martin Luther King Jr*. New York: Library of America, 1999.

Willimon, William H., ed. "Confused, Yet Curious About Jesus." In *Sermons from Duke Chapel: Voices from "A Great Towering Church,"* edited by William H. Willimon, 362–68. Durham, NC: Duke University Press, 2005.

Chapter Twelve

Preaching in American Evangelicalism
Scott M. Gibson

> *"Whatever evangelical meant, in other words,*
> *it did not mean closed minded."*
> —FREDERICK BUECHNER

Introduction

EVANGELICALISM IS PREACHING. IN fact, preachers and their preaching have formed the backbone of the evangelical movement. In these days of politicism, defining the evangelical movement might be a little fuzzy. However, what distinguishes evangelicalism is its historic commitment to the pulpit. The preaching of the Word is a distinctive mark of evangelicalism.

Readers may not be clear about the term "evangelicalism." We begin with a definition. From there we will explore the place of preaching in evangelicalism, examine the contributions of evangelical preaching, and close with words of caution and conclusion.

What Is Evangelicalism?

Evangelicalism is not easy to define. Evangelicalism is a movement not associated with any single group. One cannot point to a specific person or group and say, "That's evangelicalism," at least not in its entirety. Douglas Sweeney notes,

> Not only do evangelicals come in different shapes and sizes, but they also participate in hundreds of different denominations—some of which were founded in opposition to some of the others! The vast majority are Protestant, but even among the Protestants there are Lutheran, Reformed, and Anabaptist evangelicals. There are Anglicans, Methodists, Holiness people, and Pentecostals. There are Calvinists and Arminians....[1] There has never been—and there never will be—an evangelical denomination, despite the references one hears to the evangelical church.[2]

The spectrum of evangelicals includes Peace-churches to Black Pentecostals, men, women, multi-ethnic, and Native American, an evangelical ecumenism.[3]

Evangelicalism's roots are found over two hundred and fifty years ago in Great Britain, Germany, and America where the Wesleys and Whitfield, Edwards and Franke believed that one's Christian life was founded on the Bible, with personal rebirth through faith in Jesus Christ, the gift of the Holy Spirit, and the commitment to evangelism—persuading others to be born again.[4]

To define evangelicalism according to beliefs only limits a fully contoured understanding of the movement. Social concern has been an important part of evangelical history. Timothy L. Smith notes, "The concern for social justice has been a major contribution of evangelical faith to modern culture."[5] Derek Tidball points out that evangelicals are realis-

---

1. Sweeney, *American Evangelical Story*, 19.

2. Sweeney, *American Evangelical Story*, 20.

3. Smith, "Shared Evangelical Heritage"; Frazer, *Evangelicalism*, 12. See also Dayton and Johnson, *Variety of American Evangelicalism*; Naselli and Hansen, *Four Views on Evangelicalism*; Haykin and Stewart, *Advent of Evangelicalism*; Gerstner, "Theological Boundaries," 31–37. For a perspective on blacks and evangelicalism, see Pannell, "Religious Heritage of Blacks," 96–107; Bentley, "Bible Believers," 108–21; Wilkens and Thorsen, *Everything You Know about Evangelicals*.

4. Smith, "Shared Evangelical Heritage,"12–13. Smith considers these elements to be consistent in evangelical traditions.

5. Smith, "Shared Evangelical Heritage, 16. See pp. 16–28 where Smith details evangelical engagement with social justice. See also in the same volume, Wolterstorff, "Why Care about Justice?," 156–67. Also see for example, Spain, *At Ease in Zion*; Smith, *Revivalism and Social Reform*; Magnuson, *Salvation in the Slums*; Sweet, *Evangelical Tradition in America*; Lindner, "Resurgence of Evangelical Social Concern," 189–210.

tic: "Recognizing that conversion does not always bring about long-term or wide-scale social transformation, and that sin is located in our fallen world not just in sinful individuals, they now generally believe there are two tasks to be accomplished, that is evangelism and social action."[6] The movement is global in its reach and influence.[7]

Evangelicals run the gamut on their position and practice of education. Yet, not all evangelicals shy away from education. Evangelicals were on the forefront of establishing schools, led in inaugurating public education, and founded distinguished institutions of higher learning. From Wesley to Carl F. H. Henry up to the present, evangelicals number among the graduates of some of the most elite universities in the world.[8] In the years following the Fundamentalist/Modernist Controversy in the United States, there arose a "renaissance of conservative biblical scholarship."[9] Since then, evangelicals have found themselves on the faculties of departments of theology or biblical studies in major research universities and seminaries on both sides of the Atlantic.[10]

In the 1980s, mainline Presbyterian preacher and author Frederick Buechner was invited to teach a semester at the evangelical Wheaton College in Wheaton, Illinois. In his memoir Buechner reflected, "I knew it was Billy Graham's alma mater. I knew it was evangelical though without any clear idea as to what that meant." He continued, "Whatever evangelical meant, in other words, it did not mean closed minded."[11] Buechner further pondered his brush with evangelicalism while at Wheaton. He wrote, "The result was that to find myself at Wheaton among people who, although they spoke about it in different words from mine and expressed it in their lives differently, not only believed in Christ and his Kingdom

---

6. Tidball, *Who Are the Evangelicals?*, 132.

7. See Hutchinson and Wolffe, *Short History of Global Evangelicalism*; Lewis and Pierard, *Global Evangelicalism*.

8. Sweeney, *American Evangelical Story*, 74.

9. Stanley, *Global Diffusion of Evangelicalism*, 112.

10. Stanley, *Global Diffusion of Evangelicalism*, 93–98. A casual internet search of universities and seminaries in North America and in Britain will demonstrate the place of evangelical scholars on these faculties. As for evangelical seminaries founded in North America in the twentieth century, these include Fuller Theological Seminary, Gordon-Conwell Theological Seminary, the emergence of Trinity Evangelical Divinity School, and Regent College in Vancouver, British Columbia, among others. In Great Britain, the London School of Theology arose as a leading evangelical center of learning, among others.

11. Buechner, *Telling Secrets*, 79–80.

more or less as I did but were also not ashamed or embarrassed to say so was like finding something which, only when I tasted it, I realized I had been starving for years."[12]

John H. Gerstner observed that in contrast to the rigidness of their fundamentalist forebears, evangelicals were "not militant, schismatic, or antischolarly . . . but who are, nonetheless, proponents of the fundamentals." He continued, "They call themselves evangelicals rather than fundamentalists, not because they repudiate the fundamentals, but because they reject the image which fundamentalists acquired."[13] Evangelicals have shared biblical commitments, many are socially aware, and many have an appreciation for education.

What Is the Place of Preaching in Evangelicalism?

Preaching is the mark of the evangelical's commitment to the Bible and the spread of the movement, and arises as the unique feature of evangelicalism. The preachers of evangelicalism's first and second Great Awakenings—including Theodore Frelinghuysen, Jonathan Edwards, George Whitefield, Gilbert Tennent, Francis Asbury, Joseph Bellamy, Samuel Hopkins, Timothy Dwight, Lyman Beecher, and later Charles Finney—underscore the central role preaching played in the movement. Interestingly, although historians of evangelicalism have investigated various facets of the movement, the role and place of preaching appears to be an area yet to be explored.[14] For example, *The Oxford Handbook of Evangelical Theology* explores the Bible, theology, the church, and missions, yet none of the articles address the place of preaching in the movement.[15]

British evangelical preacher and author John Stott begins his important book on preaching with the statement of the place of preaching, "Preaching is indispensable to Christianity."[16] Preaching is also indispensable to evangelicalism.

---

12. Buechner, *Telling Secrets*, 82.

13. Gerstner, "Theological Boundaries," 30–31.

14. The histories of evangelicalism seem to presume that preaching has had an impact on the movement, citing revivals and preachers. But no one has yet to connect the dots to demonstrate the unique place of preaching in the movement.

15. McDermott, *Oxford Handbook of Evangelical Theology*.

16. Stott, *Between Two Worlds*, 1.

The Neo-Evangelical movement reflected the same commitment to preaching. Clarence Macartney and Robert Lamont of First Presbyterian Church of Pittsburgh; A. Z. Conrad and Harold John Ockenga of Boston's Park Street Church;[17] Donald Gray Barnhouse and James Montgomery Boice at Tenth Presbyterian Church in Philadelphia; Gardner Taylor of Concord Baptist Church, Brooklyn; B. M. Nottage of Berean Chapel, Detroit; Shadrach Meshach Lockridge of Calvary Baptist Church, San Diego; and Louis F. Evans of Hollywood Presbyterian Church, Hollywood, preached unwaveringly, many of whom were committed to systematic weekly exposition of different biblical books.[18] Evangelist Billy Graham, a key figure in the Neo-Evangelical movement, helped to solidify the place of present-day evangelicalism on the American and even, world stage. On the other side of the Atlantic, John R. W. Stott of All Souls and Martin Lloyd-Jones of Westminster Chapel sounded the evangelical message. The pulpit was their platform and preaching communicated their message. Preaching is indeed inseparable from evangelicalism.

Derek Tidball observes, "By tradition, evangelicals have exalted two means of conversion as primary: preaching and personal work."[19] Preaching the gospel and the Word are simultaneous commitments to conversion and growth in Christ, with preaching being the primary means of conversion. As Tidball notes, "Whatever other methods of communication are employed, most evangelicals would agree that, at some stage, there must be a verbal explanation of the gospel for people to respond to it."[20]

What is evangelical preaching like? What are the features of an evangelical homiletic? Returning to Frederick Buechner, we read what someone from the outside perceives of the movement. Buechner writes,

> Most evangelical preaching that I have heard is seamless, hard sell, and heavily exhortatory. Men in business suits get up and proclaim the faith with the dynamic persuasiveness of insurance salesmen. If there are any evangelical women preachers, I have never happened to come across them. The churches these preachers get up in are apt to be large, packed full and so

---

17. Rosell, *Boston's Historic Park Street Church*; and Rosell, *Surprising Work of God*, 55.

18. See Stanley, *Global Diffusion of Evangelicalism*, 112–16; Old, *Reading and Preaching*, 88.

19. Tidball, *Who Are the Evangelicals?*, 122.

20. Tidball, *Who Are the Evangelicals?*, 123.

brilliantly lit that you feel there is no mystery there that has not been solved, no secrets that can escape detection. Their sermons couldn't be more different from the generally low-key ones that I am used to hearing in the sparsely attended churches in New England, but they give me the same sense of being official, public, godly utterances which the preacher stands behind but as a human being somehow does not stand in. Whatever passionate and private experience their sermons may have come from originally, you are given little or no sense of what that private experience was. At their best they bring many strengths with them into the pulpit but rarely, as I listened to them anyway, their real lives.[21]

As Buechner suggests, there are stereotypes of evangelical preaching, which differ depending on one's culture, region, and background. Today, the evangelical movement is worldwide, embracing the globe.[22] Preaching is at the center for evangelicals, persuading people to receive salvation in Christ and moving them toward maturity.

The Contributions of Evangelical Preaching

Among the contributions of evangelical preaching are a commitment to the Bible, a commitment to the high place of preaching, and a commitment to scholarship.

A Commitment to the Bible

Evangelical emphasis on the Bible as the authoritative Word of God is at the heart of preaching.[23] "It was part of the evangelical genius," says Hutchinson and Wolffe, "that [with] the Bible in hand and the Holy Spirit in mind, a reflected biblical vision of the future could be worked up out of the ground almost anywhere."[24] John Stott underscores the unique place the Bible has in the ministry of preaching. He urges,

> Since God's final deed and Word through Jesus were intended for all people of all ages, he inevitably made provision for a

---

21. Buechner, *Telling Secrets*, 84.
22. Hutchinson and Wolffe, *Short History of Global Evangelicalism*.
23. Waltke, "Biblical Authority," 84–96.
24. Hutchinson and Wolffe, *Short History of Global Evangelicalism*, 276.

reliable record of them to be written and preserved. Without this he would have defeated his own purpose. As a result, today, although nearly 2000 years separate us from that deed and Word, Jesus Christ is accessible to us. We can reach him and know him. But he is accessible only through the Bible, as the Holy Spirit brings to life his own witness to him in its pages. . . .[25]

It is certain that we cannot handle Scripture adequately in the pulpit if our doctrine of Scripture is inadequate. Conversely, evangelical Christians, who have the highest doctrine of Scripture in the Church, should be conspicuously the most conscientious preachers.[26]

David L. Larsen emphasizes, "The history of preaching bears out the acute dangers of preaching out of a text rather than preaching the text." He continues, "Respect for authorial intention may be under siege currently, but it must be seen as the hermeneutical high ground which must not be surrendered."[27] The Bible indeed is the foundation for evangelical preaching.

A Commitment to the High Place of Preaching

Evangelical ecclesiology is a "proclamatory ecclesiology," observes Leanne Van Dyk.[28] The Word is preached in the power of the Holy Spirit and people's lives are changed in conversion and Christian growth. In his magisterial study of preaching, Hughes Oliphant Old devotes seven volumes to the study of preaching throughout the ages, focusing on preaching as worship as well as the place and practice of preaching in the theology of worship. He traces the contours of evangelical preaching while he explores the high place of preaching in individual preachers, suggesting the important role of preaching in the evangelical movement.[29]

There has been an emphasis on expository preaching in evangelicalism. Forebears like Birmingham's R. W. Dale advocated for systematic expository preaching.[30] G. Campbell Morgan of Westminster Chapel, London, influenced generations by his emphasis on the weekly exposition

---

25. Stott, *Between Two Worlds*, 68.
26. Stott, *Between Two Worlds*, 69.
27. Larsen, *Company of Preachers*, 14.
28. Van Dyk, "Church in Evangelical Theology," 137.
29. See Old, *Reading and Preaching of the Scriptures*, vols. 1–7.
30. Old, *Reading and Preaching of the Scriptures*, 7:451; 6:399.

of the Bible.³¹ He was followed by Martin Lloyd-Jones, John Stott, and William Still in Britain, along with Donald Grey Barnhouse and James Montgomery Boice. The practice of expository preaching remains a feature of evangelical preachers such as Calvin Thielman, Earl Palmer, William Pope Wood, Timothy Keller, Haddon Robinson, Bryan Chapell, and Tony Evans.

Preaching is central to evangelicalism despite its critics. "Preaching has stubbornly refused to acknowledge the validity of the charges against it," states Clyde Fant.³² Preaching is here to stay.

A Commitment to Scholarship

Evangelical authors on the topic of preaching range from the popular to the scholarly. Over the years, publishers like Baker, Zondervan, Eerdmans, InterVarsity, Moody, Crossway, B&H, P&R, Weaver, and Christian Focus have devoted significant portions of their catalogs over the years to the publication of evangelical preaching. The books range from popular to scholarly in content.

Several significant textbooks on preaching have emerged, including Haddon Robinson's *Biblical Preaching* (1980), Bryan Chapell's *Christ-Centered Preaching: Redeeming the Expository Sermon* (1994), and John Stott's *Between Two Worlds: The Art of Preaching Today* (1982).

In addition to scholarly publications, a professional guild called the Evangelical Homiletics Society was founded in 1997 primarily for professors in seminaries and Bible colleges who teach preaching. The society was established

> for the exchange of ideas related to the instruction of biblical preaching. The purpose of the Society is to advance the cause of biblical preaching through the promotion of a biblical-theological approach to preaching; to increase competence for teachers of preaching; to integrate the fields of communication, biblical studies, and theology; to make scholarly contributions to the field of homiletics.³³

The society publishes *The Journal of the Evangelical Homiletics Society*, which is peer-reviewed, featuring research articles and book reviews.

31. Stanley, *Global Diffusion of Evangelicalism*, 5:112.
32. Fant, *Preaching for Today*, 9.
33. The Evangelical Homiletics Society, http://ehomiletics.com.

Evangelical homileticians have gained important ground over the last fifty years and continue to make strides in writing, teaching, and scholarship, including the establishment of several doctoral programs (e.g., philosophy) in preaching and the founding of centers for preaching for preaching research.[34]

The founding of the Evangelical Homiletics Society underscores a commitment to the teaching of preaching. As part of their purpose, the society encourages the development of pedagogy by devoting conferences to the task of teaching preaching through study groups. Some evangelical homileticians who have backgrounds in educational theory developed the book, *On the Teaching of Preaching: The Use of Educational Theory and Christian Theology in Homiletics*, arising out of a Lilly Endowment grant. The book underscores the importance of informed educational pedagogy for evangelicals who teach preaching in Bible schools, colleges, and seminaries.[35]

Words of Caution and Conclusion

To be sure, there is a range of preaching in evangelicalism. The commitments listed above highlight the best of the movement. However, contemporary preaching is often driven by personality rather than the preacher having the ballast of education and maturity in the Scriptures. To evangelicalism's embarrassment, American pragmatism has distilled preaching to what works best. In his important study of evangelicalism, David Wells lamented, "Where, then, has the church lost its vision? We can only surmise from the data we have. Perhaps the disaffection is grounded in the virtual collapse of biblical preaching in the contemporary church that some have noted or in the perception that even where biblical preaching is done, it is not always sufficiently nourishing."[36] Wells wrote these words

---

34. See the websites of Southern Baptist Theological Seminary, Southeastern Baptist Theological Seminary, Southwestern Baptist Theological Seminary, Gordon-Conwell Theological Seminary (in cooperation with London School of Theology), among others that have established doctor of philosophy in preaching programs. The Haddon W. Robinson Center for Preaching at Gordon-Conwell Theological Seminary, the Kyle Lake Center for Effective Preaching at George W. Truett Seminary at Baylor and the Center for Expository Preaching at Southwestern Baptist Theological Seminary are among these newly established centers.

35. Gibson, *On the Teaching of Preaching*.

36. Wells, *God in the Wasteland*, 196. For another aspect of this concern, see Shelley, *Consumer Church*, 187–98.

over twenty years ago as he surveyed the evangelical landscape of the late twentieth century—and, sadly, they can be reaffirmed as the case today.

In spite of the detractions found within evangelicalism—the consumeristic tendencies, the threats of theological shallowness, and the pervasiveness of the cult of personality—preaching drives the movement. Evangelicalism is made up of preaching and preachers. Preaching is of great significance for evangelicalism. We can say confidently that preaching is indispensable for evangelicalism.

Bibliography

Bentley, William H. "Bible Believers in the Black Community." In *The Evangelicals: What They Believe, Who They Are, Where They Are Changing*, edited by David F. Wells and John D. Woodbridge, 108–21. Nashville: Abingdon, 1975.

Buechner, Frederick. *Telling Secrets: A Memoir*. New York: HarperCollins, 1991.

Dayton, Donald W., and Robert K. Johnson. *The Variety of American Evangelicalism*. Downers Grove, IL: IVP Academic, 1991.

Fant, Clyde E. *Preaching for Today*. New York: Harper & Row, 1975.

Frazer, David A., ed. *Evangelicalism: Saving Its Success*. St. Davids, PA: Eastern College and Eastern Baptist Theological Seminary, 1987.

Gerstner, John H. "The Theological Boundaries of Evangelical Faith." In *The Evangelicals: What They Believe, Who They Are, Where They Are Changing*, edited by David F. Wells and John D. Woodbridge, 31–37. Nashville: Abingdon, 1975.

Gibson, Scott M., ed. *On the Teaching of Preaching: The Use of Educational Theory and Christian Theology in Homiletics*. Wooster: Weaver, 2017.

Haykin, Michael A. G., and Kenneth J. Stewart, eds. *The Advent of Evangelicalism: Exploring Historical Continuities*. Nashville: B&H, 2008.

Hutchinson, Mark, and John Wolffe. *A Short History of Global Evangelicalism*. Cambridge: Cambridge University Press, 2012.

Larsen, David L. *The Company of Preachers: A History of Biblical Preaching from the Old Testament to the Modern Era*. Grand Rapids, MI: Kregel, 1998.

Lewis, Donald M., and Richard V. Pierard. *Global Evangelicalism: Theology, History and Culture in Regional Perspective*. Downers Grove, IL: IVP Academic, 2014.

Lindner, Robert D. "The Resurgence of Evangelical Social Concern (1925–75)." In *The Evangelicals: What They Believe, Who They Are, Where They Are Changing*, edited by David F. Wells and John D. Woodbridge, 189–210. Nashville: Abingdon, 1975.

Magnuson, Norris. *Salvation in the Slums: Evangelical Social Work, 1865–1920*. Metuchen, NJ: Scarecrow, 1977.

McDermott, Gerald R., ed. *The Oxford Handbook of Evangelical Theology*. Oxford: Oxford University Press, 2010.

Naselli, Andrew David, and Collin Hansen, eds. *Four Views on the Spectrum of Evangelicalism*. Grand Rapids, MI: Zondervan, 2011.

Old, Hughes Oliphant. *The Reading and Preaching of the Scriptures in the Worship of the Christian Church*. Vol. 7, *Our Own Time*. Grand Rapids, MI: Eerdmans, 2010.

Pannell, William. "The Religious Heritage of Blacks." In *The Evangelicals: What They Believe, Who They Are, Where They Are Changing*, edited by David F. Wells and John D. Woodbridge, 96–107. Nashville: Abingdon, 1975.

Rosell, Garth M. *Boston's Historic Park Street Church: The Story of an Evangelical Landmark*. Grand Rapids, MI: Kregel, 2009.

———. *The Surprising Work of God: Harold John Ockenga, Billy Graham, and the Rebirth of Evangelicalism*. Grand Rapids, MI: Baker, 2008.

Shelley, Bruce, and Marshall Shelley. *Consumer Church: Can Evangelicals Win the World without Losing Their Souls?* Downers Grove, IL: IVP Academic, 1992.

Smith, Timothy L. "A Shared Evangelical Heritage." In *Evangelicalism: Surviving Its Success*. Vol. 2, *The Evangelical Round Table*, edited by David Fraser, 12–28. St. Davids, PA: Eastern College and Eastern Baptist Theological Seminary, 1987.

———. *Revivalism and Social Reform on the Eve of the Civil War*. Nashville: Johns Hopkins University Press, 1980.

Spain, Rufus. *At Ease in Zion: Social History of Southern Baptists*. Nashville: Vanderbilt University Press, 1967.

Stanley, Brian. *The Global Diffusion of Evangelicalism: The Age of Billy Graham and John Stott*. A History of Evangelicalism: People, Movements and Ideas in the English-Speaking World 5. Downers Grove, IL: IVP Academic, 2013.

Stott, John. *Between Two Worlds: The Challenge of Preaching Today*. Grand Rapids, MI: Eerdmans, 1982, 2017.

Sweeney, Douglas A. *The American Evangelical Story: A History of the Movement*. Grand Rapids, MI: Baker, 2005.

Sweet, Leonard I., ed., *The Evangelical Tradition in America*. Macon, GA: Mercer University Press, 1984.

Tidball, Derek. *Who Are the Evangelicals? Tracing the Roots of Today's Movements*. London: Marshall Pickering, 1994.

Van Dyk, Leanne. "The Church in Evangelical Theology and Practice." In *Cambridge Companion to Evangelical Theology*, edited by Timothy Larsen and Daniel J. Treier, 137. Cambridge: Cambridge University Press, 2007.

Waltke, Bruce K. "Biblical Authority: How Firm a Foundation." In *Evangelicalism: Surviving Its Success*. Vol. 2, *The Evangelical Round Table*, edited by David Fraser, 84–96. St. Davids, PA: Eastern College and Eastern Baptist Theological Seminary, 1987.

Wells, David F., ed. *God in the Wasteland: The Reality of Truth in a World of Fading Dreams*. Grand Rapids, MI: Eerdmans, 1994.

Wilkens, Steve, and Don Thorsen. *Everything You Know about Evangelicals Is Wrong (Well, Almost Everything): An Insider's Look at Myths and Realities*. Grand Rapids, MI: Baker, 2010.

Wolterstorff, Nicholas. "Why Care about Justice?" In *Evangelicalism: Surviving Its Success*. Vol. 2, *The Evangelical Round Table*, edited by David Fraser, 156–67. St. Davids, PA: Eastern College and Eastern Baptist Theological Seminary, 1987.

Chapter Thirteen

The Significance of the "New Homiletic"

EUGENE L. LOWRY

IT WAS 1965 AT Princeton Theological Seminary during the first meeting of the Academy of Homiletics. David James Randolph, who was a professor at the Drew University School of Theology, delivered a paper at the first meeting. He began,

> A new preaching is coming to birth in the travail of our times. In the civil rights movement, in the engagement with communism, in the "secular City," in the theological school, in the parish church, in the liturgical movement and elsewhere, preaching is being rejected as a habit and affirmed as a happening. The definition of preaching which is dawning on these horizons may be stated in this way: "Preaching is the event in which the Biblical text is interpreted in order that its meaning will come to expression in the concrete situation of the hearers."[1]

And Randolph called it "The New Homiletic," drawing the connection with the New Hermeneutic. When they published the book that grew out of that lecture, he used the same words and the same paragraph. The heading was "Preaching and the New Hermeneutic toward a New Homiletic."

I do have some questions about the first paragraph. Was he referring to something that was already a movement, or something that he hoped would become a movement? Perhaps the sources utilized in the volume might provide a clue as to whether this is a current happening

---

1. Randolph, *Renewal of Preaching*, 1.

or a prophetic word. In reviewing his work, I found references to Donald Miller's *Fire in Thy Mouth*, and H. H. Farmer's *Servant of the Word*. I looked for R. E. C. Brown's *Ministry of the Word*, and did not find it—but did find a footnote on H. Grady Davis' *Design for Preaching*. I had hoped for more Davis because—much later—I finally realized that *Design for Preaching*[2] is the book of historical transition between the old and the new homiletic, a writing that has enriched so many of us.

(After a few years of preaching, I began teaching adjunctively at Saint Paul School of Theology and initially used *Design for Preaching* as a textbook in my preaching lab courses. A couple years later, I chose another text, thinking many students found Davis too deep—actually, it was really too deep for me. Some of you remember his poem comparing a sermon to a tree. It was the first time in my life I ever heard preaching related to anything alive.)

******

Whether the New Homiletic was just coming to birth or just beginning to be noticed, clearly it happened at a crisis point for North American preaching. This was a time of uncertainty and unrest, with even strange experiments of all kinds. O. Wesley Allen Jr. has noted the long tradition of homiletical form prompted by the Franciscans and Dominicans—the university sermon. Sermons were expected to offer either three points and then three subpoints (Franciscans) or three points and then more exposition of Scripture (Dominicans), but both of them deductive.[3]

Here is the way Thomas G. Long put it: "By (the) 1950s, Protestant preaching was highly didactic, instruments of instruction centered on big principles and doctrinal propositions. It sounded like term papers and academic lectures. Orderly, balanced, points and subpoints."[4]

Actually, quite a bit of time before that, it was also critiqued by Harry Emerson Fosdick. (There once was a time when secular magazines were actually interested in talking about preaching.) The critique appeared in *Harper's Magazine*,[5] with its title asking, "What is the Matter with Preaching?" Fosdick had a beginning single word for it that rather captured it.

---

2. See Davis, *Design for Preaching*.
3. Allen, *Renewed Homiletic*, 3.
4. Long, *Preaching from Memory to Hope*, 3.
5. Fosdick, "What Is the Matter with Preaching?," 133–41.

He said, "Boring." But that was not all. He continued by noting that "the text was good and the truth was undeniable. The subject was well chosen and well developed, but for all that, nothing happened. The reason for this can commonly be traced to one cause, the preacher started the sermon at the wrong end."[6] Then, Fred Craddock spoke of "The Pulpit in the Shadows."[7] Simply *An Empty Pulpit*, said Clyde Reid.[8]

Twelve years after Randolph's lecture and eight years after his book, Richard L. Eslinger published *A New Hearing*, summarizing some of what had happened in the name of the *New Homiletic*.[9] It featured five theorists who seemed to be on similar pages of thought and practice. This was not an orchestrated movement organized by anybody; instead, the publication was simply one theorist's report of the work of a few of the many writers moving in a new direction.

The five of us featured in this book did not choose to be together. Focusing on each of us in separate chapters, Eslinger placed us together. We were not totally happy with a few of the pieces of that, including our concern that perhaps people would think we are all alike. Yet, clearly, we were on the same large homiletic plate—with differing emphases. The centerpiece that Eslinger rightly sensed is in our common understanding of the sermon as an *evoked event*.

And he called this shift the "Copernican Revolution" in North American homiletics that "involves an abandonment of [the] . . . spatial paradigm." Declared Eslinger, "This new . . . revelatory paradigm relates to time rather than space."[10]

He chose Fred Craddock, David Buttrick, Henry Mitchell, Charles Rice, and myself as theorists representing this basic shift. He could have chosen a dozen others. In fact, many writers in our field believe the work of Lucy Rose belongs in the group of five. Her wonderfully researched and articulate work, *Sharing the Word*,[11] was published just prior to her untimely death. If Eslinger's work had been published five years later, who knows who else it might have been. The names that come quickly to mind would certainly include Thomas Troeger, David Schlafer, Mike

---

6. Graves, *What's the Matter with Preaching Today?*, 12.
7. Craddock, *As One without Authority*.
8. Reid, *Empty Pulpit*.
9. Eslinger, *New Hearing*.
10. Eslinger, *New Hearing*, 64–65.
11. Rose, *Sharing the Word*.

Graves, Paul Scott Wilson, Wes Allen, Jana Childers, Cleophus LaRue, Robin Meyers, Tom Long, and Barbara Brown Taylor. Many possibilities. It just happened that in 1987, he settled on these five people.

In 2007, O. Wesley Allen Jr., then Professor of Homiletics and Worship at Lexington Theological Seminary, invited the five of us to appear together for the first time in order to update our work by means of preaching in local congregations, as well as lecturing together at the seminary. This experience, along with Allen's articulate introduction of the history of this homiletical movement, was captured in his volume *The Renewed Homiletic*. Since then, Fred Craddock and David Buttrick have died, and Charles Rice and Henry Mitchell have both retired.

******

The *Foundation* of preaching for all five of us is *Scripture*. The term *Event* captures the essence of the *GOAL* of New Homiletic preaching. Fred Craddock called the goal *Evocation*. David Buttrick called it *Invocation*. Henry Mitchell called it *Celebration*. Charles Rice called it *Story*. I call it *Resolution*. The key MEANS toward achieving this event, Fred Craddock would say is *Anticipation*. David Buttrick would say homiletic *Moves*. Henry Mitchell would say *Holistic Appeal*. Charles Rice would compare sacred and secular *Story*. I would say the key means is *Plot*. (Some have called my plot the *Lowry Loop*.)

A lot has happened in the intervening years since David Randolph coined the term *The New Homiletic* in 1965. That term and the lecture at the Academy were then subsequently expanded in his publication of *The Renewal of Preaching* in 1969. In fact, within the next two years following its publication, two of the five authors later chosen by Eslinger had already been published. Hence, I will offer a fairly brief summary of the work of all five of us—in chronological order of publication. Hopefully, it will reveal the connections, the similarities, (and dissimilarities) of all five scholars.

Charles L. Rice (1970)

First was Charles L. Rice, also a professor at Drew. His first book, *Interpretation and Imagination*,[12] was published in 1970. In 1980, he joined

---

12. Rice, *Interpretation and Imagination*.

with Edmund A. Steimle and Morris J. Niedenthal to author *Preaching the Story*. In his first book, he was noting the power of story so fundamental to preaching. By *Story*, Rice, first of all, means *the* story—that is, the Scriptures. He says, "For both the New and Old Testaments, revelation is conveyed through the literary medium of story. Story expresses the Christian tradition so decisively that it becomes a normative mode of Biblical revelation. . . . [It] then interprets us and our stories."[13] Do you hear the direction?

It is crucial to understand the intent of Rice's focus. As he named it on the first page, his purpose as well as that of the others writing in this series called *The Preacher's Paperback Library*, is geared toward the "renewal of the preaching ministry. It will not stoop to providing 'sermon starters' or other 'homiletical gimmicks.'" His title declares his purpose: *Interpretation and Imagination*. Equally important is the subtitle, *The Preacher and Contemporary Literature*.

One cannot learn much from this book in one reading, which is its power. The reader is invited to an ongoing theological/literary retreat that backs off from the ordinary issues of how to preach—in order to assist in discovering how to be ready to enter the preaching moment.

Lying behind the work of Rice is the ministry of Edmund Steimle, walking midway between being a noted theological professor and a famous preacher on the long-term radio show, *The Protestant Hour*. Another former student, Morris Niedenthal, joined to produce *Preaching the Story*.[14]

Altogether their central but not limited focus is in noting that "anyone who has experienced preaching, whether in pulpit or pew, knows that it is an event—a moment, a meeting, a sudden seeing in which preacher, listener, the message, and the impinging social environment all come together."[15]

These three join together to find the central focus that can unite the several components of the sermon event: the preacher, the listeners, the churchly context, and the message. "We have chosen to concentrate our focus on that one insight or perspective which the three of us regard

---

13. Eslinger, *New Hearing*, 20.
14. Steimle et al., *Preaching the Story*.
15. Steimle et al., *Preaching the Story*, 9.

as of high importance: preaching as storytelling and the preacher as raconteur."[16]

They explain that in the first place, the dramatic form of a biblical address will affect the structure of the sermon. Each sermon should have something of the dramatic form of a play or short story—tightly knit, one part leading into and dependent upon the next, with some possibility of suspense and surprise evident in the development and the end.[17]

These conclusions grow out of the confluence of their working together. And it shows the power of the seminal focus of Rice's 1971 offering.

Fred B. Craddock (1971)

The one whose work became the turning point for the dominance of New Homiletic influence was Fred B. Craddock, who wrote *As One without Authority* in 1971. As noted previously, his opening sentence in chapter 1 declares, "We are all aware that in countless courts of opinion, the verdict on preaching has been rendered and the sentence pronounced." The second sentence then sets the stage for his writing: "All this slim volume asks is a stay of execution until one other witness be heard."[18] With that, he explains the various factors involved in the loss of power in preaching. The "Pulpit in the Shadows" is his image.

He notes that now we are bombarded by words in a way not true before; hence, the pulpit has lost its privileged position. Previously, in countless churches throughout the country, the preacher was not only the one who brought the gospel but also the outside world into the lives of the congregation. Not true anymore, and it is sad now that "Unfortunately the church has no retirement program for all words that fought well in Nicaea, Chalcedon, and Augsburg."[19] Moreover, "television has reorganized the human sensorium to image and picture, and Hellenists give ascendency to the eye."

Nonetheless, Craddock observes,

> The Bible favors the ear over the eye . . . (and) in a way unequaled by any of the other senses, the ear receives the temporal

---

16. Steimle et al., *Preaching the Story*, ix.
17. Steimle et al., *Preaching the Story*, 171.
18. Craddock, *As One without Authority*, 1.
19. Craddock, *As One without Authority*, 7.

sequence of sensations appropriate to the communication of activity and the unfolding of the history of a people. One has to raise the question whether there is involved here something so fundamental to the Christian faith that, television to the contrary, the oral must remain in the center of the field of Christian proclamation.[20]

Craddock's powerful influence on preaching as featured in *As One without Authority* focuses on his overhaul of the dominant view of sermonic shape utilized for centuries. Simply, he notes that sermons either work deductively or inductively—either beginning with general truth and ending with particulars or the reverse. "When the conclusion precedes the development, [it is] a most unnatural mode of communication. And this is precisely the authoritarian foundation of traditional preaching. . . . If the congregation is on the team, it is as javelin catcher."[21] Moreover, the deductive form lacks anticipation. "How does one get from 2b to main point II? . . . The limp phrase, 'Now in the second place,' hardly has the leverage."[22] In the inductive sermon, the preacher always provides an early promise, but the fulfillment is delayed until the folks are ready to hear it.

Craddock spoke with unusual credibility. His PhD was in New Testament studies. Hence, in a day when "preaching" was only an optional course in many seminaries, his biblical studies reputation was huge. Moreover, he already was becoming known as a powerful preacher—as well as a professor in homiletics. And he spoke articulately with a powerful mind that was both creative and accessible.

He also wrote two more books on preaching. The second was entitled *Overhearing the Gospel*[23], based primarily on the work of Soren Kierkegaard, who once said, "There is no lack of information in Christian lands; something else is lacking and this is something that one cannot directly communicate to the other."

So Craddock asks these questions: How can we teach those who already know? How can we preach to those who have already heard? He mentions how children's sermons can sometimes influence adults significantly because they do not think they are being addressed.

---

20. Craddock, *As One without Authority*.
21. Craddock, *As One without Authority*, 54–55.
22. Craddock, *As One without Authority*, 56.
23. Craddock, *Overhearing the Gospel*.

A good example of this kind of preaching is found in his sermon: "Praying through Clenched Teeth."[24] After reading the text from Galatians, Craddock began, "I am going to say a word, and the moment I say the word I want you to see a face, to recall a face and a name. . . . Are you ready? The word is 'bitter.' Do you see a face? . . . I see the face of a farmer in western Oklahoma, riding a mortgaged tractor, burning gasoline purchased on credit, moving across rented land, rearranging the dust. Bitter." Four other faces are named: a woman under a funeral canopy, a man in small grocery store, a young couple at an airport terminal, and a young minister—all bitter. Then he turns to Saul. And he never addressed anyone present and bitter until the last line that spoke of somebody's hand of love "extended to those who are bitter."

Craddock's third book focused on preaching is the classic textbook, *Preaching*. It covers every facet of preaching, including biblical work, preparation, and delivery. Published in 1985, it now has served as the centrally chosen textbook for over three decades.

Henry H. Mitchell (1977)

Next for consideration is Henry H. Mitchell, the author of at least seven works. *Recovery of Preaching* is his 1977 publication relating particularly to the shape of preaching discussed during the beginnings of the *New Homiletic*.

His focus emerges quickly as he identifies the differences involved in the context of African American preaching. He explains, "Black preaching assumes a target of whole persons. The largely cerebral appeal of most white preaching would seem to imply a primarily intellectual target . . . focusing on the production of a stimulating idea. Black preaching seeks a combination of intellectual and less rational but equally valid processes."[25]

He also notes,

> Feelings in Western culture have somehow been declared unworthy. Black culture of the masses has not progressed to the level of this lofty and ancient mistake, because its culture does not trace back through this traumatic schism of personality,

---

24. Lowry, *How To Preach a Parable*, 142–144, 148.
25. Mitchell, *Recovery of Preaching*, 12.

and so Blacks have emerged into this modern era with a kind of wholeness which is typical of so-called primitive cultures.[26]

At the same time, Mitchell does not want the term "feelings" to be interpreted as emotion without ideational content.

Citing Eliade's term "transconsciousness," Mitchell discusses the variation of meaning that might be included in the term's definition. He takes the term to include "culture-borne religious life [that] is in fact a kind of stored insight." Hence, he believes that "whatever the differences in detail, transconsciousness surely suggests the kind of multi-channel awareness and integration of which I speak in the Black religious tradition."[27]

I find this discussion quite helpful to me in trying to express my experience of the powerfully received theological thought in the African American church. In my culture, if I were to choose for my text the biblical phrase, "I was a stranger in a strange land," my culture would understand it as a biblical reference regarding the Exile. But, in the context of the black congregation, the rafters of the building might tremble upon the expressed sentence. Indeed, a deep transconscious joining of personal and historical experience would happen.

When first I learned of the inclusion of Henry Mitchell's understanding of preaching, I was struck by my wonderment about how it fits into the overarching nature of plot as the New Homiletical theorists view it. Induction, not deduction, suspense and then resolution of plot are standard features. But sometimes I have heard the black preacher announce title and theme at the beginning of the sermon. Then the preaching content sometimes even follows a kind of deductive movement. Is this narrative preaching? Why, yes, it is—with a different kind of suspense.

There is an altogether unique and powerful kind of suspense in the African-American congregation—at least, those in my experiences. With every phrase, image, and turn of thought, the congregation is waiting eagerly, energized even by the call-response of "Take your time." Of course. Gardner Taylor is right on when he tells the black preacher to start low, go slow, get high, strike fire, and retire. To tell white preachers to do so is absolutely fatal. No one will be with you by the time of the "go slow" part because most of us do not know about the *fire*, or how to manage it. Hence, the white congregation will often be content if we just conclude.

---

26. Mitchell, *Recovery of Preaching*, 13.
27. Mitchell, *Recovery of Preaching*, 16.

No wonder Henry Mitchell writes about the eyewitness account of the text and then the final celebration.

Eugene L. Lowry (1980)

Eleven years after Randolph's publication that introduced the term "New Homiletic" came the publication of my initial writing on preaching: *The Homiletical Plot*.[28] My first experience leading toward the New Homiletic came long before the term was formed, and it happened accidentally—without my knowing anything about the future. While I was away at college and seminary, my home church, First Methodist Church of Wichita, Kansas, called a new pastor by the name of Ron Meredith. Soon the pews were filled to overflowing. He could preach like nobody else. A year after my graduation from Drew Seminary, even though I intended to remain in New Jersey, I received a call to become Ron Meredith's associate. What an opportunity to find out how a great preacher worked in the pulpit and hear him explain his methodology. But, unfortunately, although he could *do it*, he had no clue about *how* he did it.

In these three years of listening, I only found this out: how he utilized illustrations was the exact opposite of what preachers typically were taught. We were told to make a point and then embody the point by illustration. Ron did the opposite, always. He would tell a story—most often a biblical one—and when completed, the point *was* made. Sometimes the story would be the whole sermon. I began to follow suit.

Later, after doing some adjunctive teaching, I happened onto Craddock's *As One without Authority*. Inductive preaching, he said. It was all the authority I needed to go to work. Soon I began to add nuances to my sermons so they could be shaped narratively . . . even showing how a non-narrative text can be shaped story-like, so that every sermon should move from itch-to-scratch. *The Homiletical Plot*, published in 1980, went beyond the principles of inductive or narrative movement. I also attempted to imagine the various steps that would be involved in a plot (drawn partly from Aristotle's *Poetica*.)

The plot has always involved five stages, even though the names associated with them have changed and their workings have been refined.

---

28. Lowry, *Homiletical Plot*.

1. "*Oops: Upsetting the Equilibrium.*" It could be termed "Conflict," or "Presenting issue" (depending on the text).
2. "*Ugh: Analysing the discrepancy.*" It could be termed "Complication." ("Analysing" often is too limiting, but "Things always get worse.")
3. "*Aha: Disclosing the clue to Resolution.*" Could be "Peripetia," "Reversal," or "Decisive Turn" (needs to mean a radical shift).
4. "*Whee: Experiencing the Gospel.*" Could be "Good News," or "Oh, Yes" (source might be out of Hebrew text, or New Testament).
5. "*Yeah: Anticipating the Consequences.*" Too negative. How about "Anticipating the Future," "Therefore," or "Denouement."[29]

The purpose in suggesting various names for the five stages of the plot has several dimensions. First, the varieties of text and purpose of the sermon require sharp yet flexible designations of purpose. Biblical texts are diverse and so are sermonic purposes. So, for example, the term for stage two, "analysing the discrepancy," was too limiting toward theological issues. What I meant is that things have to get worse, ever deeper, before a remedy can happen. Sometimes a diversity of images will do the same by contrast, not analysis. Often a story will shift gears and, once noticed, will shift direction. For example, in the Good Samaritan text, the term "neighbor" at the beginning of the story meant the one receiving help. By the end of the story, "neighbor" meant the one providing the help. How does the sermon deal with that? (And in fact, the question may be, "Who's in the ditch, anyway?")

Sometimes a shift of nomenclature will correct something I didn't actually mean. For example, in naming the final stage "Anticipating the Consequences," I neglected to remember what "consequences" meant when I was a child. I was just trying to name how life changes once the Good News of the gospel is experienced in the sermon—but in a positive, not negative, way.

In at least one case, I simply made a mistake in the text. I believe *The Sermon: Dancing the Edge of Mystery*[30] is the most comprehensive treatment of my thought. On page 81, however, I was trying to explain what to do when the "Aha" of reversal and the "Whee" of good news actually happen at once in a text. In such a case, I suggested only four steps in the plot happen (1-2-3/4-5). Apparently, some readers thought I was

---

29. Lowry, *Homiletical Plot*, 27–73.
30. Lowry, *Sermon*.

eliminating one of the steps. I didn't intend that—only that two steps might happen to merge. It was my error in description, which I made sure didn't happen in subsequent writings.

Enough of this exercise in nomenclature. The substance of early preparation, or getting ready for the shaping of the plot is what now is crucial. In preparing a sermon, all of these several steps need constant attention. The first preparation step, as one is exploring the primary biblical text, involves remembering to constantly work out loud throughout the entire preparation stage. After all, that's the way the sermon will happen on Sunday.

The greatest temptation is to miss the first preparation step altogether. What is on your mind as you read the text, think about the text, and imagine Sunday? It may be important to violate some of what you have been previously taught about reading . . . anything. If you have a text in hand and ask the question, "What's Paul's point?" or "What did Jesus have in mind?" it is the wrong question. Quickly you could be in trouble, and thereby miss the necessary biblical research that is required because, unfortunately, you think you know where the text is headed and decide immediately to go there.

No, the first step is to find something *weird* in the text, something that doesn't seem to fit the text. You'll want to ask the question, "What's weird? Is this something that Jesus always affirmed? Didn't He say something different someplace else?" To ask this type of question of the text will drive you to a deeper immersion into the text. If you just say, "I know where it's going," pity the congregation.

Oh, by the way, the lectionary doesn't like trouble. If you have a text such as verses 1 through 6, and then 12 through 16, you'd better look at the middle part they left out because that's where the important juxtaposition may be found.

Sometimes the given text will provide a minor phrase or sentence that seems unworthy of homiletical consideration. It is easy to be tempted to simply pass on to the "important" parts of the text. For example, one text said that they had to go through Samaria. But no, they didn't. There was another way. Folks knew that it was worth risking the dangerous Jericho Road down to the river to avoid Samaria. If you travel over the river and up north on the pagan side of the Jordan, and then cross over to Galilee just south of the Sea, then you never need to rub shoulders with those terrible half-breeds.

But you say, that's a minor thing. There's no sense to waste time mentioning it, unless it turns out that you want later to ask in the sermon about where Jesus is going *today*—where we never want to be—because, in fact, they didn't *have to* go through Samaria. Jesus *chose* to go through Samaria.

By the way, when I presented this material at Baylor, I mentioned this text, and wanting to note that on such a trip to Galilee everybody went on the longer route, I, at the spur of the moment, imagined an interstate highway on which they travelled. This was bad momentary imagination. That might have worked on most all roads, but not on the Jericho road. I wonder how many listeners on that day noted my ill-chosen image.

My term for the *evoked event* so central in understanding the New Homiletic is *narrative*. In my first book, the meaning of both terms *story* and *narrative* were quite close for me—too close. In *Doing Time in the Pulpit* (my best work and the least read), the key ingredients being examined were *time* (actually many *times*) *story,* and *narrative*. In the section entitled "The sermon as a form of narrative time," I stated, "If a plot is the moving suspense of story—from disequilibrium to resolution—then so is a sermon viewed from the perspective of narrative time. Any given sermon takes the form of moving suspense."[31] (*Story* is a subset of *Narrative*.)

Eighteen years *after* Craddock came out with *As One Without Authority* (and *after* Craddock followed John Brokhoff at Candler), Brokhoff published a book called *As One With Authority*, clearly attempting a rebuttal. He also had a word to say about narrative preaching. He claimed, "The problem with narrative preaching promoted today is that the whole sermon becomes nothing more than a story. There's no biblical explanation, interpretation, or application to present-day living. What each listener takes from it, if anything, is what he or she wishes."[32]

All of this is to say, beware when people speaking about narrative preaching utilize the strategy of minimalization of the term. "Narrative" will be shrunk to "story," then shrunk to "stories," lessened to "anecdotes," and finally becoming "jokes." It's easy then to be critical!

In *The Homiletical Beat*, my last book comparing preaching to performed music, I reached back to H. Grady Davis, when he stated that "a sermon is like music, not music in the score but in the live performance,

---

31. Lowry, *Doing Time in the Pulpit*.
32. Brokhoff, *As One with Authority*, 141.

where bar is heard after bar, theme after theme, and never all at once."[33] Hence, a "sermon is a movement in time. It begins at a given moment, it ends at a given moment, and it moves through the intervening moments one after another." I call it *narrative*.

David Buttrick

The best way to become acquainted with the work of David Buttrick is probably not by reading the 498 pages of *Homiletic*[34], his abbreviated compromise from the three-volume set he intended. Better to dig into the thirteen pages of "Interpretation and Preaching" in the journal *Interpretation*, January 1981. It may both thrill and shock you with his profound articulation about preaching.

Understand that he was brought kicking and screaming into the New Homiletic fold. He so disliked the term "narrative" that in his later tome, which ended with ten pages of subject indices, the term "narrative" was not even listed. Yet, in that same year of 1987, Richard Eslinger, in *A New Hearing*, seemed to know that Buttrick's work should be included. A glance at Buttrick's 1981 offering may show why.

> Since the time of the Protestant Scholastics, sermons have been designed according to an aged schema. Procedurally, a text was exegeted, interpreted, and applied—even if later was modified for briefer texts or reduced to a single topic. Throughout all the versions of this schema that were used, the result was what might be called a "method of distillation" by which passages are reduced to single propositional "truths."[35]

He gave an example of potential treatments of Luke 7:2–10, the story of the centurion's slave. (You recall—slave near death—officer vouched for by Jewish elders—"Just say the word"—Jesus does—and slave is healed.) Says Buttrick, "Usually, the preacher approaches the passage as if it were objectively 'there,' a static construct from which the preacher may get some*thing* to preach on." It becomes a topic by grabbing a verse: "Say the word, 'I am not worthy,'" or a theme chosen: "the intercession of friends," "the compassion of Jesus," or "an example of humility." In any case, Buttrick remarks, "The preacher treats the passage as if it were a

---

33. Lowry, *Homiletical Beat*, 2, 6.
34. Buttrick, *Homiletic*.
35. Buttrick, "Interpretation and Preaching," 46, 48–49.

still-life picture in which some*thing* may be found.... 'What has been ignored?' he asks. The composition of the picture, the narrative structure, the movement of the story, the whole question of what in fact the passage may want to preach."[36]

Did you notice the term "narrative?" Eslinger did. And later, Buttrick continues, "In Luke 7:2–10 we have a plotted story. Of course, non-narrative material may also be plotted ... [by means of] a sequence of ideas or images logically designed."[37]

Regarding Scripture, Buttrick makes it clear that "preaching should be a speaking *of* Scripture and not *about* Scripture." Moreover, the sermon "should favor mobile structures, forgoing fixed topics and categorical development. What we encounter in Scripture is "movement of thought or event or image by some 'logic.'"

So, it is that "language constitutes our world by naming, confers identity in the world by story. Preaching can rename God's world with metaphorical power.... Preaching constructs in consciousness a faith-world related to God."[38] Indeed, he says sermons involve ordered sequence.

So, he does work narratively but believes the term "narrative" ought not to be the primary defining term for the sermon. Instead of my term "plot," he prefers to speak about "plotted movement." Indeed, "sermons involve sequential talking." The sermon is formed by a series of "moves." Taken together, the intended purpose of the several moves is to "form conceptual understanding in communal consciousness."[39]

I certainly do not understand all he means in and by the formation of moves into sequence, but with the help of jazz improvisation I can provide an analogy (without needing any professional knowledge to grasp.)

When I mess with a tune (that is, begin to elaborate creatively!), I mess with the melody line. (Mozart did this with "Twinkle, Twinkle Little Star.") I embellish it, turn it sideways, alter the rhythm, etc. Likely, you will not lose the sense of its changing self. Its signature will stay close by. But more sophisticated pianists (progressive ones) instead will mess with the chord structures, the harmonics. They look for elaborate chordal shapes and movements. And the soloists will take us on a high ride. As

---

36. Buttrick, "Interpretation and Preaching," 49.
37. Buttrick, "Interpretation and Preaching," 51.
38. Buttrick, *Homiletic*, 11.
39. Buttrick, *Homiletic*, 23, 28, 43.

listeners, we may forget what song is being played. (Sometimes they do, too.) Finally, by the end of the performance, they will bring it all home.

I call it the difference between horizontal and vertical improvisation. And that is the difference between Lowry's *plot* and Buttrick's *moves*.

Bibliography

Allen, O. Wesley, Jr. *The Renewed Homiletic*. Minneapolis: Fortress, 2010.
Brokhoff, John R. *As One with Authority*. Wilmore, KY: Bristol, 1989.
Buttrick, David. *Homiletic*. Philadelphia: Fortress, 1987.
———. "Interpretation and Preaching." *Interpretation* 35 (Jan. 1981) 46–58.
Craddock, Fred B. *As One without Authority*. Enid, OK: Phillips University Press, 1971.
———. *Overhearing the Gospel*. Nashville: Abingdon, 1978.
Davis, Henry Grady. *Design for Preaching*. Philadelphia: Fortress, 1958.
Eslinger, Richard L. *A New Hearing*. Nashville: Abingdon, 1987.
Fosdick, Harry Emerson. "What Is the Matter with Preaching?" *Harper's Magazine* (1928) 133–41.
Graves, Mike, ed. *What's the Matter with Preaching Today?* Louisville: Westminster John Knox, 2004.
Long, Thomas G. *Preaching from Memory to Hope*. Louisville: Westminster John Knox, 2009.
Lowry, Eugene. *Doing Time in the Pulpit*. Nashville: Abingdon, 1985.
———. *The Homiletical Beat*. Nashville: Abingdon, 2012.
———. *The Homiletical Plot*. Atlanta: John Knox, 1980.
———. *How to Preach a Parable*. Nashville: Abingdon, 1989.
———. *The Sermon: Dancing the Edge of Mystery*. Nashville: Abingdon, 1997.
Mitchell, Henry H. *The Recovery of Preaching*. San Francisco: Harper & Row, 1977.
Randolph, David James. *The Renewal of Preaching*. Philadelphia: Fortress, 1969.
Reid, Clyde. *The Empty Pulpit*. New York: Harper & Row, 1967.
Rice, Charles L. *Interpretation and Imagination*. Philadelphia: Fortress, 1970.
Rose, Lucy Atkinson. *Sharing the Word*. Louisville: Westminster John Knox, 1997.
Steimle, Edmund A., et al. *Preaching the Story*. Philadelphia: Fortress, 1980.

Chapter Fourteen

Prophesying Daughters (Acts 2:17)
Women in the American Pulpit

CAROLYN ANN KNIGHT

> "The Lord speaks; many, many women spread the good news."
>
> PS 68:11 NET

> "The Lord doth give the saying, the female proclaimers [are] a numerous host."
>
> PS 68:11 YLT

> "The sermon/service is different when there is a Woman in the Pulpit!"
>
> CAROL M. NOREN

> "The twenty-first century will be the century for black women in ministry. In ever-increasing numbers they are announcing their calls to the gospel ministry and making haste to establish themselves in viable ministries throughout this country. Their presence in all levels of ordained Christian service-including preaching and pastoral ministries—promises to reshape our understanding of traditional clergy leadership roles, tilt us even more toward a neo-pentecostal fervor in the way we have church, and provide us with new and creative ways of addressing problems within the community."
>
> CLEOPHUS J. LARUE

> "As more women enter the pulpit, the men will move on to more important matters in the Church!"
>
> KELLY MILLER SMITH SR.

ON ANY GIVEN SUNDAY, in churches and synagogues around this nation, there is now the aroma of perfume and the sight of pearls and pumps in the pulpit. This aroma and sight is an indication of the powerful presence of women in the pulpit, transforming the church; enriching the preaching ministry; challenging antiquated notions and traditions about who is authorized to speak about, for, and on behalf of God; and changing the way that sermons are heard and experienced. But this is not new.

Since this symposium began, almost every presenter has suggested the presence of women as prophets, preachers (itinerant or pastoral), and evangelists. We know that from the earliest days of preaching in the church, women have ignored what the historian Edwin Gaustad calls "the restraining anchor, the unyielding institution, the bastion of male domination that had behind it the force of centuries-old traditions usually reinforced by a 'thus saith the Lord' in order to claim their right to preach."[1]

We know that the history of clergywomen in America formally dates from 1656, when British Quaker "Public Friends" Mary Fisher and Ann Austin landed in the Massachusetts Bay Colony—only to be arrested, imprisoned, examined for marks of witchcraft, and shipped back to England. We know the name of Anne Hutchinson, who in 1634 challenged the long-held principle that women must be silent. Those of us who make a steady diet of reading on this subject are familiar historically with a litany of names of preaching women—far too lengthy for this presentation—who are the bridge on which future female proclaimers have crossed.

But the path of women preachers in the twentieth and early years of the twenty-first century can best be categorized by the familiar statement: "The more things change, the more they remain the same!" To be sure, women are answering the call to preach in almost every Christian denomination and among conservative and reformed Jewish traditions. To be sure, women are enrolling in and graduating from seminary and Bible colleges in numbers equal to and in some cases surpassing their male

---

1. Gaustad, *Religious History of America*, 385.

colleagues. To be sure, in most congregations on Sunday or whenever the people gather for worship, it is no longer strange, unique, or unheard of for there to be a female presence in the pulpit.

Nevertheless, the path, position, and place of women who proclaim the gospel in this generation/century is just as challenging as those pioneering and trail-blazing women of previous centuries. It may no longer be the case that women who dare to preach in the twentieth and twenty-first centuries are imprisoned, accused of heresy, and burned at the stake; yet there are still struggles and challenges that make the calling to preach for women in this modern era a burdensome blessing.

In my preparation for this presentation, I understood that I was free to approach the topic as I saw fit. For me, that necessitates sharing some of the details of my own preaching journey. For my entire life, I have been in love with an institution that loved me as long as I stayed in my place. I have found that to be indeed true as an African American, but more poignantly and powerfully as a female.

On August 19, 2017, I marked thirty-nine years of preaching the gospel. I have not included the five years known in my memory as the "silent years"—between the time I was licensed to preach and my ordination into the Christian ministry. I call them the "silent years" because for that entire period I received no invitations to preach in any churches in Denver, Colorado, where I was born nor in Dallas, Texas, while I matriculated as the first woman in the religion department at Bishop College.

I have spent my entire life as a Baptist. I have held membership in the National Baptist Convention, U. S. A., as well as the Progressive Baptist and the American Baptist Conventions. To date, from my vantage point Baptists remain the most conservative denomination regarding the issue of women in ministry, second only to the Church of God in Christ. I remained a Baptist largely because my family has always been Baptist, but also as I grew in the church I found characteristics of the denomination that I could affirm and appreciate.

Mind you, this was all before I went to the pastor of my church to talk to him about being called to preach, which I thought it biblical to do at the age of twelve. I believed that I was doing what Jesus did. Until that time I was unaware of any prohibitions, restrictions, or hindrances regarding women preachers. Truly, I had never seen or heard a woman preach, but I was sure that there had to be women preachers somewhere in the world in other churches.

Since I was only twelve, at that time I was only allowed to ride my bicycle up and down the block. When we went to church, we went where our parents took us. However, when I went to my pastor with my big announcement and he responded "that God did not call women to preach," it was not the earth-shattering, dream-destroying news that one might think. I don't remember being crushed or upset, or feeling a sense of indignation or outrage. I simply moved on to the next profession that I had thought would be best suited for me. At the age of twelve there were a few things that I thought I would like to be in life, including a professional football player for the Denver Broncos, another dream that would be dashed. But at the age of twelve, I continued on with my life as a young girl growing up in Denver, Colorado.

On a Sunday afternoon in June, the missionaries of our church hosted a program and invited evangelist Mae Buchanan to speak. She was not called Reverend and not allowed in the pulpit, yet she still preached a sermon in every sense of the word. On that day, I heard the Word of God delivered in the form of a female, and I could not shake the voice and visual image of what I had experienced. I knew *that* was preaching. So, I sought out the counsel of M. C. Williams, who not only recommended that I attend Bishop College, but he also guided my admission process. So instead of enrolling at the University of Colorado, I headed to Bishop College. And that has made all the difference!

All of my preaching life, I have held this belief that preaching is the most important ministry of the church and thus should be its highest priority. This is not to minimize all of the other ministries of the church, but rather is to affirm that God chose "the foolishness of preaching" to save and transform individuals, churches, countries, and nations. I further believe that in doing so, from the inception of preaching, God has used both males and females.

After all of these years, I continue to have challenging and interesting experiences in preaching. In one week in August I preached before five of the female bishops in the United Methodist Church, as well as in a Baptist pulpit in Georgia where no woman had ever preached before. Such is the continued journey of women who preach. Recently, I was told by a young man whom I see every morning at LA Fitness, "You could probably get a date if you would stop telling people that you are a preacher." To which I replied, "It is going to come out at some point. Why not at the beginning?"

In 2000 Jana Childers wrote, "Preaching is a mother who conceives and gives birth to faith."[2] It's a surprising metaphor. "Preaching" and "mother" were not exactly love-and-marriage, horse-and-carriage words in the sixteenth century, nor in most of the centuries before and since. Even now, when half the students going to mainline seminaries are women, there are those who wonder about the pairing of words. What do mothers know about preaching? Do women have anything new to say about preaching? Is God really calling women to preach? I remember the days when these questions were reluctantly answered, "If God can use a donkey, He can use anybody, or as God said, the rocks would cry out!" That women are answering the call to preach is planned in the sovereignty of an almighty God, who knows far better than any male or female what is needed in the church and pulpit.

The last century and early years of this one have witnessed tremendous shifts in women's ways of preaching. Women are a richly diverse group of preachers. There is not now, nor has there ever been, "a style" that would include all women preachers, for they are richly diverse in substance, style, and delivery. Some are manuscript preachers, and others preach extemporaneously. Some preach in a still, small voice, while others whoop and holler. The way women approach preaching is through story, testimony, and biblical exposition. At the same time, however, women possess a diversity of preaching personalities.

To use the model suggested by Thomas G. Long in *The Witness of Preaching*, some women are pastoral, some are priestly, while others are prophetic. One can observe many styles of preaching when the preacher is a woman. Women, like men, are not a monolithic group in preparation or presentation. Instead, they are a diverse group. It is no longer true that one represents the whole.

I remember not long ago that when a woman stood to preach, and for whatever reason, she had a bad or off day, the sermon did not hit its intended target, or land appropriately on the ear, that was used as an indication to some that God did not call women to preach. That would certainly not be said today. Women who preach should not be exalted or condemned for being preachers. Instead, the message should speak for itself.

Now obviously, one way of noting the significance of prophesying women is by mentioning where their gifts and voices are at work in the

---

2. Childers, *Birthing the Sermon*.

church, the nation, and the world. Many women across denominational lines are gifted orators and expositors who use their preaching gifts to lead not only the local church, but also people on the national and denominational level. I feel it important in this presentation to name these women because, as in the Scriptures, women are too often left unnamed and unmentioned. Now mind you, this is my list. I am sure you have names that should be included. Just for your information, I want to especially mention two of my personal "sheroes," Barbara Jordan and Dorothy Height, both of whom throughout their careers wrote about being discouraged from pursuing the preaching ministry.

- Barbara Brown Taylor is perhaps the most gifted and celebrated woman preacher among us today. She served for many years as the rector of an Episcopal church in Atlanta before returning to the classroom to teach religion.
- Joan Brown Campbell, a gifted preacher, served as the first General Secretary for the National Council of Churches.
- Naomi Levy is the first female rabbi to lead a conservative Jewish congregation.
- Suzan Johnson Cook served as the first female president of the historic Hampton Minister's Conference.
- Sharon E. Watkins served for twelve years as the first female president of the Disciples of Christ Christian Church. She was succeeded in that by Terri Hord Owens.
- Vashti McKenzie was elected the first female bishop in the AME Church and was the first woman to serve as president of the council of Bishops.
- In 2016 the United Methodist Church significantly added to their number of female bishops by electing a historic number. These women joined Leontine Kelly and others who were elected before them.
- Traci Blackmon, the recently elected Executive Minister of Justice and Witness Ministries of the United Church of Christ, represented her denomination at the World Council of Churches.
- Jasmine Rose Smothers, a young gifted African American woman, is the lead pastor at the predominantly white historic First Atlanta United Methodist Church.

- Vashti McKenzie and Cynthia L. Hale had prominent roles in both of President Barack Obama's presidential terms.
- Gina M. Stewart is 2nd-vice president of the Lott Carey Convention and in line to become its first female president in 2021.
- Amy Butler, a graduate of Baylor University, is the senior pastor of the church that John D. Rockefeller built for Harry Emerson Fosdick, also known as the Riverside Church in New York City. All of these women, beyond what other gifts they may possess in administration, teaching and counseling, are among this nation's most gifted preachers.

And time would fail me to tell of Johnnie Coleman, Audrey Bronson, Prathia Hall, Willie Barrows, Trudie Trimm—women who were organizing pastors or stepped in and became the senior pastor of churches when their fathers or husbands passed away. Evangelist Rose Marie Rinsom-Brown once served alongside the late Bishop Gilbert E. Patterson. Evangelist Joyce Rodgers serves on the national and international level of the Church of God in Christ. Paula White, Juanita Bynum, Jackie McCullough, and Joyce Meyer are women preachers who have gained reputations in Pentecostal and Charismatic circles.

Women are now teaching preaching and serving as deans and presidents of seminaries. All of these dynamics are shaping the way that we will be doing church well into the twenty-first century. What does that mean for preaching?

Will preaching be better? Hopefully. I believe that on most days, all of our preaching is perhaps not as good as it should be and not as bad as it could be. We can all work to be better, more faithful and relevant proclaimers of this Treasure in earthen vessels.

Women in the pulpit have been transformational and relational. I believe that women should seek to be biblical and intentional in their preaching. Will it give those who listen to us preach a greater understanding of who God is, both male and female? Yes, it will. Will it expand our understanding and use of pulpit language with softer, more nurturing metaphors, similes, and illustrations? Yes, it will.

The woman who comes to ministry and preaching today has many advantages that those early voices simply did not have. For one, there is a rich repository of literature that chronicles the history, struggles, and sacrifices of pioneering women preachers. There are many, many rich biographies, testimonies, and sermons written by and about women that any person looking for a foundation on which to stand and a point of departure to launch should take advantage. There are any number of conferences that focus on preaching for women.

The woman preacher who is serious about her calling should take advantage of every occasion to read about or listen to other women preach. Barbara Brown Taylor's *The Preaching Life, Leaving Church,* and *An Altar in the World* should be required reading for any preacher, regardless of gender. *This Is My Story: Testimonies and Sermons of Black Women in Ministry,* edited by Cleophus J. LaRue, is a powerful volume of stories told by preaching women. *Birthing the Sermon: Women Preachers on the Creative Process,* edited by Jana Childers, is a helpful volume for anyone interested in understanding how women prepare sermons. *Just a Sister Away* by Renita Weems, *The Power To Speak* by Rebecca Chopp, and *Texts of Terror* by Phyllis Trible are important volumes by three female biblical scholars that are helpful for all preachers. There are sermons to be read and studied in Ella Pearson Mitchell's groundbreaking multi-volume *Those Preaching Women.* I could go on and on about resources that are written by women preachers and chronicle their many contributions.[3]

Now, for just a few moments allow me to address some of the challenges that women who preach must face even in today's ministry. I believe that the greatest challenge to preaching women is still the question of authority. The problem of full inclusion, acceptance, licensing, and ordination is still a major problem for most women. Women who are called by God are still subjected to male pastors, boards, or ecclesiastical committees that challenge their authority to serve in the local church.

As a Baptist preacher, I came to understand this problem when I understood the centrality of the pulpit in the Baptist church and the location of the Communion table. In most Baptist churches (keep in mind that my experience involves black Baptist congregations), this is what the person in the pew observes: there is the Communion table, pulpit, baptismal pool, cross. All of these are strong symbols of the Baptist faith. For far too long, the person who stood behind the sacred desk as the visible representative of God and the one authorized to speak for Him was male. Given that the language of the Bible, the hymnbook, creeds, and

---

3. See Kienzle and Walker, *Women Preachers and Prophets*; LaRue, *This Is My Story*; Schneider and Schneider, *In Their Own Right*; Taylor, *Preaching Life*; Weems, *Just a Sister Away*; Chopp, *Power to Speak*; Trible, *Texts of Terror*; Mitchell, *Those Preaching Women.*

literature were primarily masculine, the presence of the woman in the pulpit has been seen and experienced as a disruptive intrusion to the way things have always been. This is why Carol M. Noren opens her definitive work, *The Woman in the Pulpit*, with these words: "The sermon/service is different when there is a woman in the pulpit."[4]

In other words, adjustments must be made and resistance must be overcome. Far too many women have had the experience of seeing someone, male or female, walk out of the sanctuary when it is announced that a woman is the preacher for that day. In my own preaching life, I received help for this from an unlikely source. On one occasion I was listening to Joyce Meyer, a noted evangelist, on television. She was talking about how hurt and devastated she used to be when someone would walk out on her preaching. She said that she prayed and prayed about it, and the answer that she received was that she knew that she had received a word from the Lord. She knew it was a relevant word, timely word. She knew that she had studied, prepared, and prayed, so the person who was walking out was missing out on a word they needed to hear. I found that helpful in my preaching life.

The congregation experiences certain visual, aural, and oral differences when the preacher is female. So, adjustments have to be made in the way that the sermon is heard and received. In some ways, there are expectations of the woman in the pulpit that men are not asked to endure. Many times I have looked out into the congregation to see someone gesturing for me to smile. I am convinced that the female presence in the pulpit enhances and enriches Christian proclamation, but it also reveals a more complete and fuller expression of a sovereign God, a faithful church, and a more just world.

Now we all know that at its very heart—preaching is preaching. Specific rules in preaching and a structure in preaching must be followed, whether the preacher is male or female, black or white, young or old. Some clear-cut guidelines must be followed, or what we are doing is simply not preaching. Preaching must begin with God. We speak because God has spoken, and until God speaks, we simply have nothing to say. Our preaching does not cause God to show up; instead, we preach because God is already present.

At the same time, however, I believe women must be deliberate and intentional of making use in their preaching of those biblical texts in

---

4. Noren, *Woman in the Pulpit*.

which women are named and the central characters of the story. And as a matter of integrity, women must be faithful to also preach those texts that do not always cast women in a positive light.

Women preaching today have the freedom to preach on a wide range of subjects, but they should be mindful of issues men and women in the pew need to hear that can best be addressed by a female preacher. Several years ago, I served on the board of the Breast Examination Center of Harlem, whose mission it was to encourage women of color, particularly the poor, to do monthly breast exams and get annual mammograms when they were scheduled or required. As we began to take our campaign to the churches in Harlem, all of the pastors who were male were receptive to the need for such a campaign, but at the same time they were reluctant to talk about "breasts" from the pulpit. The campaign was less than successful. Who better to address breast and ovarian cancer, domestic violence, abuse of children by sexual predators, and poverty among children and youth than the woman in the pulpit?

Again, this is not to suggest that women should be restricted to preach on "women issues" or even exclusively on "women's days." Furthermore, it is not to suggest that male preachers cannot deal faithfully and adequately with these issues. Women have much to say about race, war, politics, money and sin, as well as white supremacy and misogyny in high places. They are free to preach on these issues as God so leads, but other issues have not and will not get the attention needed unless women as preachers address them. Women have something to say on every issue and in every circumstance. Thus, women should not be and must not be limited in their preaching to any subject.

The primary tool for preaching is the Bible. Women bring to the hermeneutical process a critical lens through which all texts must pass. Recently, I struggled in my seat as a male preacher preached a sermon about Job. In talking about how Job lost everything, I sensed in my homiletical stomach where this sermon was headed. And he went there indeed. When he got to the portion about Job's wife, he was critical of her remarks to Job. He called her a "foolish woman" for questioning God. I always say when I hear this passage treated this way, "Wait a minute, preacher; hold on here! This is a mother who carried and buried ten children!"

In recent days, our hearts have been torn as we have watched far too many mothers leave one child not on the college campus but in the cold cemetery. Who could blame the mother of Trayvon Martin, Sandra

Bland, or twelve-year-old Tamir Rice if they had some questions of God about how their children died?

Women bring a different hermeneutic to those biblical texts that are confusing and troubling, such as, "Women keep silent in the church. . . . Ask your husbands at home." What?! Fifty to sixty-five percent of African American women in the pews on Sunday morning have no husband at home! Or Paul says, "Women will be saved in child-bearing." What? What about the woman in the pew who cannot have children or has suffered multiple miscarriages? Indeed, women are challenged to read and discover anew a fresh meaning in these texts. Avoiding texts that we find objectionable are not helpful for the preacher or the people in the pew. We can approach these texts determined to gain and hear something meaningful from them.

Women who preach wrestle with the biblical texts from different worldviews. For some, it is a feminist worldview that tackles the issues of gender and equality in every text. For others, it is a womanist worldview that also tackles those topics but goes further in addressing issues of race, class, power, and culture as well.

Christine M. Smith, who at the time of this writing was an associate professor of preaching and worship at United Theological Seminary of the Twin Cities in New Brighton, Minnesota, authored a book in 1991 that I believe provides many helpful metaphors for understanding the significance of women's ways of preaching. I am not suggesting that men who preach cannot find these metaphors helpful, but I do believe that for women they are helpful in understanding preaching that is biblical, intentional, and relational. Although dated in some ways and far ahead of some of the situations that we are encountering in a post-911 world, I believe that what Smith suggests can be extrapolated to our homiletical needs today. In *Preaching as Weeping, Confession and Resistance: Radical Responses to Radical Evil*, Smith states that she hopes in a world filled with so much human suffering, inequity, injustice, and oppression, the preacher will see preaching as weeping—not the manipulative or condescending type of weeping, nor the despairing, hopeless type of weeping—but the type of weeping that touches the deepest passions, strongest emotions, and greatest aspirations of our lives.

This, I believe, is what Bettye Collier Thomas was speaking about in her definite work *Daughters of Thunder* when she encouraged women who preach to seek to present their audience with strategies for understanding and living with the tension between what is—human imperfection, injustice, suffering—and what God calls creation to be—a creation in which human live righteous, harmonious lives in their relations with God and with other human beings. While never denying the reality of human suffering, these preaching women offer powerful messages that all humans can overcome the imperfections, both spiritual and temporal.[5]

Wherever and whenever I observe significant, powerful preaching women, those I have observed who are doing preaching at its best understand it is preaching as weeping that engages the deepest passions, highest values, and surest convictions of those of us who preach and make them alive and present in the moment of proclamation. Again, I am not suggesting that this is not true when the preacher is male, but it is something that I look for in preaching women. What Collier noted was true of women preachers in the past, as well as the sermons preached by women today. They must speak the truth about those unnamed, unheard, and unspoken issues that men and women in the pew wrestle with week in and week out. Indeed, people come to church on Sunday and other times throughout the week expecting that the preacher has heard something from God about their situation. Women preachers must speak the truth about the reality of the ugly, horrible, terrible situation we all find ourselves in, while extending the hope that is possible.

Finally, I believe in preaching. I believe that until the Lord Jesus Christ returns for the church and we all are gathered in the "house not made with hands," there will be preaching. Women and men will continue to participate in this great fraternity/sorority until preaching is no longer necessary. Until then, it does not yet appear what we shall be.

Bibliography

Childers, Jana, ed. *Birthing the Sermon: Women Preachers on the Creative Process*. St. Louis: Chalice, 2001.

Chopp, Rebecca. *The Power to Speak: Feminism, Language, God*. Eugene, OR: Wipf & Stock, 2002.

Collier-Thomas, Bettye. *Daughters of Thunder: Black Women Preachers and Their Sermons, 1850–1979*. Hoboken, NJ: Jossey-Bass, 1998.

Gaustad, Edwin S. *The Religious History of America: The Heart of the American Story from Colonial Times to Today*. San Francisco: HarperOne, 2004.

5. Collier-Thomas, *Daughters of Thunder*.

Kienzle, Beverly Mayne, and Pamela J. Walker. *Women Preachers and Prophets through Two Millennia of Christianity*. Berkeley: University of California Press, 1998.
LaRue, Cleophus J., ed. *This Is My Story: Testimonies and Sermons of Black Women in Ministry*. Louisville: Westminster/John Knox, 2005.
Mitchell, Ella Pearson, ed. *Those Preaching Women*. Vol. 4. Valley Forge, PA: Judson, 2004.
Noren, Carol M. *The Woman in the Pulpit*. Nashville: Abingdon, 1992.
Schneider, Carl J., and Dorothy Schneider. *In Their Own Right: The History of American Clergy Women*. St. Louis: Crossroad, 1997.
Taylor, Barbara Brown. *The Preaching Life*. Cambridge, MA: Crowley, 1993.
Trible, Phyllis. *Texts of Terror: Literary-Feminist Readings of Biblical Narratives*. UK: SCM, 2003.
Weems, Renita. *Just a Sister Away: A Womanist Vision of Women's Relationships in the Bible*. Publishing/Editing Network, 1988.

Chapter Fifteen

Predicting the Next Trends in Evangelical Preaching

Retrospect and Prospect

Dennis L. Phelps

Forecasting the future is fraught with dangers, especially as a novice. Not only am I not a prophet or the son of a prophet, but I have also worked for non-profits all my life. Like Paul the Apostle, I can honestly admit that God has not given me a final word on this issue. I will leave to younger homileticians to judge my accuracy in twenty to twenty-five years. Nevertheless, I offer some reasonable speculation for our consideration—some more reasonable, some more speculative.

For this journey one could look to Canada for evangelical responses to highly secularized social contexts, South America for attraction of evangelical Pentecostal expressions, Africa for evangelical community connectedness, and Asia for evangelical responses to multi-faith challenges and political hostility. However, the following thoughts focus on American Evangelical preaching.

Who Is an Evangelical in America?

Ed Stetzer (now of Wheaton College, formerly of LifeWay Research) and Leith Anderson (of the National Association of Evangelicals) offer the three parameters used in this consideration for evangelicalism. The parameters are denominational affiliation, self-identification, and confessed personal beliefs. (Political and social views do not provide the basis for this identification as an evangelical.)[1] By this definition, approximately one-third of Christians in the USA are evangelical, with nearly 24 percent of all adults under the age of thirty (this number has increased several percentage points since 2007). It includes more than forty-five thousand congregations from over forty different denominations, and millions of Christians.[2] This is no small slice of American religious culture. Evangelicals in America distinguish themselves from traditional fundamentalists by history, views toward formal education, science, culture, and general attitude toward others.

First, we'll cover a brief review of the past seventy-five years of evangelical preaching (in other words, the retrospect part of this assignment). Haddon Robinson's survey published in the September 2006 issue of the *Journal of the Evangelical Homiletics Society* proves helpful.[3]

American Evangelical Preaching in Retrospect

In the forties and early fifties, evangelicals emphasized topical evangelistic preaching. Sunday night services were often directed toward the unconverted. In contrast to today, public invitations to receive Christ were offered at all services, including the mid-week prayer gathering. Annual week-long spring and/or fall revivals (often including early morning and even midday services) featured evangelistic preaching. Billy Graham broke through as the evangelical preacher on the national and international stage. The assumption was that many unconverted people with Protestant backgrounds were responsive to an opportunity to attend a special service with a friend or family member.

During the fifties, John Ockenga served as an institutional organizer for Neo-Evangelicalism and Carl F. Henry began articulating the theology. If Billy Graham was the pleading passionate voice (declaring, "The Bible says"), Henry was the heart and disciplined mind of American

---

1. Anderson and Stetzer, "Defining Evangelicals"; and "Who Are Evangelicals?"; National Association of Evangelicals, "NAE, LifeWay Research"; Bauder et al., *Four Views*.

2. National Association of Evangelicals, "NAE, LifeWay Research"; Strachen, "Signs of Evangelical Life"; Duduit, "Preaching"; Anderson and Stetzer, "Who Are Evangelicals?"; National Association of Evangelicals, "About NAE."

3. Robinson, "Preaching Trends," 23–28.

Evangelicalism. Preachers began to emphasize Bible teaching over evangelism. Bible churches offered a response to the totalitarian Communist threat and attracted many Christians who felt marginalized by their traditional church homes.

The shadows of World War I, World War II, Hiroshima, Nagasaki, and the threat of the Korean conflict caused many evangelicals to question the value of personal application to change the stubborn human condition. A fatalism was adopted by some. This planted seeds for an evangelical infatuation with eschatology and end-time prophecy to deliver believers from the broken and destructive world systems. This evangelical Bible preaching/teaching often followed a verse-by-verse strategy. An interpretation of the newspaper headlines and a grand scheme of deliverance (displayed with charts) and victory was emphasized, while personal application was discounted or even ignored in the sermon. Tragically, this lack of application and grappling with (rather than escaping) current issues produced an inadequate foundation to respond to the American social issues of the sixties. As Robinson notes, some of these churches could explain the will of God for a man's hair or a woman's skirt but could not apply God's Word to the walls of separation between races. Into this context, Clyde Fant Jr. and Bill Pinson released their thirteen-volume *20 Centuries of Great Preaching*, with interest on evaluating the ethical content and social application of many well-known preachers.[4]

The rejection of most forms of authority during the sixties pushed the evangelical preacher into a crisis. How could the preacher speak an authoritative message from God without an authoritative, objective outside source for the message? Religion generally and Christianity specifically became suspect. The challenge became demonstrating that the Scriptures are true, trustworthy, and relevant. Listeners needed to be brought to the Scriptures from their life experiences. The preacher was caught on the horns of a dilemma by the rise of the secular society. How could the evangelical preacher communicate as one without authority (as observed by Fred Craddock),[5] yet not surrender the evangelical affirmation of Scripture as authoritative?

The late sixties and seventies witnessed an unexpected response to these strategies. Demographics of idealistic but curious Baby Boomers fueled the so-called "Jesus Revolution." The West Coast Fuller Seminary

---

4. Fant and Pinson, *Twenty Centuries of Great Preaching*.
5. Craddock, *As One without Authority*.

(founded by Ockenga) strategy of homogenous units appealed to American pragmatism and evangelicalism, inaugurating an explosive evangelical church growth movement that moved across the nation for over a decade. However, the use of homogenous units reinforced the segmenting of evangelicals into ages, races, and cultures.

In the eighties and nineties, evangelical preaching moved toward a therapeutic model to respond to the increasing communicative and pastoral care dilemma. Was evangelical preaching finally catching up with Harry Emerson Fosdick? Felt needs became the starting point for sermons. Topical problem-solution preaching replaced verse-by-verse Bible teaching. Although previous evangelicals practiced topical preaching, their topics were primarily theological and doctrinal. The topics during this time period were life-oriented and practical. Behavioral science often supplanted theological content. Rather than answering "Is this true to the Bible?" the question became "Does this work?" Sermon "take-aways" overshadowed textual exegesis. The expectation was that the message would provide the listener with a way to make it through the next week. As David Buttrick observes, the sermon's authority shifted from the Scriptures and orthodox theology to the experience and perception of the listener.[6] Listeners determined the authority of the message based on its appropriateness and relevance for their life situations.

Into this dilemma, Haddon Robinson released *Biblical Preaching: The Development and Delivery of Expository Messages*. The result was to relocate the authority of evangelical preaching from the listener or the preacher and place it back in the Bible text.[7]

From the nineties through the early years of the twenty-first century, leadership or entrepreneurial tasks were added to the expectations of the evangelical preacher. The responsibility of preaching God's Word was called upon often to serve programmatic tasks. For too many, an office replaced the pastor's study. The latest business models replaced the biblical models. Vision and mission statements replaced theological confessions. Sermons often promoted a vision rather than expounded Scripture passages. Sermons were expected to inspire rather than apply and convict, affirm rather than teach and correct.

---

6. Buttrick, *Homiletic*.
7. Robinson, *Biblical Preaching*.

American Evangelical Preaching in Prospect

The American Culture

First, let's consider the emerging cultural context(s) in twenty to twenty-five years. Today's Millennials will be in their fifties. American culture will be led by older Busters, Millennials, and a generation of adult ZenGenners.

This will be a future with driverless electric Tesla cars (using the Google Waze app version 32.0) ordered via Amazon, with capacities monitored and adjustable through wireless software updates as needed. It is a future with roboticized factories and fast-food restaurants, iPhone watches integrated with Alexa version 18, and drone deliveries of commodities (fine-tuned for use during natural disasters).

It remains an era of tribal identity and ideology rather than individuality, rationality, or linear logic. This will increase social polarization and regionalism. Some may describe it as a period of social upheaval like the sixties. America may have traveled back to the future. However, catalytic events (such as international military conflict, economic restructuring, sectarian political upheaval from disillusionment with the historical major two-party system, or a spiritual awakening) may galvanize the culture into deeper unity. People will hunger for sanctuaries—safe places to experience community, hope, and healing.

Historically, the major cities on both coasts (e.g., New York City and Los Angeles) initiate popular trends in the USA. Those trends (during months to years) move across to the Upper Midwest and then down the Mississippi River. However, with increasing occurrence, social trends are less dependent on geography and more dependent on timeliness, creativity, visibility, and digital accessibility. This seems true for trends in evangelical preaching.

In the USA there will be no ethnic majority population.[8] We will observe the increasing secularization of social structures, but there will remain a significantly devout religious population. This religious population will reflect extreme pluralism across the religious spectrum.

---

8. Anderson, "United States of Minorities."

The Evangelical Church

What about the ecclesiastical context(s) in twenty to twenty-five years? What might our evangelical churches be like?

The pastors of current evangelical megachurches will be off the scene in twenty to twenty-five years. Most of these congregations will have struggled to navigate the leadership transition effectively because of the nature of the personal charisma of their current pastoral leaders. This has been consistent historically. Nevertheless, other leaders will have arisen and a few new megachurches will have emerged.

Evangelicalism will be more diverse theologically, ethnically, and socially.[9] It will resist withdrawing or capitulating from culture and engage other world religions. There will be less distinctions between urban and suburban churches (caused by urban regentrification).[10] More Latinos, Asians, and African-Americans will identify as evangelicals, increasing the presence of multilingual evangelical congregations.[11] Multigenerational congregations will overshadow the currently niched, generation-specific evangelical gatherings.[12] Pastoral ministry models will vary from pastor as resident theologian, pastor as community organizer, pastor as community shepherd to pastor as pragmatic executive. Could it be that the evangelical church of the future will be more like a rich Louisiana Cajun gumbo rather than a cafeteria with separated entrées? Could it be that evangelicalism will rediscover an Acts 2 model for following Jesus?

It is possible that there will be fewer total churches of any type. The number of new churches planted annually continues to be outstripped by the number of churches that close down. However, there will be an increase in mid-(two hundred to eight hundred worshippers) to large-sized (eight hundred to seventeen hundred worshippers) evangelical churches because of scales of economy, ministry options, entrepreneurial leadership, deeper sense of community, social safety, community influence, and clear faith identity.

Growing evangelical churches will have rediscovered their local communities and engaged them through redemptive expressions of

---

9. Roach, "Pew"; Scharf et al., "Homiletics Forum," 18; Zoll, "Survey"; Kim, "Three Homiletical Challenges," 10–12.

10. Anderson, "Inside Out Donut."

11. Roach, "Pew"; Anderson, "United States of Minorities."

12. National Association of Evangelicals, "Attending Church with Other Generations."

compassion. These congregations will be viewed as family redemption centers, outposts of hope in the midst of despair, and beacons of light in the midst of darkness. They will offer answers to and pathways of recovery from empty and self-destructive narcissism. These islands of personal and community refreshing will give attention to family relationships, spiritual formation, life-coaching, and character development.[13] The work will involve helping Christians look like Jesus in their daily relationships so that society will receive the good news of Jesus. They will seek to be change agents on the personal, familial, community, and international levels, offering biblical bases for social action and alternatives to totalistic government approaches. They will be seeking or experiencing another spiritual renewal in society.[14]

People will exhibit a higher expectation of evangelical churches to be places of truthfulness (not just Bible facts) and discussions about local cultural realities. They will support a high view of preaching in local church ministry. The underlying question will be, is it true? The idealism and hope of the twenty-first century was quickly hit in the gut on 9/11, followed by uncontrollable natural disasters on a massive scale, and have given way to a raw and messy realism throughout these evangelicals' lives. The missional churches led by these evangelicals will seek to be salt in a tasteless society and light in a dark world.

However, lest we break out the new wine and prepare to celebrate the revealing of the millennial reign of Christ, there are signs of a few other reasonable developments for American evangelicalism. It will struggle to separate the evangelical identity from the baggage of sectarian politics and Anglo-centered agendas. The pressure to redefine the historical core theology of the "evangelical" will grow.

Moreover, in twenty to twenty-five years, engaged evangelical missional communities will be under increasing convictional pressure from the surrounding culture. Evangelicals will be seen increasingly as nonconformists, especially with their assertion of an objective basis for moral absolutes and eternal salvation possible exclusively through Jesus Christ's work on the cross. Evangelicalism will become more of a foreign sound to the secular post-Christendom, post-modern relativism. This will feed a continued decline in nominal and cultural Christianity. The social price to identify as an evangelical Christian will continue to increase. The

---

13. Barna, "New Generation of Pastors"; Kim, "Three Homiletical Challenges," 14–15; Lane, "Training the Trainers," 24–25; Brooks, *Road to Character*.

14. Barna, "Six Megathemes."

personal inconvenience, discomfort, and even social suffering will continue. This pressure may stimulate a broader return to a more classical, pre-modern Christianity in order to offer a proven anchor in the midst of the cultural storm.

These mid-twenty-first century evangelical churches will hunger for shepherds with knowledge and wisdom to lead them. From where will these shepherds come? What might these evangelical preachers look like?

Evangelical Theological Education

There are persistent signs of a major shift in evangelical theological education and ministry preparation. These include shifts in lifestyle, demographics, accessibility, and financial models. Many of today's students bring minimal church background or experience with them to seminary. Often they've experienced fractured families and no exposure to congregational life, and came to Christ while they were university students. They come to seminary as recent converts with little Bible or theological knowledge but rather theological curiosity.

There is also an increase in bi-vocational and second-career pastors (due to an unwillingness to relocate, smaller congregations, and predictable financial security), as well as the use of collaborative preaching teams who share the responsibilities of proclamation.[15] Many of these preachers are self-taught in communicative skills and strategies, imitating models from podcasts, web streaming, conferences, and other accessible venues. Many evangelical preachers look to models like Russell Moore (cultural engagement, social and political perspectives); David Platt (missional engagement and global focus with thousands attending "Secret Church" satellite broadcasts through the night with almost unbroken linear Bible exposition); Al Mohler and John Piper (theology); and Matt Chandler and Francis Chan (daily life engagement, authenticity). This pattern of imitation is not new.

However, in twenty-five years, more evangelical pastoral candidates will develop their preaching gifts within a personal mentoring relationship with an older, experienced pastor.[16] Prospective traditional students, encumbered with increased pre-existing debt, will question the necessity,

---

15. Barna, "Aging of America's Pastors."
16. Scharf et al., "Homiletics Forum," 4–5; Barna, "Aging of America's Pastors."

relevance, and financial stewardship of formal ministry preparation.[17] This will be especially true for non-Anglo evangelicals. The number of full-time student equivalents and resident students will continue to decrease. More students who do choose to enroll will opt for the shorter, less expensive MA rather than the traditional MDiv with its core of basic theology, Bible study, and pastoral ministry instruction (including preaching). The MDiv will become the exception rather than the rule for seminary students preparing for a preaching ministry. Some schools will continue decreasing the credit hours necessary for a basic MDiv. There will be fewer seminary-trained evangelical preachers.

Pressure will continue to build for online programs and multiple delivery platforms.[18] Technology and personnel costs will continue to increase. Pressures will increase from national and regional accrediting agencies, reflecting increased involvement of the federal Department of Education in private education. There will be a scramble for increased endowments, denominational financial support, individual donors, and student scholarships. Smaller and more vulnerable institutions will merge with larger and more stable institutions. The future for the residential training of evangelical preachers will swing toward schools with strong endowments for faculty salaries, creative and flexible instructional delivery platforms, dependable and contemporary technology applications, responsive degree plans, and deep student scholarships. These challenges will move homiletical training closer to local church contexts and reduce the number of resident professors of homiletics at evangelical seminaries.

Evangelical Preaching

What about the preaching of these evangelical pastors in twenty to twenty-five years? Evangelical preaching by definition declares a basic theological core.[19] The preaching will retain a focus on the New Testament *kerygma*—the gospel without adjectives (e.g., social, prosperity, full). This includes the call to personal repentance from sin, expression of sincere faith in the person and work of Jesus, the necessity of individual

---

17. Barna, "New Generation of Pastors"; Scharf et al., "Homiletics Forum," 27–28.
18. Scharf et al., "Homiletics Forum," 27–28.
19. Scharf et al., "Homiletics Forum," 20, 23, 24–25, 29–30.

conversion to Christ, and demonstration of compassionate love toward others.[20]

The current growth in context-less social communication may challenge biblical preaching and reflect a context-less approach to the Scriptures. To address Bible illiteracy, exposition of Bible texts will continue as a method.[21] The forms will be both topical and textually consecutive. Preachers will work to stay true to the intended, plain authorial meaning and purpose, aware that the text meant *something* to the original hearers, so it cannot mean now what it never meant then. The sermon will move meaningfully between the historical and contemporary significance of the Bible text.

Linguistic philosophy will also grow in its contribution to homiletical hermeneutics, especially with the contribution of Speech-Act Theory, understanding not only the author's intended meaning but also the intended action within the original social and rhetorical context.[22] The rich textures of the Old Testament will ascend with their narrative theology, prophetic challenges, poetry for spiritual formation, and foundation for understanding Jesus and the New Testament. Preachers will continue to struggle with Christocentric interpretation, cross-centric interpretation, and application of Old Testament texts in light of the original author's intended meaning and purpose.

Prophetic preaching will rise in response to the secular hostility toward evangelical preaching. This prophetic preaching will be missional and incarnational, validated by the church's partial participation in the surrounding culture. Full participation in the culture will be resisted because it would silence the evangelical preacher's prophetic voice. In contrast, the absence of participation in the culture will be resisted because it would silence the evangelical preacher's pastoral or priestly voice.[23] The prophetic message will not be only truth spoken to power but also an invitation (even a plea) for the power to surrender redemptively to Jesus as Lord. It will work to be truth spoken with love for the intended recipient.

---

20. Scharf et al., "Homiletics Forum," 25, 30.

21. Barna, "Six Megathemes"; Scharf et al., "Homiletics Forum," 7–10, 20, 23, 26, 29–30; Roach, "Pew."

22. For example, see Kuruvilla, *Ephesians*; *Genesis*; *Judges*; *Mark*; and *Privilege the Text!*, as well as critical socio-rhetorical commentaries by Ben Witherington III.

23. Barna, "Six Megathemes"; Scharf et al., "Homiletics Forum," 21–22; Fant, *Preaching for Today*.

Otherwise, the word will be mostly judgmental—righteous and true, maybe—but still, judgmental truth spoken without love for the recipient.

The preaching will be authentic, honest, without hypocrisy, natural, relational, clear, accessible, gentle, respectful, connected to actual life, engaged redemptively with the local community, and integrated with the larger sanctification concerns of spiritual transformation, discipleship, and missions.[24]

In the midst of social intolerance, evangelical preaching will be courageous in response to perceptions of non-conformity. It will be compassionate in response to hostility.[25] In the midst of religious pluralism, evangelical preaching will emphasize the uniqueness of Jesus as the only Son of God (e.g., Virgin Birth, miracles, substitutionary atonement, and actual resurrection over death).[26] Whereas biblical theology has provided the backbone of evangelical preaching for the past fifty years, systematic theology and apologetics will provide the rib cage during the next twenty-five years. It will consider which God is valid (trinitarianism), the *imago Dei* (the definition of humanness, the consistency of human nature, and implications for medical ethics, including genetic experimentation), what is sin (beyond a legal understanding, a relational dimension, and personal brokenness), what is salvation (beyond legal, relational), and the nature of church (community over programs). The human condition will remain unchanged. The nature of the Triune God will remain unchanged. And the core of evangelical preaching should remain unchanged.

Ubiquitous technological augmentation will be seamless and almost invisible. Just as initial obsession with the television and telephone inventions faded as they became common tools of life, the obsession with current technology will fade.[27]

Effective evangelical preaching will offer a reasonable framework within which to understand individual life experiences, cultural movements, and the search for meaning in the midst of chaos.[28] It will resound

---

24. Scharf et al., "Homiletics Forum," 4, 7, 18, 22–23; Kim, "Three Homiletical Challenges," 13–15; Barna, "New Generation of Pastors."

25. Scharf et al., "Homiletics Forum," 18.

26. Kim, "Three Homiletical Challenges," 10–12; Scharf et al., "Homiletics Forum," 7.

27. Scharf et al., "Homiletics Forum," 17–18.

28. Kim, "Three Homiletical Challenges," 12–13; Scharf et al., "Homiletics Forum," 7, 17–18.

with many dialects and ethnicities, within multiple cultures.[29] It will be evaluated on the basis of the kind of faith community it forms. Examples of the future of American evangelical preaching include Jared Alcántara, H. B. Charles Jr., Charlie Dates, Matthew Kim, David Eung Ryoo, and Nick Gatzke.

Bibliography

Anderson, Leith. "The Inside Out Donut: What Churches Do When Urban Poverty and Suburban Affluence Trade Places." National Association of Evangelicals (Winter 2015/16).

———. "The United States of Minorities: No Racial Majority in 2044." National Association of Evangelicals newsletter (spring/summer 2016).

Anderson, Leith, and Ed Stetzer. "Defining Evangelicals in an Election Year." *Christianity Today* (March 2, 2016).

———. "Who Are Evangelicals and Where Are They Headed?" *Today's Conversation* podcast, National Association of Evangelicals (January 15, 2016).

Barna, George. "The Aging of America's Pastors." *Research Releases in Leaders and Pastors* (March 1, 2017).

———. "A New Generation of Pastors Places Its Stamp on Ministry." *Research Releases in Leaders and Pastors* (February 17, 2004).

———. "Six Megathemes Emerge from Barna Group Research in 2010." *Research Releases in Culture and Media* (December 13, 2010).

Bauder, Kevin T., et al. *Four Views on the Spectrum of Evangelicalism*. Zondervan Counterpoints Collection. Grand Rapids, MI: Zondervan, 2011.

Brooks, David. *The Road to Character*. New York: Random House, 2015.

Buttrick, David. *Homiletic: Moves and Structures*. Minneapolis: Fortress, 1987.

Craddock, Fred B. *As One without Authority*. 4th ed. Atlanta: Chalice, 2001.

Duduit, Michael. "Preaching, the Nones and the Future of the Church: An Interview with Ed Stetzer." Preaching.com Sermons and Articles, n.d.

Fant, Clyde E., Jr., and William J. Pinson Jr. *Twenty Centuries of Great Preaching*. Waco, TX: Word, 1971. Republished as *A Treasury of Great Preaching*. Dallas: Word Publishing, 1995.

———. *Preaching for Today*. Rev. ed. New York: HarperCollins, 1987.

Kim, Matthew D. "Three Homiletical Challenges for the 21st Century." *Journal of the Evangelical Homiletics Society* 9 (September 2009) 10–12.

Kuruvilla, Abraham. *Ephesians: A Theological Commentary for Preachers*. Eugene, OR: Cascade, 2015.

———. *Genesis: A Theological Commentary for Preachers*. Eugene, OR: Resource, 2014.

———. *Judges: A Theological Commentary for Preachers*. Eugene, OR: Cascade, 2017.

———. *Mark: A Theological Commentary for Preachers*. Eugene, OR: Cascade, 2012.

———. *Privilege the Text!: A Theological Hermeneutic for Preaching*. Chicago: Moody, 2013.

---

29. Kim, "Three Homiletical Challenges," 10; Scharf et al., "Homiletics Forum," 18.

Lane, Adrian. "Training the Trainers of Tomorrow's Preachers: Towards a Transferable Homiletical Pedagogy." *Journal of the Evangelical Homiletics Society* 9 (September 2009) 24–25.

National Association of Evangelicals. "About NAE." www.nae.net/about-nae/.

———. "Attending Church with Other Generations." Evangelical Leaders Survey (August 23, 2016).

———. "NAE, LifeWay Research Publish Evangelical Beliefs Research Definition" (November 19, 2015).

Roach, David. "Pew: Reformation Theology Waning among Protestants." *BP News* (September 6, 2017).

Robinson, Haddon W. *Biblical Preaching: The Development and Delivery of Expository Messages.* Grand Rapids, MI: Baker, 1980.

———. "Preaching Trends: A Review." *Journal of the Evangelical Homiletics Society* 6 (September 2006) 23–28.

Scharf, Greg R., et al. "Homiletics Forum: The Future of Evangelical Homiletics (and Preaching)." *Journal of the Evangelical Homiletics Society* 14 (September 2014) 4–5, 7–10, 18, 20, 23–25, 27–30.

Strachen, Owen. "Signs of Evangelical Life: A Pessimist's Optimism about the Movement's Future." *NAE Insight* (Spring 2013).

Zoll, Rachel. "Survey: White Christians Are Now a Minority of US Population." *News from the Associated Press* (September 6, 2017).

Chapter Sixteen

The Future Shapes of Preaching

Leonard Sweet

During an interview with author Kurt Vonnegut just before he died, he mentioned that "the one thing you would never see and I don't expect ever to see, is a cabinet office dedicated to the future." He continued, "Nobody sees me thinking of my grandchildren or my great-grandchildren either." Now, I'm not arguing for a cabinet-level department dedicated to the future where the worst things they'll do is bureaucratize, organize, centralize, and institutionalize it. Jimmy Carter tried this once in 1977 and got all thirteen departments, all the while saying, "I want you to focus on the future."

We're going to come out with a report in 2000. Tell me what the future is going to bring and you can actually read the report. (It's a joke.) I mean, how badly when it comes to thinking about their future, do we need to claim the future? The Native Americans did this really well. They have what's called the seven-generation rule, which says they will make no decisions until they factor in everything that they do and its impact on the seventh generation. That was as far in the future as they could think—seven generations.

We are already living in a world where five—the Native American start with three—generations are routinely present. We will soon be living in a world that is horizontal in contrast to the Native Americans, who will still be thinking vertically. You'll have seven generations present very soon.

In fact, I'm supposed to discuss the future shapes of preaching—preaching in the future. And I want us to think about the kind of future that some of you and your colleagues will see, which is not a twenty-fourth-century future but the twenty-second-century future. Because we have those here now who are twenty-second century people. Now, your ministry will continue well into the twenty-second century, but you say, "You've got to be kidding me!"

The most important influence on my life, apart from my mother, was Maria Hall, an environmentalist/philanthropist in Dayton, Ohio, who was born in 1897 and died in 2005. (Welcome to your world!) She lived in the time period of three centuries. Actuarially, if you have a male or female child born between 1990 and 2000, he or she will have a greater than 60 percent chance of living well into the twenty-second century. (Of course, this is West Virginia we're talking about here, where I'm from. Lord willing, Jesus carrying, crick not rising, and Moses not prohibiting, I could go in and out. My grandma would add some phrases to this.). Your church is norming and forming faith because you are preaching to twenty-second-century people.

Let's think about this a little bit in terms of what it means to take this future seriously. I think it's going to happen a lot quicker than some people think. Ten years ago, it was a whole different world. Half-lives are getting shorter and shorter. My oldest son got a PhD in biology, toxicology, and immunology from the University of Michigan. He got his degree in record time, but my job as his father is to make him humble. When he got his degree, I said, "You think you're so hot, Sweet, but just think: six years from now 50 percent of what you know today will be just absolutely wrong." The half-life of the scientific education is six years, and for engineering education, it's three. What's the half-life of a computer education?

Many of us are doing ministry and preaching with an information base about this culture that is so stale; it's rancid. And it's time we begin to understand the world that we're in and what God is already doing in this world so that we can be in it, but not of it. And yet, there is a biblical triangulation already in the world that is not of the world, but not out of here, either. And some of us love to be out of it in an intellectual way, but that's the particular little academic problem.

So, I want to just discuss a few things about this world that is forming. We could spend a lot of time talking about techniques, and I think that's what Dr. Gloer wanted me to do more—especially use holograms, even though it's an old concept. In fact, the prime minister of India today, Modi, was elected in 2014 because in 2012 he started appearing all around India in holographic form, and the people were so mesmerized by his speeches because it was all so real to them. It was, actually. Some say it was actually more powerful for him to speak holographically than personally.

Thus, the future's not about technology, which can come and go. Instead, it's going to have a lot of different possibilities. You'll want to be able to take your congregation different places, such as down the Emmaus road pretty soon. By the way, try to preach a three-point sermon in a world where you can take people down the Emmaus road via various sensations such as smell and touch.

If we look at this society as a missionary culture, I think that is exactly right. We're already here. Then, we need to treat the world as any missionary would in our preaching. And the first thing all missionaries do before they enter a missionary culture is learn the language or the vernacular. But this is one of the issues we have been resolutely stubborn about. We've decided not to speak the language of this culture that is forming all around us and is already here. Instead, we're determined to speak a language that we feel comfortable speaking.

The average eighteenth-century person heard seven thousand sermons in a lifetime. But each one of us receive about seven thousand sermons now every day. Somebody came up to me and said, "I want to go to church. I've never been before, so I've never heard a sermon." I replied, "Oh, you've heard sermons all the time." Approximately three to seven thousand times a day, some say more than that, we are bombarded by advertising messages. We are surrounded by communications or messages. We call them advertisements or commercials, but they are this culture's way of preaching. And a lot of them are altar calls, by the way. (The best days of altar calls are in the future, but that's another conversation.)

But notice the commercials that win an audience during the Super Bowl. You've actually got two Super Bowl games going on at the same time. Commercials aired during the game, by and large, are wordless. Think of the Budweiser commercials that only use words at the very end. This culture does not communicate in words, yet we're still talking about words. We even define *logos* as "the word," which is already the worst translation of the Greek you can come up with. We are so committed to our words in a culture that doesn't hear or speak words, yet we're still talking about words.

Now, you look at how people in our society communicate. It has two forms. This culture communicates in narrative, built around a metaphor, and this is what was missing in that entire conversation about narrative preaching in the seventies and eighties. They forgot what the root of every narrative is—a metaphor. The language of this culture is narrative and metaphor. (I combined the two terms together to make one word of it, "narraphor." I started with story and image but it came out "storage." So, I tried again.)

But now you say, "Well, that's really kind of a story." No, for the last thirty years, we've spent billions of dollars on a new frontier. During the last part of the twentieth century, we spent billions of dollars exploring outer space. In the twenty-first century, we've already spent billions of dollars supporting interspace, and we've actually mapped the microcircuitry of the brain. We know now how the brain works. One of the biggest discoveries to emerge from cognitive science, cycle neurolinguistics, and cognitive studies is that the last thing the brain comes up with is words. In fact, that happens at the end of a very long process. The mind is not made up of words, but rather metaphors which it turns into stories.

So, this is how the brain works, proved every time we dream. We will never, ever dream when we're reading. We'll never dream of us in a book because our minds don't think that way. Our minds don't think in words, but metaphors that it turns into stories or narratives. And then at the end of a very long process, we get words, but words do not have the power to change the mind. It is metaphor that brings about metamorphosis. (And by the way, this is exactly how Jesus communicated.)

So, what is this missionary culture and missionary preaching going to do for us in the twenty-first century by still trying to reach out like it's the twentieth century? The twenty-second century kids are forcing us to relearn our native tongue, which does not involve words and principles and points and propositions. The modern world began with a 95-point sermon. But we are now going back to, "The kingdom of heaven is like . . ." and then a metaphor.

Now, we also learn from Paul Ricoeur, who said he didn't do scientific research; instead, he just did linguistic studies. Ricoeur said that a narrative and metaphor are the same thing. A narrative is just an embellished and embroidered metaphor, and a metaphor is a distilled narrative. So when we discuss one, we're also discussing the other. We can't disconnect them, because they're the same thing. He's exactly right, but he's approaching it from another standpoint than brain science. But everywhere you look now, people are wondering how the brain works. And the real power to change, transform, or metamorphose comes from the "narraphor." But you've got to have a soundtrack, the hymn.

Two years ago, I started up a preaching website. Just to show people how to do this, I came up with a new story lectionary. But the two-year story lectionary tells the whole Bible as one story.

I've been involved with many church plants in my life. I have one question for those desiring membership. I ask the person, "Do you want to join this church? Stand before your brothers and sisters and tell the whole story—from Genesis to the maps. You've got ten minutes." We have so chaptered and versed, sliced and diced and chopped up everything (thank you, John Calvin and the Geneva Bible) that we all have an acute case of versitis. And you, the best preachers of the world, have versitis. Indeed, we are laboring under an alien default when we're accessing the Bible.

So, missionary preaching and the twenty-second-century culture first begins with learning the story of a culture to discover what God is already doing in that culture because He is already the future before we are. You and I don't bring Jesus anywhere. Instead, He shows up when we get there. John Wesley was insistent about this. He knew preachers who didn't want to go to the prisons, the mines, or the hovels of the poor. He said, "You will go visit the poor in their hovels, you will go to the prisoners in their cells, you will go and visit the miners in their pits. Jesus is already there and He'll be with you." In short, we don't take Jesus anywhere. Jesus is already in this future, in this world already doing great things.

So we learn the story of this culture, and then once we learn it, we listen. So the first act of preaching, in some ways, is not show and tell; it's shut up and listen. So, we're listening. Now, this is a huge assumption because even though we may know a lot of the verses, we may not know the actual story.

And so, as we listen and learn the story about what God is up to, then the second task of missionary preaching is to be able to tell that story to the satisfaction of that culture or person. I have no right to argue with you until I can first state your case to your satisfaction. If we would make that a fundamental principle, you and I can't argue with one another until I also listen to you first. Then I can say, "Okay, this is what you're arguing; this is your case," and if I state your case to your satisfaction you agree, "Yes, that's my case." Now we can enter the ring. So, part of missionary preaching involves being able to state the case to a world that is whoring after idols. We must first understand this culture that worships celebrities.

And then, third, once we have learned the story and re-stated it in ways in which we can be understood, then we show how that story is captured and critiqued. And in some ways, we are overcome by the Christian story (or, as I would put it, the Jesus story or the Redemption story). Again, this is predicated upon our knowledge of the story. (By the way, I am one who argues that this is again one story.) So, as we're learning the culture story by entering into it, we're able to recite and then capture, critique, and redeem that story by the Jesus story. Every single sermon that we hear every day—such as from Nike, who's got their story down to one swoosh—is just an image that captures the whole. That's a sermon right there.

Every single story out there, every single sermon, is telling us, "Build your life on my story. Trust my story." Preachers in this twenty-second century framework have got to find ways to tell this culture that there is only one story you can trust your life to—the Jesus story and the Jesus song. Hymn writer Fanny Crosby understood this well. One of her songs, "Blessed Assurance," was composed by two of the greatest theologians of the nineteenth century. Phoebe Palmer composed the music and Fanny Crosby wrote the words that say, "This is my story, this is my song." This is preaching in the twenty-second century. What's your story? What's your song?

We're going to learn to speak the language of the story, which also entails learning to speak the language of the song. I'm not just talking about any story, but *the* story. And we have to look at metaphors and stories as inspired and authoritative, just as we used to look at words in that way. The fact that these stories and metaphors are in the Scriptures mean that they've been put there by God. We can trust these metaphors and stories with our lives. We've been taught to trust the words but not the metaphors or stories. So, when you prescribe words and phrases and points and principles, you also prescribe metaphors and stories. The Holy Spirit is indeed the ultimate app here.

In 1996, I wrote a book called *Post Mount Pilgrims*, in which I looked at the future of preaching, and I concluded that the future belongs to the Eastern Orthodox and the Pentecostals. I actually tried to make the case semiotically. I used this acronym, EPIC, to demonstrate that the future is becoming more Experiential Participatory Imagery Connective—moving away from linear propositions and points, and moving away from performance to participation. By the way, nobody goes to a concert for this. You go to a concert to move away from merging to images, from individual to connective stuff, EPIC.

But that's just an interface. I don't know how the interface is going to play out, but it's still working. You're going to look up an interface in the operating system and discover it works. I want to hook it up to a biblical operating system through a Scriptured one. But I would change that twenty years later with one edition.

But they're both working because they're using very experiential, participatory imagery that's connective—it's just working on a different canvas. Yet I had no idea Pentecostals would sell out to mainline, or as my mentor called it, "old line." I started calling it "sideline," my students started calling it "offline," and you wonder why it's going "flat line." But I would change it a little bit today. I'd say the future belongs to Eastern Orthodox and the African Pentecostals in terms of preaching and worship. And you can't separate preaching and worship in the future. That was an isolated thing we've done. In other words, we've all got to learn and sit at the feet of the black church. That portion of the black church has sold out to modernity in this culture, but it's still kept its historic African roots. And as it ends in sing-song, and as you begin, the voice begins to sing.

So, it's time for us to be a little humble and learn from others around the world and our own context, which can teach us how to be missional in our preaching in a twenty-second century culture that doesn't speak or hear words, but is addicted to story. And every story, as we now know, is built on a metaphor.

By the way, this is why we are entrapped in such an identity crisis in the church today—because a strong identity requires narrative. My oldest son, the one who got the PhD in biology, toxicology and immunology, attended a Jesuit high school that was really excellent. They promised that they would instill in him classic Christian virtues. My other son went to a college that also promised to teach him Christian moral values. My daughter went to a school where I teach that promised to espouse the Christian worldview. And none of my kids went to the largest Christian School in the U.S. that says you've got to learn Bible verses—Liberty University.

But in my own life and the lives of my kids, in the last fifty years we've learned values, virtues, verses, and views. How has that been working for us? You can't build an identity on those things. Instead, identity requires narrative, and it's time we start building an identity. That's why we have a spiritual reproduction crisis of such huge proportion. We can reproduce the faith in our kids, communities, churches, and country, but we must understand that simply teaching values, virtues, verses, and views is the very heart of our problem.

But Jesus didn't die for a Christian worldview. He didn't die to give us virtues and values, or views and verses. Whoever you've allowed to author your life is your authority. "Authority" and "author" are actually the same word. This culture is not hungry for a worldview; it's hungry for a life story. The only one you should allow to author your life story, the only one worthy to author you, the only authority is Jesus. That's preaching in the twenty-second century.

Symposium Sermons

When Our Words Become God's
(Acts 2:32-41)

William H. Willimon

The Second Helvetic Confession brashly asserts, "The preached word IS God's word." This is an intimidating claim for us preachers and a remarkable thing to say about God. Karl Barth demonstrated at length that we can't speak of God. Sinful, limited creatures as we are, we can't speak for God. Only God can speak for God and, in preaching, *God does.* The people in our congregations—ignorant, uninformed laity that they are—think that kind of talk flatters us preachers, which shows how little they know about being a preacher!

Now, when the smoke settles at Pentecost, with Jews "from every nation under heaven" talking and hearing funny, the mocking mob in the street sneers, "They're doing what they did when Jesus was with them, they're drunk."

And Peter goes out and faces down the mob: "We're not drunk! Yet. It's only ten in the morning."

Who did Acts say preaches? Peter? Remember where we left Peter? Luke's first volume, his Gospel, says that when they were safe at the table, Peter boldly declared, "Lord, though they all desert You, I'll be there to speak up for You. You can count on me."

All it took was a powerless little serving girl to shut him up. "Weren't you with the Galilean?"

All Peter could say was, "I never really knew Him."

Now, in Luke's volume Two (Acts of the Apostles), Peter preaches—*Peter* preaches. You don't think that the same Spirit that led Jesus to speak in Luke 4, in Nazareth, has now descended on Jesus' betrayers and deniers? Then how do you explain that *Peter* preaches?

He declares to the Jewish crowd,

> This Jesus, God raised up. We are all witnesses to that fact. He was exalted to God's right hand and received from the Father the promised Holy Spirit. He poured out this Spirit. You don't believe that the Spirit was effusively outpoured? How do you explain that I'm standing here preaching? . . . God has made this Jesus, whom you crucified, both Lord and Christ. Now, let's stand for the last hymn and the benediction.

This, by my assessment, is the worst sermon in all of church history. Short, ridiculously short. No illustrations, culturally insensitive, no connections, no bridge from there to here. There's no way this sermon could get you out of Homiletics 101 at Truett.

And yet . . .

> When the crowd heard this, they were deeply troubled. They said to Peter and the other apostles, "Brothers, what should we do?" Peter replied, "Change your hearts and lives. Each of you must be baptized in the name of Jesus Christ for the forgiveness of your sins. Then you will receive the gift of the Holy Spirit. This promise is for you, your children, and for all who are far away—as many as the Lord our God invites. . . . Be saved from this perverse generation."

A judgmental, accusatory, demanding sermon. And yet. . . .

> Those who accepted Peter's message were baptized. God brought about three thousand people into the community on that day.

Take that, Truett Homiletics 101!

> "My word that goes out from my mouth . . . will not return to me empty, but will accomplish what I desire and achieve the purpose for which I sent it." (Isa 55:11)

Here's a question for you preachers: Do you think God means Isa 55:11 as a promise or as a *threat*?

Here's my thesis: the best, most frightening thing about being a preacher is not having to stand and deliver words to a bunch of losers, half of whom, according to research reported in the *Baylor Lariat*, thought it was a good idea to vote for a lying, adulterous, racist casino owner for President. No, the best, most frightening thing about preaching is the theme of this conference: *When God takes our words and makes them God's word.*

God's word shall not return empty. You'd have to be a preacher to know why that's not necessarily encouraging news.

Oh, we preachers talk a good game. Watch us! "They don't hear!" Amen. "They don't listen!" Amen. "They look like zombies sitting in pews. I'm up there giving a hundred and fifty percent, and the ushers are taking them out on stretchers."

And yet sometimes . . . I meant to get around to the sermon before Saturday, but it was first one thing and then another. So I jot down some stuff on the back of an envelope. I stand up and pull out some sappy illustrations such as, "Tie a yellow ribbon on the old oak tree," and "He ain't heavy, he's my brother"—praying to God none of them has ever been in church before.

The first person to greet me at the door is fighting back tears, gripping my hand and saying, "Good sermon, Reverend. God really spoke to me. Now I'm going to quit my job, sell the pickup, learn Spanish, and move to Honduras as a missionary."

And what is it you feel then? What's it like when your words become God's word?

"Look, uneducated, unsophisticated layperson, I was just preaching. You're not supposed to take this stuff literally. That was a metaphor! Do you think we're Baptists?"

Let me spell it out for any of you new, inexperienced preachers: Your take-away is this (write this down, it could be on the exam): Because of the God we've got, *You cannot trust preaching to be ineffective.*

Peter preaches post-Pentecost the most poorly prepared, badly delivered sermon in the Scriptures and thousands respond, "What should we do?" God made the worst sermon the most effective sermon ever preached. Three thousand were baptized!

It's enough to keep a preacher nervous.

We preachers have adequate defenses for coping with the ineffectiveness of our preaching. (The laity are idiots and biblically illiterate, half the congregation are members of the NRA, etc.). They don't hear! But many of us lack a sufficiently robust theology to account for why sometimes, despite our worst sermons, *they do hear*.

It's enough to make a preacher ask himself, *Do I really want that much power over a person's life? Do I really want the responsibility of aiding and abetting Jesus as He lays some cross on his or her back?*

I once lamented to a Duke student the scant student attendance at chapel. He attempted to comfort me with, "Hey. Go easy on yourself. I've heard you preach. I think it's a miracle you get out as many as you do. Duke is a very selective university. These students are smart. They're intelligent enough to know that if they came to the chapel, and if God used one of your sermons to speak to them, their lives would only become more unmanageable."

"That's the best reason I've ever heard for not attending church," I said.

Hey, I'm an expert and I can tell you that in forty years of teaching homiletics, despite all our efforts, nobody has ever found a sure-fire, absolutely effective way to keep the Trinity from insinuating itself into a sermon and having the last word.

Today is the anniversary of the tragedy of 9/11. Two Sundays after 9/11, I was away from Duke Chapel, and my guest preacher was Bishop Ken Carder. He preached on Jeremiah. I forget the exact passage, but it was the part where God says to Israel, "You want to know why your cities have been laid waste, your walls torn down, and you're sent into exile?"

"I'll tell you why. I sent the Assyrians. I tried to reason with you, but you refused to listen. Now, in exile, you will have lots of time on your hands, so we can talk."

Bishop Carder wondered, "Wow. What sort of God would say this to hurting, victimized people? What sort of people would have dared to be in conversation with this God? I haven't heard talk like this in the past few weeks, have you?" Ken went on to preach about a God who cares enough even to demand that victims move beyond victimization.

The next week, I called Ken and said, "I got over fifty, mostly angry, e-mails after that Jeremiad you preached in chapel. I've spent most of my week responding."

"No kidding?" said Ken. "Isn't that amazing? I didn't put that much work into that sermon. Didn't have time for proper exegesis. Wonder why God would choose to make that sermon so effective?"

In Acts 8, Philip is told by an angel to go to the desert at noon. There, he runs into an Ethiopian eunuch. Somehow, that Ethiopian has got his hands on a scroll of Isaiah. He's reading it, but there's no way he can understand it. "Like a lamb he was led to slaughter," it says. "Who's he talking about? Himself or somebody else?"

"We believe he was talking about Jesus," said Philip. "I don't have time to explain it to you. Besides you are an Ethiopian, an unclean eunuch who can't go into the temple. And the desert is nowhere to do proper Bible study."

The Ethiopian says, "What's to prevent me from being baptized in the name of the Lamb?"

Philip said, "Nothing would make me happier than to baptize you, an Ethiopian eunuch, but we need water and we're in the middle of the desert."

"Look! Water!"

And Philip muttered to himself, *Man, the saints in Jerusalem were upset about my baptizing those Samaritans. They are going to go through the roof over this!*

My point? Philip didn't do any of that. Making our words God's word is God's idea of a good time.

As Barth said, only God has the words to speak of God. But by God's grace, *aufhebung*. God lifts up our words, making them God's word.

Jonah: "Go preach to mighty Nineveh!" Go preach to Assad and Kim Il Sung put together. Jonah heads in the other direction. God sends a great fish, which swallows Jonah and then vomits him up on the beach.

"Okay, okay, I'll go preach." Jonah preaches the shortest, worst sermon, even worse than Peter's sermon in Acts 2. "In forty days, Nineveh will be overthrown. There, I've said it. Let's stand for the benediction. I did it. Now, I've got a plane to catch."

And, in response to Jonah's sulking sermon, the Ninevites repent. The people repent, the king repents, and even the cows repent.

And the world's most reluctant missionary, Jonah . . . wishes he were dead. "I knew you were a merciful God whose salvation does not stop at the U. S. border. . . . I knew!"

※※※※※※

Though I don't know her personally, recently I got a letter from someone a few of you may have met: Ivanka Trump. I don't want to violate confidences, but well, here's Ivanka's invitation to me to preach at the

White House: "You know Daddy. Poor thing, he's surrounded himself with a bunch of sycophantic, boot-licking, bogus prosperity preachers. I mean, like, who is going to tell him the truth? You know that Daddy is already truth challenged. Then there's the racism, and well, in your time at Duke Chapel you showed that you have such a gift for talking with powerful, deceitful, biblically illiterate folks. Is there any way you could come to Washington and . . ."

Later I wrote back to Ivanka. I thanked her for her kind invitation. "I'm booked every Sunday for the next three years," I lied. "How about just my coming for one of those parties at Mar-a-Lago? Not a sermon?"

You preachers know why I begged out of going and preaching the truth about God at the White House. Couldn't risk it. You know why. If I preached, and if God should take my evasive, cowardly words as an occasion to speak the Word, and if the Holy Spirit should move The Donald for the first time to hear the gospel, and hearing it, to repent, my career would never recover. I'd never be invited again to preach at Truett. Couldn't risk it.

Don't Stop Preaching

Amos 7:10–17

Jared E. Alcántara

On a cold Sunday morning in January 1827, a preacher/evangelist named Harriet Livermore proclaimed God's Word to more than a thousand people gathered at the Capitol Building in Washington D. C. She had piercing eyes and a resounding voice and wore a simple gown and bonnet. She was just thirty-nine years old. She preached without notes for more than an hour and a half before congressmen, senators, and members of the public. Even the U. S. President attended. Drawing from 2 Sam 23:3 (KJV), which says, "He that ruleth over men must be just, ruling in the fear of God," Livermore preached with truth and conviction. She corrected, rebuked, and encouraged those who listened. Many were blessed. Countless people who heard her that day wept over their sins and others were led to repentance.

But, as often happens in ministry, not everyone enjoyed Livermore's sermon. The great homiletician Fred Craddock used to say that there are two kinds of preaching people don't want to listen to: bad and good. That morning, President John Quincy Adams had to sit on the steps of the platform in order to hear Livermore preach because all the seats were taken, which probably put him in a bad mood. In a personal letter to a friend, he described Livermore as a woman filled with "the impulse of vanity and love of fame."

Several middle- and upper-class preachers also rejected her. They believed she had forsaken her femininity and modesty for acclaim and adulation. To them, she did not seem like the *right* kind of preacher: too backward, too uneducated, too unsophisticated. She was the wrong *kind* of preacher on the wrong *side* of town offending the wrong *sort* of people.[1] I wonder if they said to each other, "Surely, the Lord cannot be blessing this. Look at all these people." Rest assured that Livermore's experience was not new or unique. In fact, on that day, she joined a long company of preachers who have been misunderstood and mistreated—from Jeremiah to John the Baptist, from our Lord Jesus to American preachers like Jarena Lee.

I know another preacher who could also resonate with Livermore's experience: the prophet Amos. We read about him in Amos 7:10–17. It is the only story we have about Amos. The rest of this book contains prophetic oracles to Israel and to the other nations. It is not a well-known story. Some of you may have never heard someone preach on it. For those who are older, I doubt it ever made its way onto the Sunday school flannel-graph. But, it is an *important story*, one that should be important to all of us who preach this gospel. Perhaps you are not surprised that I chose it because it is a story about preaching.

We find two different people with two different ministry aspirations confronting one another. Let us say that Amos is the wrong *kind* of preacher on the wrong *side* of town offending the wrong *sort* of people, and Amaziah tells him to stop preaching and prophesying in Bethel. Perhaps someone has said the same thing to you at some point and, if they haven't yet, just keep on living. The response that Amos offers rings clear and remains the same for the seasoned preacher and for the first-year seminarian. Today, I would like to preach on the subject, *"Don't stop preaching."*

The short time we spend in seminary is a strange mix of the delightful and difficult. Yes, it can be *delightful*. In the span of just three short years (or for some, four years or five or more), our faith is stretched, our horizons are expanded, new ideas take root, and a broader vision of the church comes into focus. But seminary can also be a *difficult* time. The danger is subtle and subversive. Instead of knocking on our front door and announcing its intentions, it seeps its way into the ventilation systems of our souls, reconditioning the air we breathe. I find it strange and even sad that, by the time we graduate *from* seminary, we could forget the reason we came *to* seminary. The temptation is always there to quit, compromise, trade down from God's plan, nullify your calling—and yes,

---

1. For more on Livermore's sermon before Congress, see Brekus, *Strangers and Pilgrims*, 1–4.

to stop preaching. How strange that you could get a 4.0-grade point average *at* seminary and miss the whole point *of* seminary.

What we see in our text is this danger on display. We see two different ministers on two different career paths with two different ministry aspirations coming into conflict with one another. It is a good thing that ministers with different visions of ministry don't butt heads anymore like they used to in the Bible. We see Amaziah, the priest of Bethel, who is preoccupied with the burden that Amos's words will bring upon the land. By contrast, we see Amos, the prophet from Tekoa, who is more concerned about the impact God's word will have upon the people. We see Amaziah defending King Jeroboam's reputation, and we see Amos defending God's. We see Amaziah saying to Amos, "Stop prophesying. Stop preaching." But we see Amos in word and deed saying, "I cannot stop prophesying. I won't stop preaching." We hear Amaziah saying, "Go back to the land of Judah," and we hear Amos responding, "The Lord said, 'Go forward to the land of Israel.' And, if you say, 'Go back,' and God says, 'Go forward,' I am hitching my wagon to God."

Does Amaziah have a right to be upset? Whether or not we think that he does, what matters here is that *he* thinks that he does. The context reveals the reason. The Lord announces judgment in verses 8 and 9: the high places of Isaac will be destroyed, the sanctuaries of Israel ruined, and the sword of the Lord will rise against the house of Jeroboam. These are not the sorts of verses that show up in holiday greeting cards, and for good reason. Why is Amaziah so upset? He is a priest at the temple that Amos says will come to ruin. He serves the king whose house Amos says will be struck down by the sword. A prophet from the wrong side of town announces to a priest from the right side of town that the right side of town will soon become no town at all. If Amos is right, life cannot remain the way it has always been—the status quo cannot continue.

So, what does Amaziah do? He sends a message to the king of Bethel that Amos is inciting a rebellion against him. The word he uses, translated as "raise a conspiracy" (*qashar*), shows up in 1 and 2 Kings whenever people in the southern kingdom tried to overthrow people in the northern kingdom (e.g., 1 Kgs 15:27, 16:9; 2 Kgs 10:9, 15:10). When he says conspiracy, he might as well say "coup." "The land cannot bear all his words," he says to the king in his message. In the words of Patrick Miller, "Amaziah has 'de-theologized Amos' words and ignored their origin ('Thus says Amos' not 'Thus says the Lord'). Preservation of the 'house of Israel' is the issue, not the obedience of 'my people Israel.'"[2] How sad that a man whose name means "Yahweh is mighty" believes that "Jeroboam is mighty" instead. Amos must have posed some kind of threat to Amaziah and to the establishment. (It is much easier to believe that another preacher is "punking" you when most of your time is taken up with punking God.)

If we pause and reflect on Amaziah's ministry for a moment, we cannot overlook its dangerous implications for today. It is far more difficult to speak truth *to* power when you enjoy the trappings *of* power. When you are sipping the king's wine and enjoying the king's food, you are much less likely to stand up to the king when you must do so. If the prophet Nathan had been sipping wine every night in King David's house, he never would have been able to say, "You are that man, O king." If John the Baptist had been enjoying the royal food every night in Herod's palace, he would never have been able to stand up to him regarding his immoral behavior. Amaziah has become so accustomed to answering to King Jeroboam that he no longer answers to God. How swift is the declension from a ministry of influence to participation in collusion.

"Get out, you seer. Go back to the land of Judah. Earn your bread and make your living there," Amaziah says in verse 12. You can almost hear the condescension in his voice. "I'm sorry, Amos, but Bethel is for priests like me and Judah is for prophets like you. Shepherding and tree-tending are a bit too blue collar for this ministry that we're trying to build up here in Bethel. I'm sorry, Amos, but your GPA is too low, you got a C on your synagogue history paper, you failed your Hebrew mid-term, which, of course, is hard to understand since you speak Hebrew. You're not from the right family; you don't have the right accent. What good can come from Tekoa anyhow? Don't you know, Amos, that this ministry is sponsored by King Jeroboam International Corporation of Ministries? Don't you know? 'This is the king's sanctuary and the temple of the kingdom.'" That's what it essentially says in verse 13.

What a dangerous and dreadful way to engage in ministry, getting so caught up building your own kingdom that you don't have time for the kingdom of God, genuflecting before powers of an age that is passing away, advancing your agenda while forgetting about God. Gardner Taylor puts it this way, "Whenever corrupt religion and crooked government collude, Jesus Christ is crucified all over again."

---

2. Miller, "Prophetic Critique," 85.

But Amaziah is not the only character in this story. We also have the prophet Amos, the shepherd and tree tender from Tekoa. Notice that he does not hide from his humble origins. He says in verse 14, "I was neither a prophet nor the son of a prophet." Amos does not claim to be a religious and professional prophet. He knows he is not the son of a prophet, which would have meant being a member of a prophetic guild like the one that assembled around Elisha in 1 and 2 Kings. He knows that he comes from outside the inner circle. Interesting, isn't it, that God's Word often comes from unexpected places and through peculiar people?

I resonate with what Amos says here, and here is the reason. I grew up just a couple of miles away from Princeton Theological Seminary in New Jersey. My father emigrated from the Honduras in Central America in his early twenties. My mother is the daughter of a single mom from Pennsylvania. My grandfather died when she was just four years old. They have never owned a home. Somehow, in the peculiar providence of God, years later, I found myself enrolled in a PhD program just a few miles away from where I grew up, of all places, at Princeton Theological Seminary. The strangest thing happened. I started bumping into some of the people of my parents' generation, people from my neighborhood. Several of them worked the service jobs at the seminary: landscaper, custodian, or maid. Some had held me in their arms when I was a baby. They vacuumed the hallways where I went to class and mowed the lawns on the campus where I studied. I felt so guilty. Why me and not someone else from that same neighborhood?

But my thinking started to shift one Sunday morning in particular early in my first year there. I had just finished preaching a sermon at my church. An older gentleman approached me after the service, one whose face looked familiar but whose name I could not place. He told me who he was, and he said, "I don't normally come to church, but I'm from your old neighborhood. Your parents told me their youngest son was not only going to Princeton Seminary, but was also serving as a pastor at this church. I came by the church today to tell you that we're proud of you, and we are rooting for you."

"I was neither a prophet nor the son of a prophet, but I was a shepherd and tender of sycamore fig trees." You do not need to be the best, brightest, most gifted, most connected for God to use you. More than all of these, all you really need to be is willing, for if you are willing, God is able.

I imagine Amos saying to Amaziah, "I may not be a member of your prophetic establishment. I may not come from a priestly family. You may not think that God's Word can extend to the fields and orchards of Tekoa. You may not believe that God's call can reach out to the shepherds and seasonal laborers in Judah, but I am afraid you are mistaken." If I might borrow a few hymn lines, I imagine him saying, "I may not preach like Peter and I may not pray like Paul, but I can pray and I can preach. For the Lord took me, and the Lord called me to go." In Hebrew, the Lord's name is so nice he says it twice. "The Lord took me . . . and the *Lord* told me to go; and if God called me to go, I'm not going back. I can't go back. I'm sorry, Amaziah, but God's ace of hearts trumps your king of clubs. I have not come to bow before your king. I have come to warn your king. I answer to God and God alone."

Why should you not stop preaching? Amos's answer is so simple, it almost is simplistic. God has called you to this work. If God has called you to go, there's no turning back. Like the three Magi in Bethlehem, once you've been with Jesus, you *cannot* go back the way you came.

"Hear the word of the Lord," Amos says in verse 16. "You say, 'Do not prophesy against Israel, and stop preaching against the descendants of Isaac,' but God has something different to say than what you have to say." Indeed, what matters in life and in eternity is not what you have to say; it is what God has to say.

So, what does God have to say? Through Amos, God says to Amaziah: "Your wife will become a prostitute in the city, your sons and daughters will fall by the sword, your land will be divided, and you yourself will die in a pagan country." The word for "pagan" can also be translated as "unclean." Amos tells an Old Testament priest whose job centered on being clean that his life would end in an *unclean* foreign land. Not only would it impact Amaziah, but Israel would surely die in exile, away from its native land. Notice there is nothing in here about your best life now or about God's special plan for those in close proximity in power. Perhaps these words shock and disturb us, but they may not have shocked those who originally heard them. These were covenant curses as set forth in the Torah for covenant breakers who had taken advantage of covenant promises while ignoring covenant stipulations.

It takes courage to tell the truth, especially when the truth hurts. It takes courage especially since sometimes it requires a preacher to step *outside* the circle in order to name the sin that exists *inside* the circle. "Courage," Philips Brooks said in his 1877 Yale Beecher lectures, "is the indispensable requisite of any true ministry."[3] It takes courage to preach, to speak out in a world where injustice persists, falsehood reigns, and sin corrupts people in the world *and* leaders in the church. Yes, it takes courage to preach at a time in our nation's history when too many Christian leaders suffer from a severe case of allegiance confusion, when too many pastors would rather be right than be reconciled. What the church needs today is *not* more voices clamoring for the platform or craving the attention of those in power; what the church needs today, now more than ever, are voices crying in the wilderness, saying, "Prepare the way for the Lord." George Truett says it this way: "We must openly take sides with Christ, and follow with prompt and unfaltering obedience, wherever He leads. . . . Not to take sides with Christ is to take sides against Him."[4]

When you answer God's call to preach, not only do you say yes to God and yes to courage, you also join a long company of preachers who said yes to God and yes to courage, from the prophets to the present. You say "yes" with *Ireneaus,* whose faith withstood the persecution against the clergy in Lyons. You say "yes" with *John Chrysostom,* whose prophetic preaching challenged the Emperor and Empress from his pulpit in Constantinople. You join ranks with *John Wycliffe,* who spoke out against ecclesiastical abuses in England, and *John Knox,* who confronted Mary, Queen of Scots in Scotland. You stand shoulder to shoulder with women preachers of great courage like *Harriet Livermore,* who called this nation to a higher purpose, and with daughters of thunder like Jarena Lee, Julia Foote, and Harriet Baker, who said to leaders in the AME Zion church: "You say, 'Stop prophesying and stop preaching,' but God has called me to preach, so I can't stop preaching. I won't stop preaching." You come behind fearless preachers like Oscar Romero in El Salvador, who said in the last sermon he delivered before being gunned down at his church: "The Church . . . cannot remain silent before such abomination."[5] You follow in the footsteps of Gardner C. Taylor, who preached faithfully for four decades on Sunday and was willing to go to jail, if need be, to advance civil rights on Monday. You stand on the shoulders of Martin Luther King Jr., who told his congregation in Atlanta that even if they put him out of that church, nothing would change about his call to preach since his marching orders came from God.

3. Brooks, *Lectures on Preaching,* 59.
4. Truett, "Taking Sides," 184-85.
5. Oscar Romero's final sermon, March 1980, as cited in Douglass, *Nonviolent Coming of God,* 46.

Let me suggest that the prophet Amos's power to preach did not come because he was peculiarly brave or even because he was a great preacher. It did not spring from his acumen and ingenuity. No, it came from a deeper place. The spring that powered Amos's call to preach is the same spring that gives you the power to preach. "Do you not know? Have you not heard? The Lord is the everlasting God, maker of heaven and earth" (Isa 40:28a-b). We believe in a great God. We worship a great Savior, one who went to his own Gethsemane and climbed His own cross at Calvary. Then He put death to death on Sunday morning, if I might paraphrase John Donne. He brought exiles back to their citizenship and made slaves into princes and princesses in the royal house, to borrow from Gardner Taylor. Yes, Jesus is a great Savior. He is the reason we said "yes" to God in the first place.

Most of you have never heard of Antonio Montesinos. He was one of many Dominican friars sent by Spain in the year 1511 to minister on the island of Hispañiola, which is now the Dominican Republic and Haiti. When Montesinos arrived, he was shocked and appalled by how Native Americans were treated there—they were even enslaved. He was so shocked by this ill-treatment that just before Christmas in the year 1511, Montesinos, with the support of the other friars, delivered a courageous and blistering sermon on the evils of slavery in the Spanish colonies. He went on to explain that he and the other friars would no longer listen to confessions from slaveholding Spanish colonists. In the congregation that morning was a young man named Bartolomé de Las Casas. The words of Montesinos were not only a revelation to him, but they also stirred a fire in his soul that would not soon go out. He was inexorably drawn to Jesus Christ that morning, gripped by what Thomas Chalmers calls "the expulsive power of a new affection." By 1514, he had divested himself of all of his slaves and would later be known as the Great Defender of Native Americans in the Spanish colonies.

Why should you not stop preaching? You never know what will happen when God brings a fresh word with fresh fire. You never know what will happen when God takes the seeds that are planted and makes them grow. So, *don't stop preaching!* For God can take hearts of stone and make them into hearts of flesh. God can take dry bones and make them live again. You never know what will happen when you preach God's Word with truth and conviction. You never know what will happen when you listen to God's voice and speak out for those without a voice. Maybe, just maybe, justice will flow down like waters and righteousness like an ever-flowing stream. Maybe God will do what only God can do through the foolishness of preaching.

Bibliography

Brekus, Catherine A. *Strangers and Pilgrims: Female Preaching in America*. Chapel Hill: University of North Carolina Press, 1998.

Brooks, Philips. *Lectures on Preaching*. New York: E. P. Dutton, 1877.

Douglass, James W. *The Nonviolent Coming of God*. Eugene, OR: Wipf and Stock, 2006.

Miller, Patrick. "The Prophetic Critique of Kings." *Ex Auditu* 2 (1986) 85.

Truett, George. "Taking Sides." In *Follow Thou Me*, by George Truett, 184–85. New York: Long and Smith, 1932.

www.ingramcontent.com/pod-product-compliance
Lightning Source LLC
Chambersburg PA
CBHW071241230426
43668CB00011B/1539